# COLLECTOR'S ENCYCLOPEDIA OF

## Fiesta

### TENTH EDITION

Other Colored
Dinnerware,
Post86 Fiesta,
Laughlin Art China

## Bob & Sharon Huxford

### COLLECTOR BOOKS

*A Division of Schroeder Publishing Co., Inc.*

Front cover: Row 1: 12" Fiesta vase, cobalt, $1,400.00 – 1,900.00; Harlequin service water pitcher, maroon, $75.00 – 90.00; Fiesta demitasse pot, cobalt, $500.00 – 600.00; Riviera covered jug, light green, $90.00 – 110.00; Row 2: Fiesta disk pitcher, red, $550.00 – 650.00; Harlequin high-lip creamer, mauve blue, $125.00 – 165.00; Fiesta demitasse cup and saucer, ivory, $95.00 – 125.00; Row 3: Conchita individual Kitchen Kraft casserole, $90.00 – 125.00; Fiesta individual sugar bowl and creamer on figure-8 tray, colors as shown, $800.00 – 900.00.

Back cover: Post86 Fiesta — Row 1: Millennium vase; 11" round serving tray; 9½" medium vase; Row 2: hostess bowl; presentation bowl; goblet; Row 3: gusto bowl; pyramid candlesticks; napkin ring; demitasse cup and saucer. (All Post86 pieces not retired long enough to incur secondary market values).

Cover design by Beth Summers
Book design by Lisa Henderson

Fiesta is a registered trademark of the Homer Laughlin China Company of Newell, West Virginia.

COLLECTOR BOOKS
P.O. Box 3009
Paducah, Kentucky 42002-3009

www.collectorbooks.com

Copyright © 2005 Bob & Sharon Huxford

The current values in this book should be used only as a guide. They are not intended to set prices, which vary from one section of the country to another. Auction prices as well as dealer prices vary greatly and are affected by condition as well as demand. Neither the authors nor the publisher assumes responsibility for any losses that might be incurred as a result of consulting this guide.

## Searching For A Publisher?

We are always looking for people knowledgeable within their fields. If you feel that there is a real need for a book on your collectible subject and have a large comprehensive collection, contact Collector Books.

# CONTENTS

# ACKNOWLEDGMENTS

It's been thirty-one years since the *Story of Fiesta* was published, and here we are in the tenth edition. With each edition the book has expanded. We've added new photos and updated information, until the little paperback has become a hardback at least eight times its original size. We have many people to thank for that. So many collectors over the years have faithfully shared their new-found information with us, and this year was certainly no exception.

As you'll see, we've included many wonderful new photos in this edition. We could easily have added more; there were additional photos sent in and even more offered. But space quickly became an issue, and though we were reluctant to leave anyone's offerings out, we found we had to make choices. So if you sent photos that weren't used, we want you to know that we did appreciate them.

In the Fiesta color plates, you'll see some new group shots — very often a grouping of an item in every color it was produced. They're fabulous, and I know Fiesta enthusiasts everywhere will love them. They were sent to us by David Schaefer, who many of you will know from his work with the HLCCA. Besides being an art director for a publishing company, David serves on the club's board of directors and is editor of their magazine, *The Dish*. He has a very giving heart, and we can't thank him enough — not only for his wonderful photos but for promptly and graciously answering our questions, not just with short-and-to-the point answers, but answers that were detailed and full of information. David, there just aren't words to thank you properly.

In the Post86 Fiesta chapter you'll find lots of new information, provided once again by our New Fiesta guru, Joel Wilson. Joel is publisher of *The Fiesta Collector's Quarterly* and the man behind China Specialties, Inc., a company that designs and distributes dated, limited-edition lines of specially decorated Fiesta as well as some great fantasy pieces. He stays abreast of all new developments in the Post86 line, and he often sends me samples. I know I can count on him not only as a friend but also an accurate source of information. Joel, to know you is to love you, and I'm sure I speak for all your friends when I say how happy I am for you now that you have those two special ladies to share your life — daughter Kinsey and wife Charlene.

We have an exciting new Kenilworth chapter for you this time as well as tons of never-before-published Red-Striped Fiesta information. In the Kitchen Kraft/OvenServe chapter you'll find added information on the "Lady With Jug" decal. This research is all courtesy of Patrick Bunetta and J.T. Vaughn. (J.T. and Ken Blum were the photographers on these projects.) Pat has always been faithful to call me with information on his new finds (which are many — we should all be so lucky); and when I've emailed him with questions (which were also many), I could count on a patient, courteous, helpful answer immediately, even during my cancer treatment when my questions didn't always make sense. Thank you so much, Pat — you're a true gentleman.

If you're a veteran collector, I know when you hear the name Dancing Girl, you immediately connect it with Chuck Denlinger. Chuck may be retired, but Fiesta is still in his blood. For as long as I can remember, he's shared photos with me of his advanced finds. This time (though you'll see his photo credits here and there throughout the book) he sent many absolutely wonderful photos of Laughlin Art China. He's another anchor for me, always there with answers and encouragement. He and his wife Margaret are very special people. Thank you, Chuck, for years of contributions to this field of collecting.

Which brings us to the pricing section. We've always counted on collectors and dealers to give us their opinions on values, drawn from what they've bought and sold. In some editions, we had as many as fifty people send us their thoughts on the subject. This year there were only seven. This tells me that even active collectors are unsure of the market. Many vintage collections are mature by now, having been built for the most part during the heyday of Fiesta, pre-eBay, when "book price" was almost biblical. Now on about any given day you'll be able to choose from six or seven relish trays, so you no longer feel the urgency to pay whatever the dealer asks to have the privilege of taking home the "one and only" relish tray in the show. But we've done our best to suggest accurate and up-to-date pricing information, and we do appreciate those who responded to our survey: Bill Beck, Gary Beegle, Frank Dow, Diane and Brad McHenry, David Schaefer, Bill and Jo Ann Van Voorhies, and Joel Wilson. (In no way do we mean to imply that they are responsible for the pricing in this edition; we will be held accountable for that. Besides their imput, we have tried to factor in some auction values, dealer sales, and opinions of other long-time collectors.)

Because the survey didn't cover every chapter this time, we also enlisted the aid of several other collectors. (Actually, many of them were kind enough to volunteer.) In this group were: Sandra Bond, Pat Bunetta, Chuck Denlinger, Melicety Deatherage, Marjorie Duthely, Kit Fox, Jack and Treva Hamlin, Joe Keller, Heidi Kellner, Harvey Linn, Jr., Fred Mutchler, Mark Rumbolo, Becky Turner, and Ray Vlach.

Another sincere vote of thanks goes to Mick and Lorna Chase (Fiesta Plus) who conducted the survey for us this year. When I asked them to do it, I did so because I felt like I just had "too many irons in the fire," but as it turned out, there was more going on in my life than I realized. Thanks to you both for taking on this task for me and for the trip you made to the studio at Collector Books with the Post86 Fiesta shown on the back cover. It's so nice to know we can always count on you.

Murphy Creative Design and our contact there, Paula Murphy, and Renee Stark with General Mills worked together to send us professional photos of the Betty Crocker Fiesta exclusives you'll see in the New Fiesta chapter. All Betty Crocker Catalog Exclusive Fiesta® images © 2005 were used by permission of General Mills.

Becky Turner and I started corresponding several weeks after I had submitted the manuscript; but she sent me such great photos (rare Harlequin and World's Fair), we were determined to get them in, and thanks to a flexible editoral staff at Collector Books, we did. She also gave me suggestions on pricing some of the harder-to-price HLC lines. Becky, you're terrific. Thank you so much!

We love working with the great people at Collector Books, and to them we send a special thanks: Billy Schroeder, Gail Ashburn, Beth Ray, Beth Summers, Charley Lynch, Lisa Henderson, Amy Sullivan, and any others who worked on our book. You're the best.

We always appreciate the cooperation of the Homer Laughlin China Company, especially our contacts there over the years, Ed Carson (retired) and presently, Dave Conley.

These are by no means everyone we want to acknowledge; several sent in lovely pictures, but we were careful to give photo credits this edition, so watch for those. We thank each and every individual who thought enough of what we try to do to send them to us. Our list of names grows with each edition, but this book is the sum of the efforts of all of these people, and we don't want to leave one person out. Names may have changed; no doubt some of these good people have passed on. If your name is not there but should be, we apologize.

On a personal note, I want to thank all of you for your cards, good wishes, and especially for your prayers during my bout with cancer this past year. God heard those prayers and worked nothing short of a miracle in my life. I treasure the book the HLCC club sent me with a note of encouragement signed by the entire staff – thank you all so much. All the dealers at the APEC show sent me a signed card; that was very special to me. I received many cards, concerned e-mails, phone calls, and lovely flowers from Collector Books, and they all were faithful to pray for me. There just aren't words to express my feelings, they're all totally inadequate. But I want to say that I appreciate everything with all my heart.

Don and Pat Adlesperger
Joe and Char Alexander
Millie Allen
Adam Anik
Mary Apgar
Philip Azeredo
Christina Baglivi
Michael Bailey
Mike Bainter
Wayne and Laverna Baker
Sandra and Tim Baldwin
Jerry Barberio
Rita Barg
Bill Beck
Dave Beck
Gary Beegle
Michael and Lisa Belcher
  (Sit-a-Spell Antiques)
Rick Benning
Gabriele Benson (Memory Lane)
Deane Bergsrud
Dennis Bialek
Donald G. Biellier
Sue Lynn Bishop
Ken Blum
Sandra Bond
  (Secretary/Treasurer HLCCA)
Dave Bowers

Robert Bowers
Greg and Kristen Bowman
Dennis Boyd
Paul Brache
Noel and Jennifer Brodzinski
Joyce Brooks
Ken Brown
Sharon C. Browning
Ben Brian C. Buckles
Patrick Bunetta
Gloria and George Burkos
Dave Burrows
Jim Campbell
Tom Chanelli
Mick and Lorna Chase
  (Fiesta Plus)
Emily Chipps
Phillip and Joyce Clover
Don and Gail Contrell
Gary Crafton
Doug Dann
Melicety Deatherage
Mary Delagardelle
David Delaune
Mildred Delaune
Chuck and Margaret Denlinger
  (Dancing Girl)
Michael Desjardins

Bob and Michelle Detterick
Carolyn Dock
Steve Douglas (HLCCA)
Frank Dow (Fiesta and More)
Mike Drollinger
Marjorie Duthely (Pres. HLCCA)
Glenn Edmond
Robin and Bud Fennema
Darcy Fitspatrick
Mary Flick
Steven P. Fonder
Kit Fox (Vice Pres. HLCCA)
Terry Franks
Dale Gallis
Cinda Gambil
Kathy Garrels
Jo Ann Giovannelli
Leona Gonzales
Philip L. Gray
Robert Green
William and Donna Griglock
Gus Gustafson
  (chromatics@Buttzville Center)
Mike Haas
  (chromatics@Buttzville Center)
Jack and Treva Hamlin
David Hanrahan
Ted Haun

# Acknowledgments

Derrick Henry
Mark Hoaglin
Jeff Howe
Margaret and Charles Huddleston
Jill Hughes
George and Mary Hurvey
Shel Izen
Lynette Janssen
Jim Jenkins
Troy Jenkins
Edward and Linda Jennings
Doug Jensen
Everett and Gladys Johnson
 (Blue Spruce Antiques)
Phillis and Ray Johnson
Paul Joyner
Alice Kahn
Patt Hart Keats
Joe Keller
Shirley Keller
Heidi Kellner
Florence and Leo Keopple
Ann Kerr
Thomas Kiehl
Jack and Norma Kinion
 (White River Red's Antiques)
Diane Kirk
Lori Kitchen
Jean Kocmond
Frank and Liz Kramer
Hardy Kristopher
Ruth Kulhanek
Jack Kunberger
Kathy Lange
Lois Lehner
Sandy Levine
Gena Lightle (As Time Goes By)
Ron and Joan Lillquist
Harvey Linn, Jr.
Annette Littman
Juliana Lloyd
Patricia Logan
George and Deanna Longnecker
Mrs. M.J. Lucas
Craig Macaluso
Jack and Norma Majewski
Arlene and Shirley Manning
Grant and Carole Martin
Donna Matherly
Thomas Maybury
 (Maybury's Antiques)
Cathy McCulty
Brad and Diane McHenry

Jim Mederios
Richard and Diane Megyese
Margaret Merryman
Jane Millett
Ronna Miltmore
Mary Mims
Laura and Christopher Monley
John Moses
Hugh Mosher
Donald and Lela Mutch
Fred Mutchler
Larry and Bonnie Newlin
Ida Bonner Newman
Bob Novak
Donna Obwald
Florence and Lyle Ohlendorf
Janet Parks
Judie Perez
Ron Perrick
Jill Peterson
Diane Petipas (Mood Indigo)
Mary Petrone
Leonard Pilch
 (Yesterday's Rainbows)
Stephen Ponder
Lori Pratt
Dave Prichard
 (Gray Barn Photography)
Steven Prickett
David Reardon
Charles and Pam Reed
Jim Rodgers
Charles Roehm
Mark Rumbolo
Frank Sargent
Linda Saridakis
Randy Sauder
Thomas G. Schafer
David Schaefer
Barbara Seimsen
Robert Sell, Jr.
Steve Sfakis
Terry Sfakis
Peter Shalit
Kathleen Shields
Greg and Rose Shinkel
Janet Showers
Bob Shriner (ABC Antiques)
Ronald Sidel
Rick and Joanne Simpson
Sam and Jennifer Skillern
Helen R. Skinner
Sam Smith

Susan Soultanian
Jean Stack
Marlyn Stampados
Dennis Stasiak
Tom and Toni Staugh
George Stecker
Randy Stephens
Joyce and Dan Stevens
William Straus
Ora Strock
Mike Sullivan (As Time Goes By)
Jan Sweet
Lois Szemko
J. Taylor
Tom Taylor
Terry Telford
Les and Brenda Tesch (III)
Gregory Thompson
Lorna Thornton
David Tiedman
Charles Tomlinson
Geri and Dan Tucker
Ernest Tucking
Becky Turner
 (Financial Consultant, HLCCA)
Aural Umhoefer
Kay and Joe Vahey
Bill and Jo Ann Van Voorhies
J. T. Vaughn
Ray Vlach
Joan Vermette
Dr. Geraldine Vest
Vance and Amy Vogeli
Elaine Walls
Lorraine Walker
Charles Walter
Christine Walter
Carole Watkins
Clyde Watson
Harry Weitkemper
Gail Wical
Joy Willems
Donald Williams
Austin and Lucille Wilson
Joel Wilson (China Specialties)
June Wilson
Rod Wilson
Ann Wise
Ronnie and Jean Woods
Michael and Carol Wowk
Catherine Yronwode

## Collector's Clubs and Tradepapers

***The Fiesta Collector's Quarterly Newsletter***
P.O. Box 471
Valley City, OH 44280

Sample copy on request and receipt of long SASE. For collectors of old and new Fiesta. Features regular updates of new colors and items added to the new Fiesta line.

***Homer Laughlin China Collector's Association (HLCCA)***
P.O. Box 721
North Platte, NE 69103-0721
Toll free: 877-874-5222
www.hlcca.org; e-mail: info@hlcca.org

A non-profit 501(c) volunteer organization committed to the education of collectors of all HLCo. product lines. Dues, $25.00 single; $40.00 couple. Includes *The Dish*, a 16-page quarterly magazine published by HLCCA with color photographs, historical information, newly discovered information about various vintage and contemporary HLC lines, and articles from collectors, plus yearly conference and exclusives.

## Sources for New Fiesta

*Saks Dept. Store Group:*
Carson Pirie Scott
Younker's
Bergner's
The Boston Store
Herberger's
Proffitt's
McRae's

*May Dept. Store Group:*
Filene's
Kaufmann's
Hecht's
Strawbridge's
Foley's
Famous-Barr
The Jone Store
L.S. Ayres
Marshall Field's
Robinson's May
Mier & Frank

*Federated Dept. Store Group:*
Macy's East
Macy's West
Rich's/Macy's
Lazarus/Macy's
Goldsmith's/Macy's
Burdine's Macy's
The Bon/M
Macy's.com

*Other Dept. Stores:*
Elder-Beerman
The Bon Ton
Gotchalk's
Beall's
American Home Furnishings

*Other Sources:*
Amazon.com
eBay
Various other Internet sites

# THE LAUGHLIN POTTERY STORY

The Laughlin Pottery was formed in 1871 on the River Road in East Liverpool, Ohio, the result of a partnership between Homer Laughlin and his brother, Shakespeare Laughlin. The pottery was equipped with two periodic kilns and was among the first in the country to produce whitewares. Sixty employees produced approximately 500 dozen pieces of dinnerware per day. The superior quality of their pottery won for them the highest award at the Centennial Exposition in Philadelphia in 1876.

In 1879 Shakespeare Laughlin left the pottery; for the next ten years Homer Laughlin carried on the business alone. William Edwin Wells joined him in 1889, and at the end of 1896 the firm incorporated. Shortly thereafter, Laughlin sold his interests to Wells and a Pittsburgh group headed by Marcus Aaron.

Under the new management, Mr. Aaron became president, with Mr. Wells acting in the capacity of secretary-treasurer and general manager.

As their business grew and sales increased, the small River Road plant was abandoned, and the company moved its location to Laughlin Station, three miles east of East Liverpool. Two large new plants were constructed and a third purchased from another company. By 1903 all were ready for production. A fourth plant was built in 1906 at the Newell, West Virginia, site and began operations in 1907. In 1913 with business still increasing, Plant 5 was added.

The first revolutionary innovation in the pottery industry was the continuous tunnel kiln. In contrast to the old batch-type or periodic kilns which were inefficient from a standpoint of both fuel and time, the continuous tunnel kiln provided a giant step toward modern-day mass production. Plant 6, built in 1923, was equipped with this new type kiln and proved so successful that two more such plants were added — Plant 7 in 1927 and Plant 8 in 1929. The old kilns in Plants 4 and 5 were replaced in 1926 and 1934, respectively.

In 1929 the old East Liverpool factories were closed, leaving the entire operation at the Newell, West Virginia, site.

At the height of production, the company grew to a giant concern which employed 2,500 people, produced 30,000 dozen pieces of dinnerware per day, and utilized 1,500,000 square feet of production area. In contrast to the early wares painstakingly hand fashioned in the traditional methods, the style of ware reflected the improved mass-production techniques which had of necessity been utilized in later years. The old-fashioned dipping tubs gave way to the use of high-speed conveyor belts and spray glazing, and mechanical jiggering machines replaced for the most part the older methods of man-powered molding machines.

In 1930 W.E. Wells retired from the business after more than forty years of brilliant leadership, having guided the development and expansion of the company from its humble beginning on the Ohio River to a position of unquestioned leadership in its field. He was succeeded by his son, Joseph Mahan Wells. Mr. Aaron became chairman of the board; his son, M.L. Aaron, succeeded him as president. Under their leadership, in addition to the successful wares already in production, many new developments made possible the production of a wide variety of utilitarian wares including the oven-to-table ware, OvenServe, and Kitchen Kraft. Later, the creation of the beautiful glazes that have become almost synonymous with Homer Laughlin resulted in the production of the colored dinnerware lines which have captured the attention of many collectors today — Fiesta, Harlequin, and Riviera.

On January 1, 1960, Joseph M. Wells became chairman of the board, and his son, Joseph M. Wells, Jr., followed him in the capacity of executive vice president.

Homer Laughlin continues today to be one of the principal dinnerware producers in the world.

# THE STORY OF FIESTA

In January of 1936, Homer Laughlin introduced a sensational new line of dinnerware at the Pottery and Glass Show in Pittsburgh. It was Fiesta, and it instantly captured the imagination of the trade — a forecast of the success it was to achieve with housewives of America.

Fiesta was designed by Fredrick Rhead, an English Stoke-on-Trent potter whose work had for decades been regarded among the finest in the industry. His design was modeled by Arthur Kraft and Bill Bersford. The distinctive glazes were developed by Dr. A.V. Blenininger in association with H. W. Thiemecke.

This popularity was the result of much planning, market analysis, creative development, and a fundamentally sound and well-organized styling program. Rather than present to the everyday housewife a modernistic interpretation of a formal table service which might have been received with some reservation, HLC offered a more casual line with a well-planned series of accessories whose style was compatible with any decor and whose vivid colors could add bright spots of emphasis. Services of all types could be chosen and assembled at the whim of the housewife, and the simple style could be used compatibly with other wares already in her cabinets.

In an article by Fredrick Rhead taken from the *Pottery and Glass Journal* for June 1937, these steps toward Fiesta's development were noted: first, from oral descriptions and data concerning most generally used table articles, a chart of tentative sketches in various appealing colors was made. As the final ideas were formulated, they were modified and adjusted until development was completed. Secondly, the technical department made an intensive study of materials, composition, and firing temperatures. During this time, models and shapes were being studied. The result was to be a streamline shape, but not so obvious as to detract from the texture and color of the ware. It was to have no relief ornamentation and was to be pleasantly curving and convex, rather than concave and angular. Color was to be the chief decorative note; but to avoid being too severe, a concentric band of rings was to be added near the edges.

Since the early '30s, there had been a very definite trend in merchandising toward promoting color. Automobiles, household appliances and furnishings, ladies' apparel — all took on vivid hues. The following is an excerpt from Rhead's article:

**THE HOMER LAUGHLIN CHINA COMPANY**

*Extends to Buyers a cordial invitation to inspect the famous Homer Laughlin Line and to view for the first time our attractive Shapes and Patterns for 1936*

Including "Fiesta", a Revolutionary New Line of Pottery in Solid Colors.

❧

**ANNUAL POTTERY and GLASS EXHIBIT**

PITTSBURGH,    PA.
JANUARY 9th to 17th
WM. PENN HOTEL          SUITE 735

❧

THE  HOMER  LAUGHLIN  CHINA  COMPANY
Newell,                      West Virginia

Pacific Coast Representative—M. Seller Co., San Francisco, Calif.
Chicago Office—Room 15-104 Merchandise Mart.

Full page invitation in Jan., 1936 *China, Glass and Lamps* magazine, introducing buyers to "Fiesta – a Revolutionary New Line of Pottery in Solid Colors." Photo courtesy David Schaefer.

> The final selection of five colors was a more difficult job because we had developed hundreds of tone values and hues, and there were scores which were difficult to reject. Then there were textures ranging from dull mattes to highly reflecting surfaces. We tackled the texture problem first. (Incidentally, we had made fair-sized skeletons in each of the desirable glazes in order to be better able to arrive at the final selection.)

We eliminated the dull mattes and the more highly reflecting glazes first, because in mass production practice, undue variation would result in unpleasant effects. The dull surfaces are not easy to clean, and the too highly reflecting surfaces show "curtains" or variations in thickness of application. We decided upon a semi-reflecting surface of about the texture of a billiard ball. The surface was soft and pleasant to the touch, and in average light there were no disturbing reflections to detract from the color and shape.

We had one lead with regard to color. There seemed to be a trade preference for a brilliant orange-red. With this color as a keynote and with the knowledge that we were to have five colors, the problem resolved to one where the remainder would "tune in" or form appropriate contrasts.

The obvious reaction to red, we thought, would be toward a fairly deep blue. We had blues ranging from pale turquoises to deep violet blues. The tests were made by arranging a table for four people; and, as the plate is an important item in the set, we placed four plates on various colored cloths and then arranged the different blues around the table. It seemed that the deeper blues reacted better than the lighter tones and blues which were slightly violet or purple. We also found that we had to do considerable switching before we could decide upon the right red. Some were too harsh and deep, others too yellow.

With the red and blue apparently settled, we decided that a green must be one of the five colors. We speedily discovered that the correct balance between the blue and the red was a green possessing a minimum of blue. We had to hit halfway between the red and the blue. We had some lovely subtle greens when they were not placed in juxtaposition with the other two colors, but they would not play in combination.

The next obvious color was yellow, and this had to be toned halfway between the red and the green. Only the most brilliant yellow we could make would talk in company with the other three.

The fifth color was the hardest nut to crack. Black was too heavy, although this may have been used if we could have had six or more colors. We had no browns, purples, or grays which would tune in. We eliminated all except two colors: a rich turquoise and a lovely color we called rose ebony. But there seemed to demand a quieting influence; so we tried an ivory vellum textured glaze which seemed to fit halfway between the yellow and the regular semi-vitreous wares and which cliqued when placed against any of the four colors selected. It took a little time to sell the ivory to our sales organization; but when they saw the table arrangements, they accepted the idea.

In the same publication a month earlier, Rhead had offered this evaluation of the popularity of the various colors with the public:

When this ware first appeared on the market, we attempted to estimate the preference for one color in comparison with the others. As you know, we make five colors ... Because the red was the most expensive color, we thought this might affect the demand. And also, because green had previously been a most popular color, some guessed that this would outsell the others. However, to date, the first four colors are running neck and neck, with less than one percent difference between them. This is a remarkable result and amply bears out...that the "layman" prefers to mix his colors.

Company price lists have always been our main source of information. Over the years as more and more have been found, we have been able to pinpoint important production changes more accurately. Lists found as recently as this decade have clarified some misconceptions that resulted simply from not having them available for our original study. Our earliest is dated May 15, 1937; it lists fifty-four items. An article in the August 1936 issue of *China, Glass, and Lamps* reported new developments in the line since it had been introduced in January:

> New items in the famous Fiesta line of solid-color dinnerware include egg cups; deep 8" plates; Tom and Jerry mugs; covered casseroles; covered mustards; covered marmalades; quart jugs; utility trays; flower vases in 8", 10", and 12" sizes; and bowl covers in 5", 6", 7", and 8" sizes.

By the process of elimination, then, in trying to determine the items original to the line, these must be subtracted from those on our May '37 price list. A collector who has compiled the most complete assortment of company price lists that we are aware of tells us that the 10-ounce tumbler, the 6-cup (medium) teapot, and the 10½" compartment plate that are listed on our May '37 pamphlet were not yet listed on the fall 1936 issue which he has in his collection; so these would also have to be eliminated. These items remain, and until further information proves us wrong, we assume that they comprised the original assortment: coffeepot, regular; teapot, large; coffeepot, A.D.; carafe; ice pitcher; covered sugar bowl; stock-handled creamer; plate, 10"; plate, 9"; plate, 7"; plate, 6"; compartment plate, 12"; teacup and saucer; coffee cup and saucer, A.D.; footed salad bowl; nested bowls, 11½" to 5"; cream soup cup; covered onion soup; relish tray; compote, 12"; nappy, 9½"; nappy, 8½"; dessert, 6"; fruit, 5"; ashtray; sweets compote; bulb-type candleholders; tripod candleholders; and salt and pepper shakers.

Adding to the selling possibilities of Fiesta, in June 1936 the company offered their Harmony dinnerware sets. These combined their Nautilus line decorated with a colorful decal pattern, accented and augmented with the Fiesta color selected for that particular set. N-258 featured yellow Fiesta accenting Nautilus in white decorated with a harmonizing floral decal at the rim; N-259 used green Fiesta to complement a slender spray of pine cones. Red Fiesta, in N-260, was shown in company catalogs with Nautilus decorated with lines and leaves in an Art Deco motif (see Kitchen Kraft, OvenServe for matching kitchenware items); and blue (N-261) went well with white Nautilus with an off-center flower-filled basket decal. These sets were composed of sixty-seven pieces in all. Of the Nautilus shape there were 9" plates (eight), 6" plates (eight), teacups and saucers (eight), 5½" fruits (eight), a 10" baker,

*Homer Laughlin China Ad.* Feb. 1936, from *China, Glass and Lamps* magazine. Photo courtesy David Schaefer.

and a 9" nappy. Fiesta items included 10" plates (eight), 7" plates (eight), 6" plates (eight), a 15" chop plate, a 12" compote, one pair of bulb-type candlesticks, a pair of salt and pepper shakers, and a creamer and sugar bowl. Retail price for such a set was around $20.00. This offered a complete service for eight and extra pieces that allowed for buffet and party service for as many more in the contrasting items.

For some time during the earlier years of production, beautifully accessorized "Fiesta Ensembles" were assembled — you will see a picture of a display ad showing such a set in the color plates. It contains 109 pieces, only forty of which are Fiesta: 9" plates (eight), 6" plates (eight), teacups and saucers (eight), and 5" fruits (eight). Accessories included a 24-piece glassware set with enameled Mexican motifs. There were eight of each of the following: 10-oz., 8-oz., and 6-oz. tumblers; color-coordinated swizzle sticks; and glass ashtrays. A flatware service for eight with color-coordinated Catalin handles, a red Riviera serving bowl, a 15½" red Riviera platter, and a sugar and creamer in green Riviera completed the set. The flatware and glassware in these ensembles were manufactured by other companies and merely shipped to HLC to be distributed with the ensemble. Records fail to identify the company that may have manufactured these complementary accessories. Included in the packing carton was a promotional poster advertising this set for $14.95.

Originally all five colors sold at the same price; bud vases and salt and pepper shakers were priced in pairs. But on the May '37 price list, red items were higher than the other colors. For example, a red 12" flower vase was priced at $2.35; in the other colors it was only $1.85. A red onion soup was $1.00, 25¢ higher than the others. New to the assortment at that time were the three items mentioned earlier — the 6-cup (medium) teapot, the 10½" compartment plate, and the 10-ounce tumbler. Bud vases and salt and pepper shakers were priced singularly.

A few years ago a mid-1937 price list told us that the sixth color, turquoise, was added then and not in early 1938 as we had previously reported. There is a 5" fruit on the May list; however, by mid-1937 the listing shows a 5½" and 4¾" fruit. Possibly the 5" and the 5½" are the same size fruit, with the so-called 5" listed actual size in mid-1937 due to the addition of the 4¾" size. (In comparing actual measurements to listed measurements, we have found variations of as much as ¾".) At this point, the first item had been discontinued; the 12" compartment plate was no longer available. The covered onion soup (evidently much more popular with today's collectors than it was then) was the second item to be dropped; by late that year it, too, was out of production. Two new items were added in the fall of 1937: the sauce boat and the 11½" low fruit bowl. The assortment remained the same until the following July when the disk water jug and the 12" oval platter made their first appearance on company listings. No further changes were made until October 1939, when the stick-handled creamer was replaced by the creamer with the ring handle.

From 1939 through 1943, the company was involved in a major promotional campaign designed to stimulate sales. This involved several special items or sets, each of which was offered for sale at the price of 75¢ to $1.00. An ad from the February 1940 *China, Glass, and Lamps* magazine provides us with the information concerning the campaign.

> ...dollar retailers in Fiesta ware include covered French casserole; four-piece refrigerator set; sugar, creamer, and tray set; salad bowl with fork and spoon set; kitchen set; casserole with pie plate; chop plate with detachable metal holder; and jumbo coffee cups and saucers in blue, pink, and yellow.

But it also presents us with a puzzling question: what were the jumbo coffee cups and saucers? Sit 'n Sips perhaps? (See "Commercial Adaptations and Ephemera.") The colors mentioned, though dark blue and yellow were in production in 1940, sound pastel with the inclusion of pink. Anyone have an answer? We don't!

Another item featured in the selling campaign is described in this message from HLC to their distributors:

JUICE SET IN FIESTA . . . To help increase your sales! Homer Laughlin is offering an unusual value in the famous Fiesta ware . . . a colorful, 7-piece Juice Set, calculated to fill a real need in the summer refreshment field. The set consists of a 30-ounce disk jug in lovely Fiesta yellow, and six 5-ounce tumblers, one each in Fiesta blue, turquoise, red, green, yellow, and ivory. Sets come packed one to a carton, and at the one dollar minimum retail price are sure to create an upward surge in your sales curve. Dealers who take advantage of this Juice Set in Fiesta will find it a potent weapon in increasing sales of other Fiesta items. At a nominal price, customers who have not yet become acquainted with Fiesta can own some of the ware which has made pottery history during the past few years. The result? They'll want to own more!

Although the other promotional items are relatively scarce, the yellow juice pitcher is very easily found. This flyer is the only mention of it being for sale during this period; neither it nor the juice tumblers were ever included on Fiesta price lists. A few pitchers have been found in red, and only recently has evidence surfaced to explain that at least some of them were special ordered by the Reliable Tea Company, who offered the juice sets (red pitcher and six assorted juice tumblers) as premiums to their customers during the '40s. In 1952 the promotion was repeated — the juice pitcher in gray, the tumblers in dark green, chartreuse, and Harlequin yellow. Either this issue was not extensively promoted or proved to be a poor seller, judging from their scarcity in these colors. Juice tumblers in rose are not at all rare, yet they were not mentioned in this color in any of these promotions. A factory spokesman explained this to us: while rose was not a standard Fiesta color until the '50s, it had been developed and was in use with the Harlequin line during the '40s. Since it was available in the dipping department, it was used to add extra color contrast to the juice set.

The French casserole, individual sugar and creamer on the figure-8 tray, and the 9½" salad bowl were also never listed except in this promotion. Each is standard in a specific color; on rare occurrences when they are found in non-standard glazes, their values soar! (See Suggested Values in the back of the book.) French casseroles were all to have been yellow; however, two dark blue bases and two complete casseroles have been reported, and a lid and base have been found in light green. Before the fifth edition was published, we received a letter telling us that an ivory one existed, and since then the owners have written to us to verify its existence. Yellow was also standard for the 9½" salad bowl, but a very few rare examples have surfaced in dark blue, red, ivory, and light green. The individual sugar and creamer in the *China, Glass, and Lamps* ad

*Homer Laughlin China ad.* May 1939. Photo courtesy David Schaefer.

were described as both being yellow on a cobalt figure-8 tray, but in a jobber's catalog dated spring 1940 that was discovered since the eighth edition, this set is described as containing a red creamer, a yellow sugar bowl, and a cobalt tray. This explains the few red creamers that have been found over the years. One sugar and at least two creamers have been found in turquoise, a cobalt creamer has been reported, and trays in yellow and turquoise exist as well, but these are very rare.

One of the most exciting discoveries of this decade is the three-piece Fiesta Kitchenware Set referred to in the promotions as "casserole with pie plate." See the Fiesta color plates for a look at this exciting set photographed with its original carton. We're sure it's authentic, since it was originally found in the unopened carton in exactly the colors described in the ad: casserole body — green, casserole cover — red, 9½" plate — yellow.

Other items that have never been included on any known price list are the syrup pitcher and the very rare flat 10" cake plate. It was only recently that we found a list containing the four smaller sizes of the nested bowl lids that were mentioned in Rhead's article. A butter dish was never listed with Fiesta, but the consensus of opinion after so many years of collecting is that the Jade Riviera butter dish (see Plate 251 for more information) was dipped to go with the Fiesta line as well, since it may be found in cobalt and ivory, both standard colors in only one of HLC's lines, Fiesta.

More changes occurred in the fall of 1942. Items discontinued at that time included the tripod candleholders, the A.D. coffeepot, and both the 10" and 12" flower vases.

In 1943 our government assumed control of uranium oxide, an important element used in the manufacture of the Fiesta red glaze. As a result, it was dropped from production — "Fiesta red went to war." Perhaps the fact that Fiesta red had been listed separately and priced proportionately higher than the other colors was due to the higher cost of raw material plus the fact that the red items required strict control during firing; losses that did occur had to be absorbed in the final costs.

The color assortment in 1944 included turquoise, green, blue, yellow, and ivory. The nested bowls, no longer were listed. The rate of price increases over the seven years Fiesta had been on the market is hard for us to imagine: ashtrays were still only 15¢, egg cups were up to 35¢ from 30¢, relish trays were up only 15¢ to $1.80 complete.

Although the colors are listed the same on the 1946 price list, the following pieces were discontinued: bud vase, bulb-type candleholders, carafe, 12" compote, sweets compote, 8" vase, 11½" fruit bowl, ice pitcher, marmalade and mustard, 9½" nappy, relish tray, footed salad bowl, large teapot, 10-ounce tumbler, and utility tray.

A price list from November 5, 1950, helps us pinpoint the time of the radical color change that had taken place by October of 1951. Though the 1950 price list still offered the original colors, by fall of 1951 light green, dark blue, and old ivory had been retired; their replacements were forest green, rose, chartreuse, and gray. Turquoise and yellow continued to be produced. These four new colors have been dubbed "'50s colors," since they and the listed assortment remained in production without change until the end of the decade.

Prices listed in 1956, twenty years after Fiesta was introduced, were higher, of course; but still the increase is so slight as to be quite noteworthy to us in the twenty-first century. Ashtrays sold for 40¢, teacups that were 25¢ were up to 65¢. Dinner plates had little more than doubled at 90¢, and coffeepots sold for $2.65. They, too, had about doubled in price.

The big news in 1959 was, of course, the fact that Fiesta red was reinstated. It was welcomed back with much ado! The Atomic Energy Commission licensed the Homer Laughlin China Company to again buy the depleted uranium oxide, and Fiesta red returned to the market in March of 1959.

In addition to red, turquoise, and yellow, a new color — medium green — was offered. Rose, gray, chartreuse, and dark green were discontinued; and the following items were no longer available: 15" chop plate, A.D. coffee cup and saucer, regular coffeepot, 10½" compartment plate, cream soup cup, egg cup, 4¾" fruit bowl, and 2-pint jug. A new item made an appearance — the individual salad bowl.

By 1961 the 6" dessert bowl was no longer listed. Aside from that change, the line and the color assortment remained the same. Though retail prices had risen in 1965, by 1968 some items stayed the same while others actually dropped slightly.

In the latter months of 1969 in an effort to meet the needs of the modern housewife and to present a product that was better designed to be in keeping with modern day decor, Fiesta was restyled. Only one of the original colors, Fiesta red — always the favorite — continued in production (see chapter on Fiesta Ironstone).

The big news of 1986 was the exciting new line of Fiesta ware that was introduced in the spring. How better to celebrate its fiftieth birthday! We'll tell you all about it in one of the following chapters.

# THE RADIOACTIVE RED

Exactly when the first rumors began circulating, hinting that the red Fiesta could be hazardous to your health, is uncertain. In most probability, it was around the time that Fiesta red was reintroduced after the war and was no doubt due to the publicity given to uranium and radioactivity during the war years. Clearly another case where "a little learning can be a dangerous thing."

In any case, this worry must have remained to trouble the minds of some people for several years. Even today the subject comes up occasionally and remains a little controversial, though most folks in this troubled age of acid rains, high unemployment, cholesterol-free diets, and constant reminders that "cigarettes are hazardous to your health" don't really seem too upset by it anymore.

The following letter appeared in the *Palm Beach Post Times* in February 1963. It was written tongue-in-cheek by a man who had evidently reached the limit of his patience. HLC sent it to us from their files; it has to be a classic.

> Editor:
>
> After reading about the radioactive dishes in your paper, I am greatly concerned that I may be in danger, as I had a plate with a design in burnt orange, or maybe it was lemon.
>
> This plate was left to me by my great-grandmother, and I noticed that whenever she ate anything from it, her ears would light up; so we all had to wear dark glasses when dining at her house.
>
> I first became suspicious of this dish when putting out food for my dog on it I noticed the dog's nose became as red as Rudolph's; and one day a sea gull fed from it, and all his feathers fell off; then one night when the weather was raw I placed it at the foot of my bed, and my toenails turned black.
>
> Using it as a pot cover while cooking eel stew, the pot cracked; and reading the letters in your paper last week have concluded I am not the only person having a cracked pot in the house; so perhaps some of your other readers used a plate for a cover.
>
> I finally threw this plate overboard at a turn in the channel, now a buoy is no longer needed there, as bubbles and steam mark this shoal.
>
> Will you please ask your Doctor or someone if they think this plate is radioactive, and if so am I in any danger, and if so from what?
>
> (Name Withheld)

Several years ago we were allowed the opportunity to search through old company literature in the event that some bit of pertinent information had escaped our notice. It was obvious from letters contained in these files that HLC had always been harassed with letters from people concerned with the uranium content of the Fiesta red glaze. Their replies were polite, accommodating, and enlightening. Here in part is one of their letters:

> Before 1943 the colorant (14% by weight of the glaze covering the ware) is uranium oxide (U-308), with the uranium content being made up of about 0.7% U-235 and the remainder U-238. Between 1943 and 1959 under license by AEC, we have again been producing a red glazed dinnerware. However the colorant now used is depleted technical grade U-308 with the uranium content being made up of about 0.2% U-235 and the remainder U-238.

Studies were conducted for us by Dr. Paul L. Ziemer and Dr. Geraldine Deputy (who is herself an avid Fiesta collector) in the Bionuclionics Department of Purdue University. The penetrating radiation from the uranium oxide used in the manufacturing of the glaze for the red Fiesta ware was measured with a standard laboratory Geiger Counter. All measurements are tabularized in units of milliroentgens per hour (mR/hr).

| Item | Surface Contract | 4" Above Surface | Along Rim |
|---|---|---|---|
| 13" Chop Plate | 0.8 | 0.35 | 0.1 |
| 9" Plate | 0.5 | 1.5 | 0.07 |
| Fruit Bowl | 1.5 | 0.5 | 0.1 |
| Relish Tray Wedge | 0.8 | 0.2 | 0.02 |
| Cup | 1.3 | 0.2 | 0.03 |

In order to compare the above values to familiar quantities of radiation, we calculated the exposure of a person holding a 13" chop plate strapped to his chest for twenty-four hours. This gives 20 milliroentgens per day. Safe levels for humans working with radiation is 100 milliroentgens per week for a five-day week or 20 milliroentgens per day as background radiation.

Some other measurements of interest for comparison purposes are:

| Item | Radiation |
|---|---|
| Radium Dial on a Watch | 20mR/hr |
| Chest X-Ray | 44 mR per film |
| Dental X-Ray | 910 mR per film |
| Fatal Dose | 400,000 mR over whole body |

Back in May of 1977 on an eastern television station, an announcement was made concerning the pros and cons of the safety of colored-glazed dinnerware. Fiesta was mentioned by name. We contacted the Department of Health, Education, and Welfare, FDA, in Chicago, Illinois. This in part is their position, and it is supported by HLC:

> The presence of lead, cadmium, and other toxic metal in glaze or decal is not in itself a hazard. It becomes a problem only when a glaze or decal that has not been properly formulated, applied, or fired, contains dangerous metals which can be released by high-acid foods such as fruit juices, some soft drinks, wines, cider, vinegar, and vinegar-containing foods, sauerkraut, and tomato products.

The FDA report continues:

> Be on the safe side by not storing foods or beverages in such containers for prolonged periods of time, such as overnight. Daily use of the dinnerware for serving food does not pose a hazard. If the glaze or decal is properly formulated, properly applied, and properly fired, there is no hazard.

Note: Testing is ongoing on vintage dinnerware, and some scientists believe the threat of lead, cadmium, uranium, and other metals leaching out of the glazes is enough to cause concern. They especially warn against putting it in the microwave, since this may accelerate the process.

# IDENTIFICATION OF TRADEMARK, DESIGN, AND COLOR

Fiesta's original design, colors, and name are the registered property of the Homer Laughlin China Company. Patent No. 390-298 was filed on March 20, 1937, having been used by them since November 11, 1935. These four seem to be the most common.

Photo courtesy David Schaefer.

The indented trademark (the first three illustrated above) was the result of in-mold casting; the ink mark (on the far left) was put on with a hand stamp after the color was applied and before the final glaze was fired.

As many other manufacturers were following the trend to toward brightly colored dinnerware, the wide success and popularity of the Fiesta ware line resulted in its being closely copied and produced early on by another company. Homer Laughlin quickly brought suit against its competitor and forced the imitation ware to be discontinued. To assure buyers they could buy with complete confidence, "Genuine" was added to the ink hand stamp sometime before 1940. See the sweets comport below for an example of the ink stamp before the word "Genuine" was added.

There are some items in the Fiesta line which were never meant to be marked — juice tumblers, demitasse cups, salt and pepper shakers, teacups, and some of the Kitchen Kraft line (though a rare few have been found with the ink stamp). Sweets comports, egg cups, ashtrays, and onion soups may or may not be marked, and many plates that are normally stamped by hand carry no mark either. Never pass up an unmarked item if you can verify that it is genuine Fiesta. As you become more aware of design and color, you will be able to recognize it quite easily.

Fiesta's design is very simple and therefore very versatile. The pattern consists of a band of concentric rings graduating in width, with those nearer the rim being more widely spaced. The rings are repeated in the center motif on such pieces as plates, nappies, platters, and desserts. Handles are applied with slight ornamentation at the base. Vases and tripod candleholders, though designed without the rings, are skillfully modeled with simple lines, geometric forms, and stepped devices that instantly relate to the Art Deco mood of Fiesta's clean, uncluttered shapes. Flat pieces and bowls are round or oval; hollow ware pieces are globular, and many are styled with a short pedestal base decorated with the band of rings.

But, of course, it's Fiesta's vivid colors that first capture your attention. The wide array of color provides endless possibilities for matching color schemes and decor. And if you find you love all eleven, you'll surely enjoy collecting a place setting in every color — Fiesta red, yellow, rose, old ivory, gray, dark blue, turquoise, forest green, light green, medium green, and chartreuse.

*Example of sweets comport with the HLCo USA ink stamp.* Photo courtesy Philip Gray.

# DATING CODES AND ENGLISH MEASUREMENTS

Many HLC lines often carry a backstamp containing a series of letters and numbers. The company has provided this information to help you in deciphering these codes:

---

In 1900 the trademark featured a single numeral identifying the month, a second single numeral identifying the year, and a numeral 1, 2, or 3 designating the point of manufacture as East Liverpool, Ohio.

In the period 1910 – 1920, the first figure indicated the month of the year, the next two numbers indicated the year, and the third figure designated the plant. No. 4 was "N," No. 5 was "N5," and the East End plant was "L."

A change was made for the period of 1921 – 1930. The first letter was used to indicate the month of the year such as "A" for January, "B" for February, "C" for March. The next single digit number was used to indicate the year, and the last figure designated the plant.

For the period 1931 – 1940, the month was expressed as a letter; but the year was indicated with two digits. Plant No. 4 was "N," No. 5 was "R," No. 6 and 7 were "C," and No. 8 was listed as "P." During this period, E-44R5 would indicate May of 1944 and manufactured by Plant No. 5. The current trademark has been in use for more than seventy years, and the numbers are the only indication of the specific years that items were produced.

---

Collectors have long been puzzled over the origin and meaning of such terms as oval "baker" and "36s bowl" — not to mention the insistent listings of 4" plates, when it has become very apparent that 4" plates do not exist! We asked our contact at HLC for an explanation. He told us that each size bowl was assigned a number. Smaller numbers indicated larger bowls, and vice versa. The word "baker" as used to describe a serving bowl was an English potting term. It was also the English who established the unfortunate system of measurements based on some rather obscure logic by which a 6" plate should be listed as 4". The 7" "nappies" (also an English term) actually measure 8¾"; 4" fruits are usually 5½"; and 6", 7", and 8" plates are in reality 7", 9", and 10".

This practice continued through the '50s (though more in connection with other HLC lines than Fiesta) until it became so utterly confusing to everyone involved that actual measurements were thankfully adopted. However, these may vary as much as ¾" from measurements listed on company brochures. For instance, 9" and 10" plates actually measure 9½" and 10½", and the 13" and 15" chop plates are 12¼" and 14¼".

The small incised letters and/or numbers sometimes found on the bottom of hollow ware pieces were used to identify a pieceworker — perhaps a molder or a trimmer — and were intended for quality control purposes. More likely to appear on Harlequin, these are sometimes seen on Fiesta as well.

# FREDRICK HURTEN RHEAD

The Rhead family was prominent among the finest ceramists of nineteenth-century England. Fredrick Hurten Rhead came from a long line of English Stoke-on-Trent potters and must without doubt be considered one of the most productive artisans in the history of the industry. At the age of 19, he was named art director at the Wardel Pottery. After leaving his home in Staffordshire in 1902, he worked at the Vance/Avon Faience Co. in Tiltonville, Ohio, for a term of about six months before moving on to the Weller Pottery in Zanesville, Ohio. By 1904 he was awarded the position of art director at the nearby Roseville Pottery. The many lines of artware he produced for these companies earned him widespread recognition. Inspired by nature and influenced by both Art Nouveau and the Arts and Crafts Movement, he became well known for dramatic sgraffito work, which he executed in intricate detail. An element he often favored was a stylized tree, variations of which he used frequently throughout his career. In later years, he designed a set of nested mixing bowls for Homer Laughlin; they were decorated with embossed trees reminiscent of his earlier work.

Leaving Roseville in 1908, he went to the William Jervis Pottery on Long Island. In 1909 he accepted the post of instructor in pottery at the University City Pottery in St. Louis. From 1911 to 1913 he was associated with the Arequipa Pottery in Fairfax, California. There, with the assistance of his wife, Agnes, he taught ceramics to patients at the Arequipa Sanatorium. Leaving Arequipa, he organized the Pottery of the Camarata in Santa Barbara, later to be incorporated as The Rhead Pottery. Never a confident thrower, Rhead involved himself fully with developing new glazes. One of his finest achievements was Mirror Black, a re-creation of the sixteenth-century black-glazed pottery of the Orient, which earned him a Gold Medal at the 1915 San Diego Exposition.

In December of 1916, Rhead published *The Potter*, a monthly magazine dealing with the progress of the industry. The editor of the historical department was Edwin A. Barber, whose death was reported in the third issue (February 1917). With that, the paper was abandoned.

Freed of the pressures he had felt at the commercial potteries in Ohio, Rhead utilized this time to develop his creative capabilities to their fullest, but as a business man he was unable to keep his pottery afloat. He

encountered financial difficulties, and his pottery failed. Returning to Zanesville in 1917, he joined the American Encaustic Tiling Company. Loiz Whitcomb, a fellow artisan from his California pottery (with whom he had fallen in love after his first marriage was annulled), came back to the Midwest to join him; they soon married. Rhead served at AE Tile as director of research. In 1927 he moved to the Homer Laughlin Company where he designed his famous dinnerware line, Fiesta. He remained there until his death in 1942. No other ceramic artist made more of an impact on this country's pottery industry. From the early days of his career to the last, Rhead's work evolved effortlessly, leaving behind a legacy still enjoyed by thousands today.

Shown are examples of only two of the lines Rhead developed for Roseville and Weller, Della Robbia on the left, and Jap Birdimal above.

**Plate 1**

*Ashtray.*

Shown here in dark green, these were made from 1936 until the Fiesta Ironstone line was discontinued in 1973, and they can be found in all of the old colors plus the Turf Green and Antique Gold of Ironstone. They measure 5½" in diameter.

**Plate 2**

*Covered Onion Soup Bowl (left foreground).*

Imagine a lifestyle that required a soup bowl with a lid! Just one of the little amenities that have gone by the wayside since "stay-at-home" moms went to work. They're very scarce today, so even back in the more formal '30s they probably were never good sellers. They're found in ivory, red, light green (shown), dark blue, turquoise, and yellow. (See an example of each in Plate 3.) Since they were discontinued by fall of 1937, only a few weeks after turquoise was added to the color assortment (mid-1937), they're very scarce in that color. Across the handles, they measure 6" (quite a bit larger than the sugar bottom that new collectors tend to confuse them with.) (See Plate 103 for a cream soup bowl in ivory with a red-stripe decoration.) *Dessert Bowl (upper left).* This was also in the original line. Shown here in dark blue, these were produced in 1961 in all colors, but they are scarce in medium green. Note that unlike the fruit bowls in this picture, there is no flat rim flange. It's rather shallow with vertical sides, and 6" in diameter. *Individual Salad Bowl (center back).* A later addition, these were not produced until 1959 and were, of course,

only made in the colors of that period — red, turquoise, yellow, and medium green. They're easier to find in red and medium green; nevertheless expect to pay a premium for medium green, regarded by collectors as Fiesta's most desirable color. Occasionally you may find one with no rings in the bottom, probably produced toward the transition into Fiesta Ironstone when such modifications were finalized. Collectors are also reporting bowls in all four colors as well as the brighter Harlequin yellow with no inside rings at all. *Fruit Bowl, 5½" (upper right).* Probably the bowl listed as 5" in the original assortment, this item was made until the restyling in 1969 and is available in all eleven colors. One example has been reported in the blue of the Skytone line and you will see one in Plate 512 in a glaze its owner likes to call "mystery green" in the Experimentals chapter. *Fruit Bowl, 4¾" (right foreground).* This was probably the bowl that was added to the assortment in mid-1937. We have price lists that are dated 1956 and 1959; they show it as still available in 1956, but it does not appear on the price list for 1959 when medium green was introduced, and only a few have been found in that color. It's rather scarce in red as well; here you see it in the rose of the '50s assortment.

**Plate 3**
*Onion Soup Bowls.*
This is the complete color assortment of the covered onion soup bowl. Some are unmarked; others are marked "Fiesta" in the mold. The marked ones were produced first. They have the same flat surface inside that you see in the cups in Plate 30 and the sugar bowl in Plate 60. These bowls were revised early in 1936 with modifications that allowed them to be made in one piece, and therefore less expensive to manufacture. Bowls made after the revision were not marked, and the inside well was no longer flat in the bottom but rounded and bowl-like. The lid was also modified; the earlier lid has a vertical flange about ⅜" in length. The flange on the later version measures about ⅛". Turquoise onion soup bowls are hard to find, since that color wasn't introduced until mid-1937, only a few months before these bowls were dropped from production. Mysteriously, collectors report finding a turquoise example now and then with the indented mark — evidently stockpiled greenware was pulled from the shelf and dipped in the newly introduced color.

**Plate 4**
*Onion Soup Bowls.*
Alongside the standard onion soup bowl is a one-of-a-kind example of what is probably the first model. It was replaced less than a year later by the one more familiar to us. Shown here in light green, it differs from the regular version in several ways: note that the handles are flat rather than rolled under, the bowl flares at the rim above the handles, and the foot is wider and shorter. The lid is less rounded and ½" wider. It's marked "Fiesta HLC" in the mold, and it's the only example of its kind to have ever surfaced; it was never put in mass production.

**Plate 5**
*Cream Soup Bowl.*
These were part of the original line and continued to be made until sometime in 1959. They're found in all colors but are extremely rare in medium green, the newcomer to the color assortment that year. So rare, in fact, that many otherwise complete collections are missing the medium green soup bowl. (One is shown in Plate 68.)

**Plate 6**
*Mixing Bowls.*
Stacked together, a set of seven weighs just about twenty pounds. These bowls were made in only the original six colors, since they were just in production from 1936 until around 1943. Each bowl is numbered in sequence on the bottom: #1 being the smallest at 5"; #2, 6"; #3, 7"; #4, 8"; #5, 9"; #6, 10"; and #7, 11½". An ad dated December 1938 indicated that as a Christmas season promotion, for $2.50 you could purchase a Rainbow Mixing Bowl Set — a four-piece assortment that contained a yellow 7", a green 8", a dark blue 9", and a red 10". Collectors tell us that the #7 (11½") bowl is difficult to find, perhaps because it wasn't included in this promotion, or simply because fewer sold, since its size likely made it unwieldy to use. The #1 (5") bowl is also scarce, and that might also be contributed to size. It might have been just right for storing leftovers, but as a mixing bowl, it would be very small! The only bowl lids ever officially offered on a company price list were the four smaller sizes, 5", 6", 7", and 8". Although the list we refer to is undated, we can place it after August 1936 (our price list bearing that date makes no mention of them — though Rhead's August 1936 *China Glass, and Lamps* article did) and before mid-1937 (because turquoise was not yet being offered on the list in question).

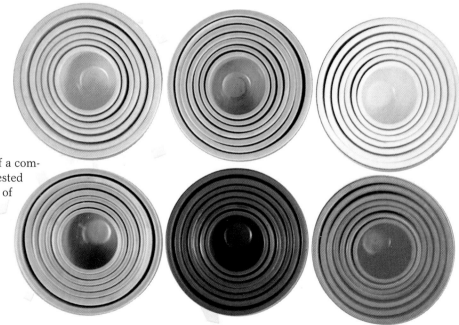

**Plate 7**
*Mixing Bowls.*
Here's a fantastic view of a complete collection of the nested bowl sets, one in each of the six original colors.

**Plate 8**

*Bowl Lids.*

They're extremely rare in any size! The #5 nested bowl lid remained undiscovered until just before our 1994 update. Since then, one more #5 and at least three #6s, have finally been unearthed, including the one in this fantastic, pristine all-red set. Is there a #7? According to old HLC records, there may just be! There are rumors that suggest that somewhere there are two ivory test lids, but it is generally agreed that the #7s were never marketed.

**Plate 9**

*Bowl Lids in the Metal Rack.*

The lids were made in the four colors shown here and in ivory. These have been turned over so that you can see the rings on the back. Photo courtesy Chuck Denlinger.

**Plate 10**

*Nappy, 9½" (left).*

This bowl was part of the original assortment and was still listed on our 1944 price list, but by fall of 1946, it was no longer available. You'll find it in only the first six colors. *Nappy, 8½" (center).*

Shown here in medium green, these bowls were made from 1936 until the line was restyled in 1969, so they come in all eleven colors. *Unlisted Salad Bowl (right).* Although this salad bowl (3¾" deep by 9½" in diameter) was never listed on the company's price pamphlets, a trade paper from 1940 reported on the Homer Laughlin sales campaign that offered this bowl accompanied by the Kitchen Kraft spoon and fork for only $1.00 — another of the promotionals. See page 12 for information concerning the promotionals. The ad copy indicated that these bowls were offered in only yellow. They're very scarce even in the standard yellow glaze, but a rare few have been reported in ivory, red, light green, and dark blue (see Plate 11).

**Plate 11**
*Salad Bowl.*
This is a very rare example of the unlisted salad bowl, shown here in dark blue — it's just as rare in ivory, light green, and red.

**Plate 12**
*Footed Salad Bowl (left).*
According to our survey, these handsome bowls are scarce and becoming rare. They were made from the time Fiesta was introduced until 1946 in only the first six colors (this prize is Fiesta red, of course), and if one color is any harder to find than the others, it is probably ivory. Though they're listed on company material as being 12" in diameter, they're actually only 11¼". *Fruit Bowl (right).* These are hard to find, especially in red. They were made from 1937 until sometime between 1944 and 1946 in only the six original colors. They're shallow, only 3" deep, and 11¾" in diameter.

**Plate 13**
*Tripod Candleholders.*
Their very distinctive Art Deco lines have made these tripod candleholders very desirable additions to any collection. They've always been scarce and are even more so today. They were made in only the first six colors, since they were discontinued around 1942 or 1943. Though these are virtually always found with the wet (glazed) foot, very rarely you'll find an example with a dry, unglazed base. One set has been found in a most unusual deep aubergene.

**Plate 14**
*Bulb Candleholders.*
What a magnificent lineup! Both these and the tripod candleholders were part of the original line; this style was discontinued sometime between 1944 and 1946. They were made in these early colors and are relatively easy to find. We've also heard from a collector who has these in Harlequin yellow. Photo courtesy David Schaefer.

**Plate 15**

*Carafe.*

The carafe was part of the original line but was no longer listed by 1946. Its wonderful Deco lines make it a favorite among collectors. These were made in the first six colors only, with ivory being the most difficult to find. The company lists its capacity as three pints.

**Plate 16**

*Casserole.*

Considering that production of the "covered casserole" (as it was always referred to on HLC price lists) continued uninterrupted from 1936 on, they're not especially easy to find. They were made in all eleven colors (this one is dark green), but the medium green example tops the charts as far as value and desirability. In December 1942, McClurgs department store offered a "Fiesta Holiday" assortment; most noteworthy in their ad was #44, an "8" footed handled salad bowl." The item pictured was the bottom of this casserole. (See Plate 436.)

**Plate 17**

*Tricolator Bowl.*

This is simply the casserole bottom without the standard applied foot. When we did our original research, there was nothing in the material we were given to verify that HLC had made it; in fact, the company spokesmen felt sure the company had not! These are always marked "Tricolator," a company that specialized in combining a piece such as this one with a warmer base, a metal frame, etc. It was common practice for a pottery to make items such as this to fill a special order — not just for Tricolator, but for similar companies as well. You can also find coffeepots that were made for Tricolator by Hall, some of which bear the marks of both companies. Tricolator bowls have been reported in ivory, yellow, red, turquoise, green, dark blue, and Harlequin yellow. When found, they're normally open, though one collector tells us his was bought at an estate sale topped with the standard Fiesta casserole lid. By the

way, the company finally conceded that it was produced at HLC!

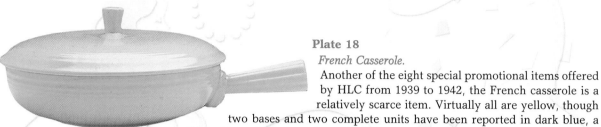

**Plate 18**

*French Casserole.*

Another of the eight special promotional items offered by HLC from 1939 to 1942, the French casserole is a relatively scarce item. Virtually all are yellow, though two bases and two complete units have been reported in dark blue, a lid and base have been found in light green, and one complete unit has been reported in ivory. The lid differs significantly enough from the one on the casserole in Plate 16 that you'll easily be able to tell which lid you have, should you find a spare. The French casserole lid measures 9" in diameter compared to 8" for the regular casserole lid, and the finial is ⅞" across the top compared to 1¼".

**Plate 19**

*Promotional Casserole and Pie Plate.*

Though not marked and for some time lacking documentation to verify their origin, collectors nevertheless suspected that these casseroles had been made by Homer Laughlin, since they kept turning up in colors identical to several of HLC's standard glazes. But being guided by information provided to us by HLC, for years we had no choice but to exclude them from the Fiesta line-up. Finally, several years ago, evidence surfaced to the contrary. A company

representative discovered an old order sheet showing its "#600 Gift Assortment of Colored Ware" — and there it was, our mystery casserole! Then this set was found, still sealed in its original unopened carton which is stamped Fiesta on the side not shown. Note the colors are exactly as described in the promotional campaign we mention on pages 12 and 13. The casserole is 3" deep and measures 8" in diameter. See Plate 388 in the "Go-Alongs" chapter for another view. Most of them are red, turquoise, yellow, light green, and mauve blue, though dark blue, Harlequin yellow, and spruce green have also been found, as well as one base in maroon. The Fiesta Kitchen Kraft pie plate is 9¾"; it's shown again later in the Fiesta Kitchen Kraft section. In Harlequin colors, these items are very rare.

**Plate 20**
*Promotional Casserole with Label.*
This pristine promotional casserole in mauve blue still sports its original paper label: Oven-Tested Colored Ovenware Laboratory Tested at 450 (degrees) for Three Hours. The label is the same shape as the Royal Chrome label in Plate 50. Photo courtesy Geri and Dan Tucker.

**Plate 21**
*Coffeepot.*
The coffeepot can be found in all of Fiesta's colors except medium green. It was in the original line but was not made after mid-1956. Unless you're one of those collectors who has to have every piece in every color (or you personally know someone who does), here are more coffeepots that you've probably never seen in one group before or ever will again — one in each of the ten colors.

**Plate 22**
*Comport.*
These were made from 1936 until sometime between 1944 and 1946. They're 12" in diameter and can be found in only the six original colors as shown in this spectacular photo. Photo courtesy David Schaefer.

**Plate 23**
*Sweets Comport.*
We found that the sweets comport, part of the original assortment, was discontinued between 1944 and 1946, making it available in only the six early colors. They're 3½" tall, and only about one out of four examples is marked with the ink stamp, "HLCo." See page 17 for a marked example.

**Plate 24**
*Stick-Handled Creamer.*
This creamer was made from 1936 until late 1939, when it was replaced by the ring-handled creamer shown in Plate 25. They were made in the six early colors and are hardest to find in turquoise. Photo courtesy David Schaefer.

**Plate 25**
*Ring-Handled Creamers.*
Shown here in all eleven colors is the creamer (collectors call it the regular creamer) that replaced the original stick-handled version in the fall of 1939 and continued in production until restyled for the Ironstone line. Photo courtesy David Schaefer.

**Plate 26**

*Creamer and Sugar Bowl, Individual; Figure-8 Tray.*

This set is from the 1939 – 1943 sales campaign. Nearly all sets are found with the creamer and sugar bowl in yellow on a dark blue tray; however, occasionally you'll find a red creamer and once in a while a turquoise tray. (This one is in my collection; it's marked Fiesta with an ink stamp. I bought it during the very early days of our collecting in that wonderful shop in Newell where I also bought two 12" vases for $7.00 each.) Though very few have been reported, creamers and at least one sugar bowl were found in turquoise, and a creamer was found in dark blue — well before the new line was introduced in 1986. A 1944 McClurg's catalog page that was reproduced on the cover of *The Fiesta Collector's Quarterly,* Winter 1998, featured the dark blue figure-8 tray with a Harlequin sugar bowl and creamer.

**Plate 27**

*Cups and Saucers.*

Cups and saucers in all eleven colors. On an interesting note, a collector sent us a photo of his cup showing evidence of saggar pin marks, even though the foot had been wiped clean of glaze, as they all are. Photo courtesy David Schaefer.

**Plate 28**

*Teacup, Demitasse Cup.*

Teacups and demitasse cups are rarely ever marked (neither are mustards, juice tumblers, or salt and peppers), but a few have been reported bearing the HLCo USA ink stamp. These may have been some that were earmarked for export to Canada. Photo courtesy Pat Bunetta.

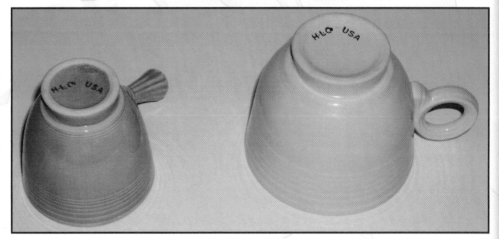

**Plate 29**

*Teacups.*

Here are three distinct styles of teacups — those with the inside rings (left) are the oldest. They also have a hand-turned foot. Only a few have been found in medium green which would seem to indicate that it was sometime around 1959 when the inside rings disappeared and the foot was modified to no longer require expensive hand trimming. The teacup on the right represents the second style. Note that the third style (center back), though produced in the color assortment available through the '60s, has the "C" handle of Fiesta Ironstone — evidently manufactured near the time of the restyling. Though cups are rarely ever marked (neither are mustards, demitasse cups, juice tumblers, and salt and pepper shakers), a few have been reported bearing the HLCo USA ink stamp. See examples of the teacup and demitasse cups with this mark in Plate 28. These may have been some that were earmarked for export to Canada. (If your cup has a molded-in mark, it's new, made post-1986.) Photo courtesy Pat Bunetta.

**Plate 30**

*Flat-Bottomed Cups.*

Cups like these are so rare, this is the first time we've been able to actually show you an example. This is Rhead's original cup. Note the flat interior. The foot was thrown separately and then attached to the body, just like his original demitasse cup, sugar bowl, stick-handled creamer, and covered onion soup bowl. One collector has these flat-bottomed cups in all six original colors. (See the caption Plate 3 for information on the revision.) The saucers that go with these cups are flatter than normal, so they don't stack well with the regular style, and they have a series of several rings around the rim of the bottom and foot. Photo courtesy Philip Gray.

**Plate 31**

*Demitasse Pot; Demitasse Cups; Saucers.*

If you've never been sure of the meaning of the terms demitasse and "A.D.," they simply refer to small cups of strong black coffee meant to be slowly sipped and lingered over after a lovely dinner. Designed to serve after-dinner coffee with elegance and flair, demitasse pots and cups were included in the original line. The pot was discontinued before 1944; you'll find it only in the six original colors, with turquoise examples being especially hard to find. The cups and saucers were supposedly made in just ten colors — no medium green, since they were discontinued in 1956, three years before the color was introduced — but four sets in medium green were discovered just before the eighth edition. For you skeptics, we show the green lineup in Plate 32. Of the ten standard colors, the '50s colors are hardest to find. A collector has reported finding one in brick red. Virtually never marked, a rare few have been found with the HLCo USA mark. (See Plate 28.)

**Plate 32**
*Demitasse Cup and Saucers.*
Here's that medium green demitasse cup and saucer! Four sets have been in the same family since the '50s — and they're not even collectors! These are definitely medium green, not a heavy application of light green. If we've learned one thing about Fiesta over the past thirty years, it's that there are no absolutes. Just about anything is possible. Of the four, one saucer is marked Fiesta, two are unmarked, and the other has written under the glaze the following code: "1/3 (over) C-FY-FG." There is also a medium green demitasse pot at the East Liverpool, Ohio, Ceramics Museum. Plates in the background are forest green, light green, medium green, and chartreuse. Photo courtesy Joel Wilson.

**Plate 33**
*Demitasse Pots.*
This breathtaking lineup contains an example of all six of the colors in which the demitasse pot was made. Note the vent hole in the lid of the yellow example. These were put in by hand and evidently most of the time regarded as a dispensable option.

**Plate 34**
*Egg Cups.*
These were not part of the original line; they were added in mid-1936. They were discontinued between January and September of 1956 and are available in ten colors as shown (no medium green). Collectors report that chartreuse and gray are the hardest to find. Photo courtesy David Schaefer.

**Plate 35**
*Marmalade and Mustard Jar.*

Marmalades (the yellow one) and mustards (shown here in red) were two of the items mentioned in Rhead's August 1939 magazine article quoted in the chapter entitled "The Story of Fiesta." He wrote that these were new to the line at that time. They were discontinued between 1944 and 1946, so they're found in the first six colors only.

**Plate 36**
*Mustard Jars.*
Here are all the colors of the mustard jars. Marked examples are extremely rare; when they are marked, it is with the HLCo USA stamp in gold or blue-black ink stamp. See information in Plate 29; for a photo of a marked example, see Plate 391. Photo courtesy David Schaefer.

**Plate 37**
*Disk Water Pitchers.*
Not original but added to the line in 1939, the disk water pitcher continued to be made until the end of production. It's very scarce in medium green and chartreuse and rather hard to find in the '50s colors. Photo courtesy David Schaefer.

**Plate 38**
*Disk Juice Pitcher; Juice Tumblers.*
Of all the promotional items, this set is the only one that is fairly easy to find. Nearly every pitcher you'll see will be yellow (collectors report a high incidence of the use of Harlequin yellow, a slightly brighter shade than Fiesta yellow), but once in awhile you may find one in red. The red pitchers, according to a recent report by a couple who discovered some of the original coupons, were offered as a promotion by the Dayton Spice Mills, the Old Reliable Coffee Company. "Yours for only three coupons and $1.19," one says, "six tumblers in lovely colors" (it lists turquoise, green, yellow, blue, ivory, and red) "and a superbly shaped red Fiesta jug. High quality both in material and texture...designed and executed with artistic skill of the first order." Though juice tumblers were discontinued before the '50s, rose tumblers are not uncommon. (See Plate 41 for comments.) The pitcher holds 30 ounces and is 5¾" tall. The tumblers vary in size notoriously; they range in height from 3⅜" to 3½" and from 2⅜" to 2½" in diameter and vary in thickness as well. The juice tumblers in Plate 44 with the HLCo USA mark may well be the rarest of the "never marked" items. (The others are the demitasse cup, mustard, teacup, and salt and pepper shakers, listed in order of decreasing scarcity.) See Plate 491 ("Experimentals" chapter) for what may have been an experimental design for the promotional juice tumbler.

**Plate 39**
*Disk Juice Pitcher; Juice Tumblers.*
A sales promotion offered in 1952 is represented here — the very rare gray juice pitcher along with a tumbler in each of these colors: dark green, Harlequin yellow, and chartreuse. These are seldom found. One collector's theory, and it may well be fact, is that this set was dipped to go with Rhythm. The dates coincide, and one tumbler in maroon (the fourth Rhythm color) has been reported, lending more credence to the theory. It seems to be the consensus of opinion that since the new gray juice pitcher hit the market, collectors are less in awe of the old one.

**Plate 40**
*Disk Juice Pitcher; Juice Tumblers.*
This juice set was glazed in the Jubilee colors — another sales promotion. The gray tumbler is especially interesting to collectors, since it is exactly like the standard Fiesta gray from the '50s.

**Plate 41**
*Tumblers.*
Though you might expect that the rose and gray tumblers (the pair to the right) were from the '50s, since those colors were standard '50s fare, you must remember that these tumblers were discontinued well before then. Instead, the gray is actually Jubilee's mist gray and the rose a standard Harlequin color of the late '30s, "borrowed" to add a seventh color to the seven-piece juice set. The pair to the left is glazed in Jubilee's shell pink and cream beige.

**Plate 42**
*Juice Pitchers.*
This turquoise juice pitcher shown alongside the disk water pitcher for comparison is a one-of-a-kind example (as far as we know), a legend among Fiesta collectors everywhere. It sold for a staggering sum several years ago!

**Plate 43**
*Tumblers.*
The water tumblers were discontinued between 1944 and 1946, having been made since the onset of production, so they're found in the original six colors only, with turquoise perhaps being a little scarce. This spectacular grouping displays both water and juice tumblers in the original six colors. Photo courtesy David Schaefer.

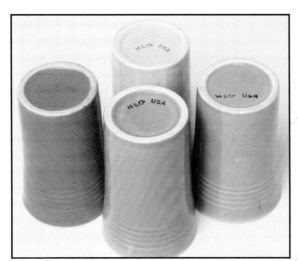

**Plate 44**
*Juice Tumblers.*
Very rare signed juice tumblers with the HLCo USA stamp mark. The color of the stamp varies from piece to piece, color to color. At this time, six tumblers are confirmed to have been found. Photo courtesy Pat Bunetta.

**Plate 45**
*Ice Pitchers.*
Made from 1936 until sometime between 1944 and 1946 in the original colors only, the ice pitcher is a little hard to find in ivory; it's red and turquoise that top the price scale. Though its looks seem to suggest otherwise, it does not have a lid. Photo courtesy David Schaefer.

**Plate 46**
*2-Pint Jug.*
The 2-pint jug was part of the original assortment. It was produced until mid-1956, so it only stands to reason that it was never made in medium green. But here, along with all the other lovely Fiesta colors it came in, is a very rare example in medium green — as far as we know, the only one that has ever been found. Photo courtesy Sandra Bond.

**Plate 47**
*Relish Trays.*
Five individual sections fit into the base of the relish tray. Its round center is often mistaken for a coaster, and though we thought for years that the company never produced them with that use in mind (coasters were never listed on price brochures), at least once they did! *The Fiesta Collector's Quarterly* once reproduced a '40s ad that offered a 13-piece beverage set: pitcher, six tumblers, and six coasters! Color make-up is important in determining the value of a relish tray. Red and dark blue are the desirable base colors, and today's collectors seem to prize examples that contain a piece in each of the original six colors. Photo courtesy David Schaefer.

**Plate 48**
*Relish Tray Inserts.*
There are variations on the relish tray inserts; the most obvious is in the thickness of the walls. If you order one of these by mail, be sure to specify which you prefer, as they don't mix well and won't fit together properly. The thicker inserts are molded, so they usually carry the cast-indented mark — an integral part of the mold itself. The thinner ones were pressed by machine (a quicker and more economical method of production) and are usually not marked, though you will find some that are ink stamped. No doubt the thick ones are a little older, but this will have no bearing on value, at least to most collectors.

**Plate 49**
*Cake Plate.*
The 10" cake plate is completely flat and very, very rare. We've never found it mentioned in any of the company's literature, but since it has only been found in the original five colors, it has to be an early piece. They're not marked, but one was reported bearing an original "Cake Kraft" label, and another bore the label shown in Plate 50.

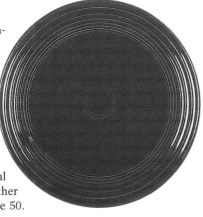

**Plate 50**
*Royal Chrome Label.*
This is the label that was found on one of the cake plates — you may remember it from a very exciting eBay sale! Royal Chrome was an assortment of Fiesta ware items

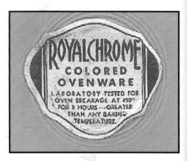

with chrome fittings. Included in the line were Kitchen Kraft casseroles, pie plates, and platters, as well as several pieces from the dinnerware line. See the "Go-Alongs" section for other examples.

**Plate 51**
*Handled Chop Plate.*
This is how the chop plate was marketed in the 1939 – 1943 selling campaign (so we're showing it here instead of in the "Go-Alongs" chapter). It was offered along with seven other items/sets at $1.00 or less each. The rattan-wrapped handles were of course manufactured by another company and shipped to HLC where they were fitted to these plates. They have been found in sizes to fit the 7", 9", and 10" plates (this size also fits the relish tray) as well as the 13" and 15" chop plates.

**Plate 52**
*Compartment Plate, 12".*
These were made from 1936 until mid-1937. They're not mentioned on the May 1937 price list and have never been reported in turquoise. They measure 11½" (actual measurement for a 12" plate). Some of these are thicker and weightier than others, and not all are marked.
*Compartment Plate, 10½".*
Not quite as scarce, this size replaced the larger one in mid-1937. It was dropped in 1956, three years before the advent of medium green. These measure very close to the listed size. *Chop Plate, 15".* Both chop plates were in the original assortment. This one was discontinued early in 1956, so it is found in all colors except medium green. Actual measurement is 14¼". *Chop Plate, 13".* This size continued to be made until the restyling and can be found in all eleven colors, though it's rare in medium green. *Plates, 10", 9", 7", 6".* Plates have always been in good supply, however the 10" size is becoming harder to find. The number of rings within the foot area on the back of any Fiesta plate will vary; these identified the particular jigging machine that made it and were used for quality control purposes. Occasionally you may notice when you stack your plates that not all are the same depth. If there was a purpose for this variation, we're not aware of it. From the 10" down to the 6" size (they actually measure 10⅜", 9½", 7½", and 6½"), they're available in all eleven colors. Harlequin spruce green 10" and 6" plates have been found; the 6" plate is marked "Fiesta."

**Plate 53**
*Deep Plate.*
The deep plate was an August 1936 item that continued in production until the restyling — it's 8¾" in diameter and found in all eleven colors. Most of us would call it a soup or salad bowl, though it is fairly shallow.

**Plate 54**
*Unlisted Plate.*
Discovered at an estate sale in Minnesota, this unlisted plate measures 11½". It's not from the new line. We're showing you the back — note the glazed foot ring, the saggar pin marks, and the old trademark. The appearance from the front is line-for-line, ring-for-ring Fiesta, and the color is a perfect match for the vintage yellow.

**Plate 55**
*Sauce Boat.*
The sauce boat (gravy boat) was produced from 1937 until 1973 in all of Fiesta's colors, with red and the colors of the '50s most difficult to find. *Platter.* The 12½" platter was first listed in July 1938 and remained in production through the Ironstone phase. Though it was listed in the vintage line as 12" and in Ironstone as 13", collectors tell us the actual size never changed. It's easy to find in all eleven colors. *Utility Tray.* Added to the line in mid-1936, the utility tray (referred to as "celery tray" on Western price lists) was dropped from the line sometime between 1944 and 1946, so you'll find them in only the first six colors with red perhaps a bit hard to find. *Syrup.* Syrups rate very high with collectors. You'll find them in only the first six colors, and they're scarce in ivory. The lids are plastic and some will fade with age; those in dark blue are especially bad as they tend to fade out to purple. Though it's a little hard to believe, considering the careful attention he paid to detail throughout the line, the syrup is the only piece of Fiesta that Rhead didn't design. The mold was bought from the DripCut Company, who made the tops for HLC as well. Other potteries, Vernon Kilns for one, also used this mold. Decades ago, a tea company filled syrup bases with tea leaves, added a cork stopper and their label, and unwittingly contributed to the frustration of today's collectors who have only a bottom. (See the chapter entitled "Commercial Adaptations and Ephemera" for a photo of two.) *Salt and Pepper Shakers.* These were made during the entire production period and can be found in all the Fiesta colors. Aside from the larger Kitchen Kraft shakers, this is the only style made in the Fiesta line. You may find a good imitation with holes on the side, but they are not genuine. Remember that Fiesta was widely copied, not only the bright glazes but often the band of rings as well. Virtually all are unmarked; only a very few have been reported with the HLCo USA mark, generally believed to indicate ware that was exported to Canada.

**Plate 56**
*DripCut Syrup Pitcher.*
Here's a shot of the predecessor of the Fiesta syrup pitcher. The bottom is marked "DripCut Heat Prof LA CAL." Photo courtesy Chuck Denlinger.

**Plate 57**
*Salt and Pepper Shakers.*
Note the center holes on every shaker in this great photo. Though most are pierced in the center, you'll find a few that are not. Photo courtesy David Schaefer.

**Plate 58**
*Sauce Boat and Stand.*
The sauce boat in this photo is from the original line, and may be found in all eleven colors. But the stand (underplate) didn't become available until the Ironstone line was introduced in 1969. Collectors pay dearly for one in Mango Red (shown here), since it makes a very desirable addition to any Fiesta collection. It measures 9" x 6½".

**Plate 59**
*Sugar Bowls.*
The sugar bowl remained basically the same from 1936 on, though the bases of earlier examples are flared out as compared to those made in the late '40s in the original colors and those made in the '50s colors, when a slight change in the mold resulted in a base with a rather stubby appearance. They're shown here in all eleven wonderful colors. What a perfect demonstration of the perfect union between Fiesta's shapes and colors. Photo courtesy David Schaefer.

**Plate 60**
*Sugar Bowls.*
The sugar bowl on the left is the original model, when the base and the body were molded as two separate pieces; the other is the standard sugar bowl. There are three distinct differences between them; the early example has a raised base and the inside bottom is flat; the width of the vertical lid flange is twice as wide as the standard version; and the mark is Fiesta, "HLC USA." Because the style on the right could be molded in one piece, they were much less expensive to manufacture.

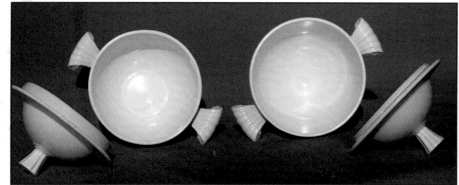

**Plate 61**
*Teapots, Medium.*
This size was added to the line in 1937 and was available throughout the entire production period. You'll find it in all these eleven colors, though it's rare in medium green. Photo courtesy David Schaefer.

**Plate 62**
*Teapots, Large.*
This was in the original assortment. It was made only until sometime between 1944 and 1946 so it's found in just the first six colors as shown here. You will find some lids that have no vent holes.
Photo courtesy Craig Macaluso, Metairie, LA.

**Plate 63**
*Tom and Jerry Mugs.*
These are sometimes referred to as coffee mugs; they were reported in Rhead's article (mid-1936) as being new to the line and continued in production until the end. They were made in all eleven colors, though ivory examples are scarce. Note the trademark ring handle. You'll find these will vary in thickness of the walls as well as height. The example in Plate 64 is in maroon — one of a set of fifteen found with a matching "punch" bowl (the footed salad bowl, of course). It belonged to the widow of a former HLC manager who, in addition to this unique Tom and Jerry set, also owned a very large collection of Harlequin in maroon. This set was made to order to match her Harlequin dinnerware.
Photo courtesy David Schaefer.

**Plate 64**
*Tom and Jerry Mug.*
Very rare in maroon.

**Plate 65**
*Flower Vases, 8", 10", and 12".*
All three sizes of the flower vase were introduced in mid-1936 according to Rhead's magazine article we referenced back in the chapter entitled "The Story of Fiesta." They're all very scarce and highly valued by collectors. The 8" vase continued longest in production — it was dropped between 1944 and 1946. The 10" and 12" vases were made only from mid-1936 until fall of 1942. All of these vases are available in only the first six colors. Photo courtesy David Schaefer.

**Plate 66**
*Bud Vases.*
Part of the original line, the bud vase was discontinued between 1944 and 1946. It's fairly easy to find and was made in the first six colors. It's 6¼" tall. Normally these all have a dry foot (no glaze on the foot ring), but we heard from a collector who has one entirely glazed over on the bottom.

**Plate 67**
*Medium Green Pieces.*
We thought you'd enjoy seeing this full-page shot of some nice medium green items. This color is scarce and is considered very desirable by collectors today. Prices continue to increase for even the smallest items. Some pieces of Fiesta are very rare in medium green, for instance: the cream soup (see Plate 68), 6" bowl, 4¾" fruit, disk pitcher, casserole, and medium teapot. And, of course, since it was not introduced until 1959 and many pieces had been discontinued by then, some items are simply not available in this color. Even to the most experienced eye, the difference between a heavy application of light green and an average coverage in medium green is sometimes a bit tricky to discern.

**Plate 68**
*Cream Soup.*
This is a very rare, very desirable item — the most valuable of any medium green piece; in fact, in the entire Fiesta line it is surpassed only by the covered onion soup in turquoise!

**Plate 69**
*Variations in Green Colors.*
Over the past few years, we've had many newcomers who have asked for some help in sorting out all the greens. Here they are (left to right): chartreuse, light green, medium green, and dark green.

## Kitchen Kraft

Since the early '30s, the Homer Laughlin China Company had been well known as a manufacturer of a wide variety of ceramic kitchenwares. In 1939 the company introduced a bake-and-serve line called Fiesta Kitchen Kraft as an extension of the already popular genuine Fiesta ware. This was offered in four original Fiesta colors — red, yellow, green, and blue. The following pieces (compiled from the April 1941 price list) were available:

Covered jars: small, medium, and large
Mixing bowls: 10", 8", and 6"
Covered casseroles: 8½", 7½", and individual
Pie plate, 10"
Salt and pepper shakers, large

Covered jug, large
Spoon, fork, and cake server
Refrigerator set, four-piece
Cake plate, 11"
Plates: 6" and 9"

These were chosen from the standard assortment of kitchenware items which had been the basis of the many Kitchen Kraft and OvenServe decaled lines of years previous; none were created especially for Fiesta Kitchen Kraft. This line was in production for a relatively short period — perhaps being discontinued sometime during WWII prior to 1945.

In addition to the items listed on page 44, there are at least three more to add. These may have been offered in the original assortment and discontinued by the 1941 listing. They are the oval platter in a chrome holder (which was shipped as a unit from HLC), a 9" pie plate, and a variation in size of the covered jug. The difference is so slight, even side by side it could go unnoticed. Collectors report as many of one size as the other. If you really want to label yours large or small, check the circumference. The larger one measures 21½" while the smaller one is 20".

The 6" and 9" plates listed on the 1941 illustrated brochure were used as underplates for the casseroles. When we visited the morgue at HLC, we saw examples of these. What we remembered was that they were of a thinner gauge with a moderately wide, slightly flared rim and seemed to have been taken from one of their other lines, since the style was not typically Kitchen Kraft. There are probably more questions raised about these underplates by collectors today than concerning any other item. In the eighth edition, we showed what seemed to be the elusive 6" underplate for the first time, not realizing then that it was the small Carnival plate. It looked perfectly correct; the double rings under the rim of the casserole complemented the double rings at the rim of the plate very well. The fact that there were three other reports of collectors buying the individual casserole with this plate seemed to reinforce the possibility that these actually were the elusive underplates for which we'd all been looking for so long. But now we're convinced otherwise. For one thing, no 9" Carnival plates have been reported to us — surely matching plates would have been used for both sizes. I searched through all our old research material to see if we had a photograph of the plates we saw in the morgue. And we did! They're like the ones on the Fiesta Kitchen Kraft brochure and exactly like the underplates in the decaled Kitchen Kraft lines — all of which are Nautilus. Of the collectors I discussed this with, most agree that the correct underplate would be Nautilus (because of the two reasons I just mentioned), but since anyone has yet to see one in the Fiesta Kitchen Kraft colors, the consensus is that for some reason they were never actually marketed. Perhaps someday someone will have better answers, but after more than thirty years of research and study, we don't!

Over the years, collectors have reported finding the stacking refrigerator set, mixing bowls, 8½" casserole, salt and pepper shakers, pie plate, and other items in the ivory glaze. Just before the ninth edition came out, a large covered jar was reported. This time we have documentation for you — see Plate 86. Ivory pieces are so rare that even a veteran collector who has spent twenty years concentrating on the more unusual items says that he has yet to see some of the items that have been reported to us. Collectors are split on the issue of whether

the glaze is truly ivory or more of a cream color (some describe the glaze as ranging from a butterscotch ivory to a very light ivory — others see it as a perfect match to Fiesta ivory); whatever your viewpoint, this was never listed as a standard Kitchen Kraft color, but at some point, an ivory line must have been produced, either separately or in conjunction with Fiesta Kitchen Kraft. No information exists to answer this question, at least that we're aware of. There is a white Kitchen Kraft line as well; it's more often encountered than ivory. Of the four standard colors, dark blue is most in demand. Along with red, it represents the high side of the price range.

**Plate 70**
*Mixing Bowls.*
The mixing bowls measure 10", 8", and 6" and have proven rather difficult to find. Note the original sticker on the large one (it's reproduced on page 45). They've been found in ivory as well as Harlequin, Jubilee, and Rhythm colors. They may or may not be marked. The 6" bowl was once used as an advertising piece for Wm. Jameson, Inc., N.Y., producers of "Shorewood, 90 Proof Maryland Straight Rye Whiskey, the finest name in rye."

**Plate 71**
*Cake Plate (left).*
These may or may not be marked — once in awhile you'll find one bearing a gold ink stamped "Fiesta HLCo." The only hint of decoration is the narrow band around the edge formed by one indented ring. These are much easier to find than the regular, very rare Fiesta cake plate. *Pie Plates.* These come in two sizes: 10" and 9". Actually, they measure 10¼" and 9¾". (Read the chapter "Dating

Codes and English Measurements" if this confuses you.) These lack rings both inside and out and are usually not marked, though very rarely they'll carry the gold mark as well. The 10" size has been reported in the maroon and spruce green of the Harlequin line. In the chapter called "Go-Alongs," you'll see the metal frame (similar to the one in Plate 401) that was sometimes shipped along with the pie plates directly from the factory. It is very unusual to find the small size in the Fiesta Kitchen Kraft colors; it is more often found in ivory or white decorated with decals.

**Plate 72**
*Gold Fiesta Ink Stamp.*
This mark was photographed on a red pie plate. As its new owner (who very recently sent me this picture) puts it, "Rather neat: is it a Kitchen Kraft pie plate or a Fiesta pie plate?" I say "new owner," because at some point during the past many years, I'm sure this plate was in my collection! If you look at past editions, the description reads, "though we have one with a gold Fiesta stamp." I can't even remember selling it, but I checked out my Fiesta "wall," and ours is not there. Not surprising, since we've sold most of our collection over the years. It's had time to go from coast to coast, and has ended up, for now anyway, no more than eighty miles away from home.

**Plate 73**
*Casseroles.*
These come in three sizes: 8½", 7½", and individual. All are scarce. In Plate 74 you'll see the lid in greater detail.

**Plate 74**
*Casserole Variations.*
This 8½" casserole has a base with variations from the standard mold in that the lip is recessed, and this one has no mark. A variation on the individual casserole was reported as well: the two rings under the rim of the bowl are placed higher, and the knob on the lid is more recessed. This one has the usual embossed mark.

**Plate 75**
*Covered Jars.*
To determine the size of your covered jar, measure the circumference. The large jar measures 27½", the medium, 22", and the small one, 17½". Lid detail is evident in Plate 76.

**Plate 77**
*Covered Jug.*
There are two sizes of these jugs, but the differences are subtle. The circumference of the larger is 21½"; the smaller jug measures 20".

**Plate 76**
*Covered Jar.*
Here you'll see the lid in better detail. These are becoming hard to find in mint condition.

**Plate 78**
*Platter.*
This is the 13" oval platter, shown in Harlequin spruce green, not a standard Kitchen Kraft color. They're very, very rare in this color. A few have been found in Harlequin yellow, and one has been reported in mauve blue (see below). Even in the regular four colors, they're scarce, and they're not usually marked. The metal holder is an HLC issue, though, of course, not all of these platters were sold in a frame.

**Plate 79**
*Platter.*
Here's proof that the platter actually exists in mauve blue! Photo courtesy Chuck Denlinger.

**Plate 80**
*Servers: Spoon, Cake Lifter, Fork.*
These are hard to find, especially in mint condition. Their handles are embossed with the same flowers as one of the OvenServe lines. One has been found in ivory, not to be confused with the white spoons regularly found in the OvenServe lines. If you find one of these marked "CS" on the back, it is from a line of limited edition collectibles called OvenServe Style Utensils, made for a private company, China Specialties, Inc. These were made in colors to match both old and new — old turquoise, old ivory, forest green, rose, and lilac. Other colors may follow. These were not made by Homer Laughlin. *Salt and Pepper Shakers.* Look familiar? These are larger versions of their Fiesta dinnerware counterparts, although by no means are they as plentiful. These have been found in Harlequin yellow as well, but such a find is very unusual.

**Plate 81**

*Servers: Spoons, Cake Lifters, Forks.*
Here's how the complete set looks — something you certainly don't see everyday! A spoon has been reported in dark green and a cake lifter in turquoise, both extremely rare.

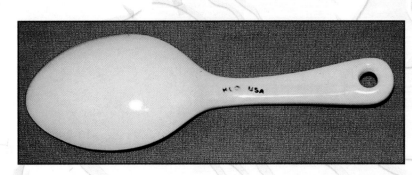

**Plate 82**

*Spoon Variation.*
Here's another version of the serving spoon — very rare indeed. It's slightly more narrow than the standard style and 11½" long. As far as we know, there are very few of these in ivory and white, one with decals, and another in turquoise which the owner says came from the Wells' estate. He also tells us that he has seen a brochure from Homer Laughlin that shows a light green example.

**Plates 83 and 84**

*Spoon.*
How's this for a pristine example? This spoon not only has the elusive paper label in mint condition, but it's also marked on the back: "HLCo USA." In this condition and with the label, expect to pay at least double the suggested book value — add even more for the ink stamp — if you're ever lucky enough to find one like this! On top of all these attributes, one of our advisors in this survey is convinced that these are hard to find in yellow.
Photo courtesy Chuck Denlinger.

**Plate 85**
*Stacked Set (Refrigerator Jars).*
The covered refrigerator stack set consists of three units and a flat lid and is usually made up of all four Kitchen Kraft colors. See the most unusual example in Plate 86!

**Plate 86**
*Stacked Set (Refrigerator Jars.).*
Certainly better than word of mouth...here's the proof that somewhere the large covered jar does exist in ivory, as does the stacking refrigerator jar and the Kitchen Kraft salt shaker in Plate 87! These are extremely rare.
Photo courtesy Chuck Denlinger.

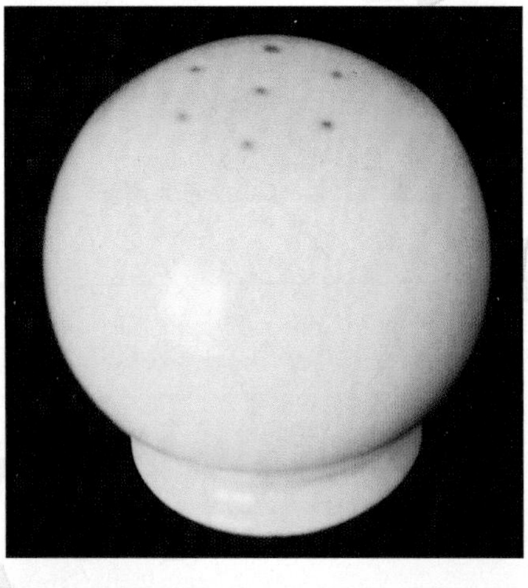

**Plate 87**
*Salt Shaker..*
The very rare ivory salt shaker.
Photo courtesy Chuck Denlinger.

# *Ironstone*

In 1969 much of the original line was restyled. The number of available pieces was drastically reduced. A company flyer dated July 1, 1969, illustrated with photos of the entire Fiesta Ironstone assortment (now nineteen items in all), indicates that the line hit the market several months sooner than we once thought.

There were many factors that of necessity brought about this change. Labor and production costs had risen sharply. Efforts to hold these expenses down influenced the selection of colors. Fiesta red was retained but now called mango red. To complement the red, two additional colors were selected, antique gold and turf green, both of which were being used at that time in several other lines of dinnerware HLC was producing. These three colors were fired at or about the same temperature, a significant cost-saving measure in contrast to the separate firings required for the older Fiesta colors. (It was pointed out to us as we toured the factory that since each of the old colors were fired at various temperatures, orders were running ahead of production for Fiesta as well as other lines.) These pieces were offered in antique gold only: covered casserole, tea server (teapot), water jug (disk pitcher), coffee server, and 10¼" salad bowl. To further economize, all markings were eliminated. (You will very seldom find a piece of Ironstone with the Fiesta stamp; the few that are marked were probably made during the transition from the original line to Ironstone.)

The restyled pieces had a more contemporary feeling — bowls were flared, and applied handles were only partial rings. The covered casserole had molded, closed handles, and the handles had been eliminated entirely from the sugar bowl. The covered coffee server made a return appearance after an absence of several years. Four additional items quickly supplemented the original nineteen for a total of twenty-three. The oval platter that was listed as 12" in the original line was now listed as 13". (In reality, actual measurement was always 12½".) New items included the soup/cereal bowl, the sauce boat stand, and the 10" salad bowl.

Finally in November 1972, all production of mango red Fiesta was discontinued because many of the original technicians who developed this color and maintained control over the complicated manufacturing and firing processes had retired, and modern mass-production methods were unsuited to produce it successfully. On January 1, 1973, the famous line of Fiesta dinnerware was discontinued altogether.

Because Ironstone was made for a relatively short time, it is not easy to find. Red mugs and the sauce boat stand in any color are regarded as "good pieces." Red is the most difficult color to find; green is scarce in some pieces; and gold, being the only color the complete assortment was made in, is the most available. You may find cups with the Ironstone handle in Fiesta yellow, medium green, and turquoise. (For a complete listing of available items, see "Suggested Values" in the back of the book.)

**Plate 88**
*Ironstone Grouping.*

**Plate 89**
*Examples in Unusual Two-color Glaze.*
This 10" jumbo salad bowl and these mugs are from standard Ironstone molds but have a very unusual glaze treatment. The colors used here are antique gold on the outside and an eggshell on the inside. Only one other 10" jumbo salad bowl in this color combination has been reported. Photo courtesy Pat Bunetta.

**Plate 90**
*Ironstone Coffee Mugs.*
Here is the elusive coffee mug in all three of the Ironstone colors as well as Amberstone (center) and an example of the two-color glaze (at the lower left). No literature or sales promotional material has been found to date offering this variation. Photo courtesy Pat Bunetta.

# Amberstone

Amberstone was introduced in 1967, three years before the Fiesta line was restyled; yet the illustration on an old order blank shows that the sugar and creamer, cup, teapot, soup/cereal, casserole, and coffee server were from the same molds that were later used for Fiesta Ironstone. Only on the pieces that had relatively flat areas large enough to permit decoration do you find the black, machine-stamped underglaze pattern. The remaining items were simply solid brown. Some of the hollow ware pieces are found with the familiar Fiesta cast-indented trademark.

Sold under the trade name "Genuine Sheffield" dinnerware, Amberstone was produced by HLC exclusively for supermarket promotions, and several large grocery store chains featured Amberstone as a premium. (For a listing of items offered, see "Suggested Values" in back of book.)

Plate 91

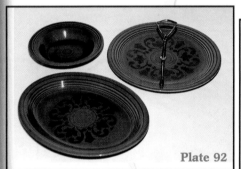

Plate 92

Plate 93

Plate 94

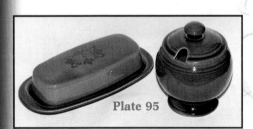

Plate 95

Plate 96

Plate 97

*Additional Amberstone Shapes.*
The marmalade is shown in Plate 95 and the mustard (alongside salt and pepper shakers for size comparison) in Plate 94. Note the Ironstone pieces: casserole, flared fruit bowl, salad bowl (in Plate 98), mug, and sauce boat stand. We'd reported in previous editions that the elusive mug had a Fiesta ring handle, based on line drawings in a brochure the company gave us years ago. In Plate 96 you can see that we were in error. There's an oddity in Plate 97, an Amberstone cup with an old Fiesta handle; we've also had a report of a Nautilus cup in Amberstone brown. The sauce boat is sometimes marked Fiesta, and an unusual 13" chop plate has been found without the decal.

**Plate 98**
*Salad Bowl.*
This is the Amberstone salad bowl — very few have been found. Photo courtesy Harvey Linn, Jr.

## Casualstone

In 1970 Homer Laughlin produced a second line of dinnerware to be sold exclusively through supermarket promotions. This dinnerware was called Casualstone and was presented under the trade name "Coventry." The antique gold of the Fiesta Ironstone was decorated with an intricate gold machine-stamped design which, like Amberstone, appeared on only the shallow items. An old order blank shows that it was less expensive than the Amberstone of three years previous, possibly because a color already in production was used. (For a listing of available items, see "Suggested Values" in back of book.)

**Plate 99**
*Casualstone Grouping.*

## Casuals

There were two designs produced in the beautiful Fiesta Casuals, and although they are both relatively difficult to find, often when they are found the set will be complete, or nearly so. They were introduced in June 1962; and as sales were only moderately active, they were discontinued around 1968. The Plaid Stamp Company featured both lines in their illustrated catalogs during these years.

GENUINE
*Fiesta*
H. L. Co. USA
CASUAL

The Hawaiian 12-Point Daisy design, shown below, featured a ½" turquoise band at the rim and turquoise daisies with brown centers on a white background. The other pattern was Yellow Carnation which featured the yellow flowers with a touch of brown on a white background. A yellow rim band completed the design. In each line, only the dinner plates, salad plates, saucers, and oval platters were decorated; the cups, fruit dishes, nappies, sugar bowls, and creamers were simply glazed in the matching Fiesta color. The designs were hand sprayed and overglazed using a lead mask with the cut-out motif. A complete service consisted of six place settings: dinner plate, salad plate, cup, saucer, and 5½" fruit. A platter, 8½" nappy, sugar, and creamer were also included. (For a listing of available items, see "Suggested Values" in back of book.)

**Plate 100**
*Hawaiian 12-Point Daisy Design.*

**Plate 101**
*Yellow Carnation Design.*
The correct cups to use with these lines are those without the inside rings!

## Fiesta with Stripes

Red-striped Fiesta is an extremely rare variation of the original Fiesta. The simple addition of three graduated red stripes to vintage ivory achieves a sharp Deco look. The stripes are well done and are applied over the glaze; they're located outside and below the rim of hollow ware shapes such as the cup, bowl, mustard, and casserole, and near the outside edge of saucers, plates, and lids. A variation of the pattern of applied stripes has been discovered on the bud vase and the 10" flower vase. On occasion, a lid will be found that does not have the thin applied stripe at the base of the finial.

Advanced collectors speculate that because of the very few pieces of red-striped Fiesta found, Homer Laughlin may have produced for a client or customer a one-time production-run dinnerware service for twelve that included extra serving pieces. Collectors and dealers need to seriously consider the plausibility of this scenario.

Determining a production date is difficult. At best we can only establish approximate dates, because no sales brochures or literature illustrating red-striped fiesta has been found. No notes are found in Rhead's journals or HLC's modeling log. However, we do have a few clues to help us address this question. We feel confident from our research that this line was produced at some point during a six-month window between February/March

**Plate 102**
*Coffeepot.*
Until recently, this blue-striped example was the only one known to exist; but finally a red-striped coffeepot has surfaced as well.

and July/August 1936. This narrative contains all the research from which this conclusion was reached.

First, look at the Fiesta shapes that were modified soon after going into production in November 1935. These shapes include the onion soup, sugar bowl, teacup, after-dinner cup, and stick-handled creamer. All five of these shapes originally had a flat inside bottom; the lid to both the onion soup and the sugar bowl had a 5/16" deep flange.

In February of 1936, after three months of production, the covered onion soup became the first Fiesta shape to undergo modifications. The lid was changed to incorporate a 1/8" deep flange; the inside bottom of the bowl was rounded out, hand turning was added to the foot, and the indented mold mark was omitted.

Recently, a slip-cast and signed red-striped covered onion soup was discovered. The lid has a 5/16" deep flange; the body has a flat inside bottom and is signed with an indented mold mark.

In March of 1936 after four months of production, the covered sugar bowl became the second Fiesta shape to undergo modifications. The lid flange became shorter — 1/8" long, the inside bottom was rounded out, and hand turning added shape to the foot. Today the sugar bowl may be found either signed or unsigned. The only red-striped covered sugar bowl ever found incorporates a slip-cast lid (with the 5/16" deep flange), a modified body with the round inside bottom, a hand-turned foot, and no indented mold mark.

Very few Fiesta shapes can contribute directly to Fiesta's history as well as the red-striped covered sugar bowl and the signed red-striped covered onion soup incorporating a slip-cast lid and body. This is because both experienced modifications soon after going into production, and both can strongly point to an early 1936 production date for red-striped Fiesta.

Modifications made to the Fiesta teacup in August 1937 and the Fiesta after-dinner cup in September 1937, and the replacement of the stick-handled creamer in July 1938 also provide clues. The modifications made to the two cups include a rounded inside bottom and a hand-turned foot. Since no Fiesta teacup or after-dinner cup with red stripes incorporating the 1937 modifications has been reported, August/September 1937 seems too long a production cycle for red-striped Fiesta. Only one creamer has been reported, and it has a stick handle. We must therefore conclude red-striped Fiesta production definitely ended well before 1938.

Because we find only two of the fourteen Fiesta shapes that were added to the line between mid-June to August 1936 with the red-stripe decoration, we can conclude that it was produced sometime between February/March and July/August 1936. These fourteen shapes include the first four sizes of mixing bowl lids, deep plate, egg cup, 2-pint jug, mustard, marmalade, coffee mug, utility tray, and all three sizes of the Fiesta flower vase. Of these, only the mustard and the 10" flower vase have been reported with red stripes. The mustard and marmalade were introduced into production at the same time in June 1936. Though two mustards with red stripes have been reported, no marmalade has ever been found. The 10" flower vase was introduced into production in August 1936 — only two have been found with red stripes.

Collecting red-striped Fiesta will be very challenging and expensive. Whether on eBay or at a live auction, red-striped Fiesta always commands a lot of interest and high-dollar values. Check the "Suggested Values" section for a complete list of confirmed red-striped Fiesta shapes. Please write and share if you have any information regarding red-striped Fiesta.

We want to thank Pat Bunetta and J. T. Vaughn for the research they have done on striped Fiesta.

**Plate 103**
*Covered Onion Soup Bowl.*
A total of only nine red-striped onion soup bowls have been found to date. A few years ago, a complete set of eight was found – how exciting! The red-striped onion soup has an estimated minimum value of $10,000 and is considered as rare, if not rarer, than the turquoise onion soup. Experts believe that no more than a dozen of these rarities ever went into production. This number is far less than the estimated thirty-five to forty-five turquoise onion soups that have been reported.

**Plate 104**
*Assorted Grouping.*
Partial service with extra serving pieces: relish tray; covered casserole; nappies: 6", 8", and 9"; cream soup bowl; plates: 6", 7", 9"; chop plates: 13" and 15"; teacup and saucer; mustard jar; and salt and pepper shakers.
Photo © Adam Anik.

**Plate 105**
*Ashtray.*

**Plate 106**
*Mixing Bowls.*
Here's proof that at least one set of the red-striped mixing bowls was produced. Five of the seven have been found. Shown here are #1, #2, #3, #4, and #7. Photo courtesy J.T. Vaughn and Ken Blum.

**Plate 107**
*Sugar Bowl; Demitasse Cup and Saucer; Chop Plate, 13"; Bud Vase; Covered Onion Soup Bowl.*
Two red–striped demitasse cups and saucers have been found, and one red-striped demitasse coffeepot has been reported. In 2003 a blue-striped demitasse coffeepot and six matching demitasse cups and saucers were auctioned off on eBay. Blue-trimmed items are extremely rare. Three bud vases with variations to the applied red stripes have been found. Photo courtesy J.T.Vaughn and Ken Blum.

**Plate 108**
*Comport.*

Photo courtesy Steve and Mary Patrone.

**Plate 109**
*Bud Vase, 10".*
Two 10" flower vases have been found as well — one is decorated with three graduated stripes near the base. Here you see the second (a one-of-a-kind) that has been decorated with three gold bands of varying widths, seven graduated red stripes near the base, and a date in gold: 1887 May 17 1937. (This one has been estimated to be worth a minimum of $15,000.00.)

Photo courtesy J.T. Vaughn and Ken Blum.

**Plate 110**
*Plate, 10".*
You'll find these in two sizes, the dinner plate and the 7" plate. Besides ivory, they've also been reported in yellow, and the stripes may be dark red or green. They were made sometime during the '40s and sold through Sears as a cake set, either as a service for four or for eight. They nearly always show wear. Some collectors believe the stripes were applied by another company, since they don't display the high-quality workmanship we connect with HLC production. Others still believe they were done by Homer Laughlin, but are the result of the company using shortcuts to save time, money, and resources. Does anyone know for sure? At any rate, they've never been regarded as very desirable by Fiesta collectors.

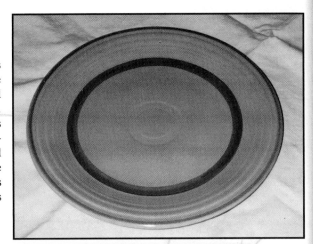

## Decals

Here and on the following pages are examples of Fiesta with decals. You'll find many other examples as well. They may have been decorated by HLC, but more than likely the work was done by smaller decorating companies — there were several in the immediate vicinity.

**Plate 111**
*Turkey Plates.*
We are sure that these were decorated by Homer Laughlin. Shown are the 9" plate with a maroon band, a 13" chop plate with the yellow band, and Kitchen Kraft cake plate that is trimmed in gold. The 15" chop plate has also been reported with the turkey decal, as has a Rhythm platter. All are very rare.

**Plate 112**
*Butterfly Tidbit Tray.*
With the addition of the center handle, the chop plate is converted to a tidbit. Eight gold butterflies and gold stripes complete the look.

**Plate 113**
*Relish Tray.*
Relish trays seem to have been a favorite item to decal, as we have seen several; this one is especially attractive.

**Plate 114**
*Demitasse Cup and Saucer.*
Items with this decal are becoming an area of collecting interest all their own, regardless of which company's mark they carry — it was used not only to decorate some of HLC's lines but other companies' as well. Much of this ware was decorated by Royal China, who often added its mark to that of the pottery company. HLC's Georgian line has been found with this decal, so have items marked "W.S. George," and there are others. In past editions we have featured cake sets made up of the 15" Fiesta chop plate and six matching dessert plates — one set in ivory, a second in yellow. This decal has not been limited to dinnerware; you'll often see lamps, vases, and other assorted pieces with variations of this theme. The gold work on this piece is not typical; usually the background is left undecorated, and sometimes rim stripes or wide gold bands are added.

**Plate 115**
*Ashtray.*
Shown in the blue of Skytone with the Stardust pattern. Blue lines were popular during the '40s and '50s.

**Plate 116**
*Sweets Comport Plate.*

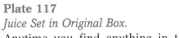

**Plate 117**
*Juice Set in Original Box.*
Anytime you find anything in the original carton it's a special treat! Not only is this the hard-to-find Jubilee color assortment, but each piece is decaled as well.

**Plate 118**
*Tom and Jerry Set.*
This is the large footed salad bowl and the Tom and Jerry mugs — a set that is hard to find complete. HLC made another set as well, but on shapes other than Fiesta. Values for the set shown here are listed in the Fiesta lineup; a picture of the second set we mentioned is shown in the "Miscellaneous" chapter (Plate 707).

**Plate 119**
*Calendar Plates.*
HLC issued calendar plates for a number of years, using whatever blanks were available. In 1954 and 1955, the company just happened to use Fiesta. The 9" plate in the center is the rare size; it may be found for either year. The 1954 plate has been found in ivory only; the 1955 may be green, yellow, or ivory.

## Lustre

Every now and then over the past twenty-five years a piece or two of Fiesta with all-over lustre decoration has been reported. Several small firms in the vicinity of HLC specialized in decorating ware from the area's several potteries and china companies — no doubt one (or more) of them is responsible for these pieces. We have file photos of a 2-pint jug and an egg cup that both sport silver lustre treatments. Other collectors told us about a dinnerware set they had acquired that they were able to trace back to 1948. It was in cobalt with gold bands and consisted of 7" plates, dinner plates, 4" fruits, teacups, and a

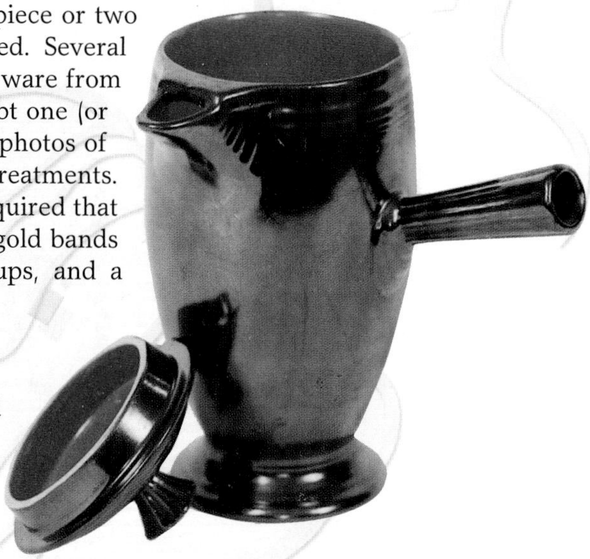

**Plate 120**
*Demitasse Pot.*
This was originally Fiesta red as you can see inside but it's now glazed in a copper-bronze lustre, and we know of another with silver over its original green.

**Plate 121**
*Relish Tray.*
The tray itself was once ivory, the inserts dark blue — now the entire tray is glazed in silver. All but one piece is impressed with the Fiesta trademark.

**Plate 122**
*2-Pint Jug.*
Silver lustre again, this time over turquoise.

## New Fiesta — Post86

After a thirteen-year absence, Fiesta was reintroduced to the market on February 28, 1986. Its Art Deco style, which had looked somewhat dated in 1973 when the Fiesta Ironstone line was discontinued, had again become the rage in home decoration. Only a short time before this, several lines of solid-color dinnerware had been introduced by competitors (including Moderna by Mikasa and a line-for-line interpretation of Fiesta by Rego China made for the restaurant trade). Sample items were produced and dipped in a number of colors to gauge consumer preferences at a Chicago trade show in December 1985. Gray and yellow were also tested in addition to the five winning colors of cobalt blue (darker and denser than the original), rose (a true pink), white, apricot (a pale, tannish peach), and black. Interest was deemed great enough to begin production. In order to appeal to the restaurant trade, HLC made a last-minute decision to go with a vitrified body (as opposed to the semi-vitrified body used for the original Fiesta). While vitrified china is denser and will not absorb moisture, it also has to be fired at a higher temperature and shrinks more during firing. Because of this, new molds had to be designed for the dinner plates to keep them at 10½". The higher firing also caused some shapes to have a tendency to deform or sag. Thus the Ironstone-style casserole, sugar bowl, coffee server, and flat teapot lid had to be redesigned. The original brochure (see Plate 124) had photographs of the semi-vitrified samples and showed a casserole with handles in the Ironstone style. But this particular item was never produced in the new line; instead it was restyled into the covered casserole shown in Plate 125. The coffee server was replaced by the restyled version. (See Plate 126 for both styles — the restyle is in the foreground.) Today the original (old style) coffee server has a market value of approximately $250.00. Note the differences in the finials. The original has the Ironstone-type knob, while the restyle has the more familiar flared, fluted knob from the old Fiesta line. This fluted knob eventually became standard on virtually every item in the line that took a lid. The sugar bowl was replaced with one made from the old marmalade mold (without the notch for the spoon) in the first few months of production. See the 1987 brochure which shows the actual shapes of the new Fiesta casserole, sugar bowl, coffee server, and teapot lid in Plate 125.

THE HOMER LAUGHLIN CHINA COMPANY: A FIESTA OF AMERICAN DINNERWARE is the Department of Culture and History's celebration of a major West Virginia industry.

A leader in design and production in the nation for more than a hundred years, the company's achievements stem from 1870 when the Laughlin brothers, Homer and Shakespeare, dared to produce American dinnerware fine enough to challenge English imports.

The culmination of the latest in design and technology, Homer Laughlin Company's Fiesta provided brightness and flair in a Depression-weary world, and was affordable to everyone. Energetically sought by collectors today, its color, design and uniqueness make Fiesta collectible at any price.

*Note:* The term now accepted within the collecting community is Post86. This encompasses all Fiesta items produced after February 1986. We use "Post86" and "new Fiesta" interchangeably throughout our text.

**Plate 123**
*Invitation.*
Less than three hundred of these invitations were sent out for the exhibition that unveiled the new Fiesta line. They were from the governor of West Virginia, Arch A. Moore, Jr. Imagine the thrill of receiving one!

**Governor Arch A. Moore, Jr.**

invites you to share in the opening festivities of

**"The Homer Laughlin China Company: A Fiesta of American Dinnerware"**

a major exhibition presented by the Department of Culture and History
**Saturday, March 9, 1985**
**8:00 p.m.**

The Cultural Center
State Capitol Complex
Charleston, West Virginia

Reception immediately following ribbon-cutting

R.S.V.P.                                    Entertainment

## Post86 Fiesta Colors

Fifteen new colors have been added over the years to the 1986 assortment of white, black, rose, apricot, and cobalt blue. The year of introduction of each is shown below. The second date indicates when that color was discontinued.

Yellow (very pale and creamy) . . . . . . . . . . . . . . . . . . . . . . . . . . . . . . . . . . . . . . . . . . . .1987 . . . .2002
Turquoise (darker, with more of a green cast than the old color) . . . . . . . . . . . . . .1988
Periwinkle blue (pastel gray-blue) . . . . . . . . . . . . . . . . . . . . . . . . . . . . . . . . . . . . . .1989
Sea mist green (pale mint or "Jadite" green . . . . . . . . . . . . . . . . . . . . . . . . . . . . . .1991
Lilac (a rich, deep lavender tone, a limited two-year color) . . . . . . . . . . . . . . . . .1994 . . . .1995
Persimmon (a reddish coral shade) . . . . . . . . . . . . . . . . . . . . . . . . . . . . . . . . . . . .1996
Chartreuse (brighter than the old, a limited two-year color) . . . . . . . . . . . . . . . . .1997 . . . .1999
Pearl gray (only slightly lighter than vintage gray) . . . . . . . . . . . . . . . . . . . . . . .1999 . . . .2001
Juniper (a deep teal green, a limited two-year color) . . . . . . . . . . . . . . . . . . . . . .2000 . . . .2001
Cinnabar (a deep brownish maroon) . . . . . . . . . . . . . . . . . . . . . . . . . . . . . . . . . . .2000
Sunflower (a bright, Harlequin-like yellow) . . . . . . . . . . . . . . . . . . . . . . . . . . . . .2001
Plum (a deep purple) . . . . . . . . . . . . . . . . . . . . . . . . . . . . . . . . . . . . . . . . . . . . . . .2002
Shamrock (a bright green, slightly more yellow than the old medium green) . . . . .2002
Tangerine (a medium to light orange, reminds many of orange sherbet) . . . . . . . .2003
Scarlet (a bright primary red) . . . . . . . . . . . . . . . . . . . . . . . . . . . . . . . . . . . . . . . .2004
Peacock (bright turquoise — due out in October) . . . . . . . . . . . . . . . . . . . . . . . . .2005

The entire assortment of pieces which were in the line at the respective times were produced in the colors listed above. In addition to these colors, a very limited color, sapphire (a bright blue, slightly lighter and more brilliant than the 1930s cobalt) was produced exclusively for Bloomingdale's during the winter of 1996 in a narrow selection of pieces. Unlike the lilac, chartreuse, and juniper, which were produced for two full years, sapphire was limited to 180 firing days, and sapphire was only available in the following items: five-piece place settings, 13½" oval platter, 32-oz. serving bowl, large disk pitcher, 6½-oz. tumblers, medium flower vase, wall clock, handled serving tray, and the newly restyled carafe. In addition, the jumbo 18-oz. cup and saucer from the Fiesta Mates line were also dipped in sapphire. To collectors' consternation, no sugar and creamer or salt and pepper were ever officially produced in sapphire.

There is one more color, raspberry, which was officially produced in only one item, the presentation bowl pictured on page 78. Five hundred raspberry presentation bowls were produced by HLC in December of 1997 to celebrate the 500 millionth piece of Fiesta that had been manufactured since 1936. The bowls were presented to owners and shareholders of this private, family-held company. Fifteen of the bowls were donated to three charity auctions to benefit education scholarship funds in the Newell/East Liverpool area in June and August of 1998. And while the bowls at these charity auctions went for $5,000.00 + , it should be remembered that many purchasers were not collectors of Fiesta, but wealthy benefactors with ties to the town, the local college, or the Aaron and Wells families, and the prices realized at these particular auctions did not necessarily reflect the values of the bowls themselves but were in actuality donations to the towns' scholarship funds. Subsequent sales between private individuals that may have taken place at lower amounts do not reflect a decline in the value of the raspberry presentation bowls but an elimination of the dollar value of the substantial "charitable donation layer" found on the ones sold at the charity auctions.

Homer Laughlin discontinued apricot in December 1997, and we already see apricot trading for a significant premium over currently produced colors, even though it was made in large amounts over the course of eleven years. HLC tells us that black is on "non-stock status," meaning it will only be produced to order several times a year and will require a longer lead time for orders, rather than being produced and carried in stock; and HLC officials tell us black may be put on hiatus at some point in the future. This indicates an important change in nomenclature from "discontinued" to "put on hiatus" for glaze colors which may be dropped due to low sales. While limited edition colors would not be reissued, some regular-line colors that fall from favor in the marketplace (as Fiesta follows home fashion trends, and the hot color this year may be a generally disliked one five years from now) might be put on hiatus but reintroduced if that color starts to be used in home decoration, creating a demand for it from the average consumer. Dave Conley, National Retail Sales Manager of Homer Laughlin China, provided the following sales levels by color for Fiesta in 2003. It should be noted that Tangerine, the newest color at the time, was introduced in late 2003 and thus actual sales figures for 2003 shown on page 65 under-represent the popularity of that color.

*Fiesta Sales rankings by color for calendar year 2003*
1. *Cobalt blue, 15.3%*
2. *Sunflower, 14.0%*
3. *Shamrock, 13.5%*
4. *Cinnabar, 10.0%*
5. *Plum, 8.8%*
6. *Persimmon, 8.1%*
7. *Tangerine, 7.7%*
8. *Turquoise, 5.5%*
9. *White, 4.9%*
10. *Periwinkle blue, 4.5%*
11. *Sea mist green, 2.9%*
12. *Rose, 2.5%*
13. *Black, 2.2%*

It should be noted that as of this writing, Homer Laughlin is anticipating that scarlet, the new color for 2004 (see Plate 186), will be the largest introduction of any color of Fiesta up to this point. Brilliant red glazes have always been the most difficult of all colors to achieve and have been absent from the marketplace for many years. The perfection of a brilliant red glaze on a fully vitrified china product is seen as a major technological achievement by the industry, especially in a high-volume production pottery. Homer Laughlin has committed to buying all the glaze pigment available from its one source for all of 2004 into 2005 in order to satisfy the projected demand for this remarkable color.

## New Fiesta Shapes

Many new items and shapes have been added to the line since 1986, some of them designed for the restaurant trade. The original 1986 assortment of pieces as well as some (not all) subsequent additions are shown on the company flyer on pages 71 and 72. To help identify the new colors, we've also shown the flyer front.

The following items, along with their official item code numbers, make up the full Fiesta assortment as of the summer of 2004.

| Item No. | Description | | |
|---|---|---|---|
| 0098 | Chili Bowl, no handle, 18-oz. (*) (Jumbo Cup with no handle) | 0448 | Carafe with Handle, 60-oz. |
| 0149 | Jumbo Cup, 18-oz. (*) | 0450 | Bouillon, 6¾-oz. |
| 0293 | Jumbo Saucer, 6¾" (*) | 0451 | Rim Soup, 9", 13¼-oz. |
| 0409 | Oval Serving Bowl, 12" | 0452 | Cup, 7¾-oz. |
| 0412 | Bread Tray, Oval, 12" | 0453 | Mug, 10¼-oz. |
| 0417 | Small Pie Baker, 6⅜" | 0455 | Bowl, Extra Large, Serving, 2-qt. |
| 0418 | Cappuccino Mug | 0456 | Platter, 9⅝" |
| 0419 | Medium Pie Baker, 8¼" | 0457 | Platter, 11⅝" |
| 0421 | Small Mixing Bowl, 7½", 44-oz. | 0458 | Platter, 13⅝" |
| 0422 | Medium Mixing Bowl, 8½", 60-oz. | 0459 | Fruit, 5⅜", 6¼-oz. |
| 0424 | Pedestal Mug, 18-oz. | 0460 | Bowl, Small, 5⅝", 14¼-oz. |
| 0439 | Spoon Rest | 0461 | Bowl, Medium, 6⅞", 19-oz. |
| 0440 | Small Vase, 8" | 0462 | Rim Pasta Bowl, 12", 21-oz. |
| 0443 | Senorita Embossed Trivet | 0463 | Plate, Bread and Butter, 6⅛" |
| 0446 | Tumbler, 6½-oz. | 0464 | Plate, Salad, 7¼" |
| 0447 | Utensil Crock | 0465 | Plate, Luncheon, 9" |
| | | 0466 | Plate, Dinner, 10½" |
| | | 0467 | Chop Plate, 11¾" |

| Item No. | Description |
|---|---|
| 0470 | Saucer, 5⅞" |
| 0471 | Bowl, Large Serving, 8¼", 40-oz. |
| 0472 | Stacking Cereal Bowl, 6½", 11-oz. |
| 0475 | Mini Disk Pitcher, 5-oz. |
| 0477 | Saucer, A.D., 4⅞" |
| 0479 | Sugar Packet Holder (*) |
| 0482 | Bowl, Large, Mixing, 9½", 70-oz. (same as covered casserole base) |
| 0484 | Disk Pitcher, Large, 67¼-oz. |
| 0485 | Disk Pitcher, Small, 28-oz. |
| 0486 | Sauce Boat, 18½-oz. |
| 0487 | Deep Dish Pie Baker, 10¼" |
| 0488 | Round Candlestick Holder, 3⅝" |
| 0490 | Bud Vase, 6" |
| 0491 | Medium Vase, 9⅝" |
| 0492 | Individual Creamer, 7-oz. |
| 0494 | Covered Butter |
| 0495 | Covered Casserole, 70-oz. |

| Item No. | Description |
|---|---|
| 0496 | Covered Teapot, 44-oz. |
| 0497 | Salt and Pepper Set |
| 0498 | Individual Covered Sugar, 8¾-oz. |
| 0499 | Relish Tray, 9½-oz. |
| 0505 | Pizza Tray, 15" |
| 0549 | Cup, A.D., Ring Handle, 3-oz. |
| 0565 | Royalty Vase, 4⅞" |
| 0566 | Monarch Vase, 9½" |
| 0568 | Ramekin (French Baker), 8-oz. |
| 0570 | Java Mug, 12-oz. |
| 0723 | Gusto Bowl, 23-oz. |
| 0753 | Hostess Tray, 12¼" |
| 0756 | Range Top Salt and Pepper, Handled |
| 0760 | Snack Plate with well, 10½" |
| 0764 | Teapot, 2-cup |
| 0765 | Pedestal Bowl, 9⅞", 64-oz. |
| 0821 | Sugar and Creamer on Tray Set |

* Originally part of the Fiesta Mates line, now part of Homer Laughlin's official Fiesta catalog.

The following shapes have been added to the regular line subsequent to 1986 but have already been retired:

| Item No. | Description |
|---|---|
| 0468 | Round Serving Tray, 11" |
| 0469 | Napkin Rings, 4-Piece Set |
| 0473 | China Face Wall Clock |
| 0476 | Cup, A.D., Stick Handle, 3-oz. |
| 0493 | Restyled Covered Coffee Server, 36-oz. |
| 0766 | Tripod Bowl |

Except for the discontinued items, each piece is pictured individually on the official Homer Laughlin Fiesta page on the Internet at www.hlchina.com/fiestaitems.htm should you have access to the web and wish to see each item in detail. A line drawing of each can be found in Plate 139.

In addition, a boxed child's set, called "My First Fiesta®" was available in the following color assortment (see Plates 150 and 151.)

(1) Teapot, yellow (2-cup, same as 0764)
(2) Teacups, rose and periwinkle (demitasse cups with ring, rather than stick handles)
(2) Saucers, rose and periwinkle (same as adult size A.D. saucer 0477)
(1) Creamer, turquoise
(1) Sugar Bowl, turquoise
(2) 6" plates, yellow (same as bread and butter plate 0463)

With the original light yellow glaze having been discontinued from the regular line in late 2002, Homer Laughlin took the opportunity to revamp the color lineup of the "My First Fiesta®" set to reflect the more popular bright colors. The new version has the assorted colors of shamrock, plum, sunflower, and tangerine.

A number of items were "borrowed" from the restaurant line and dipped in Fiesta colors to fulfill the needs of the food-service industry. These were named *Fiesta Mates*, and lack the concentric rings or other elements of typical Fiesta styling. They will be marked with the Homer Laughlin backstamp rather than the Fiesta mark shown on page 67. They include the Tower mug, the Denver mug, Seville 3½-oz. ramekin, 10" oval baker, skillet server, Irish coffee mug, 18-oz. Colonial teapot, and 5-oz. jug creamer. Items in the list that started on page 65 (sugar packet holder, jumbo cup and saucer, chili bowl) marked with an asterisk (*) are from the Fiesta Mates line which have been incorporated into the official Fiesta assortment since late 1999.

Other Fiesta items will no doubt be designed and introduced as retailers request them. All of the pieces on pages 65 and 66 are marked Fiesta (including cups) with the exception of the four Fiesta Mates indicated with the asterisk. The cast-indented mark is very similar to the old; the ink-stamped items are marked with a newer version that is shown here. Notice that all letters are upper case — contrast this with the original Fiesta script marks on page 17.

## New or Old? — Vintage or Post86?

Because there was so much variation in the old vintage turquoise glaze and because the new pearl grey is so close to the vintage gray, these two colors, pearl gray and turquoise (and to a lesser extent, shamrock, sapphire, and new cobalt), are the ones most likely to cause confusion to a collector of the old. Only those pieces that are still being made from the old, original molds will carry the old-style, in-mold mark (such as the disk water and juice pitchers, medium, and bud vases, pyramid and bulb candleholders, and sauce boat). In response to collectors' concerns about the similarity of the old and new grey glaze colors, concurrent with the introduction of pearl grey in 1999, Homer Laughlin has added a raised "H" to the underside of those items which shared the old-style molds with the old-style marks to distinguish them from vintage ware. This was added to the mold and thus is found on all colors of these items made in 1999 and later, but it can sometimes be obscured by a heavy application of glaze. In addition, turquoise, cobalt, and sapphire were produced for a number of years prior to the "H" being added, so newer collectors may need to compare some items (such as the new medium vase to a vintage medium vase) to verify the age of such an expensive piece before purchase. All the new items will be slightly smaller and feel relatively heavier than the old, due to the more dense vitrified clay body used since 1986. (Vitrification relates to the temperature of firing — new Fiesta is fired hotter, thus the clay particles tend to fuse together and become more glasslike. Less air is captured in the clay body, making each item slightly heavier, smaller, and more durable. Because it is more dense, it does not absorb moisture or bacteria, thus making it suitable for restaurant use.)

If you can't compare colors and sizes when shopping, remember that saggar pin marks and a fully glazed foot always indicate old Fiesta. (Homer Laughlin just doesn't use saggar pins anymore.) To clarify, old Fiesta plates, for instance, always had a fully glazed foot (the part of the plate that touched the table), and in the firing process, the old plates had to be propped up on three little pins called saggars so they would not fuse themselves to the kiln shelf when the glaze melted during firing. This left the three little scars (or saggar pin marks) on the underside of the plates and under the rims of the vintage bowls with which we are all so familiar. New Fiesta pieces all have a dry or wiped foot; there is no glaze covering the area that touches the table. Old tripod candlesticks almost always had a fully glazed foot and three saggar pin scars on the underside; new ones will always have a dry, wiped foot. Even compared to those items which in the vintage line had a wiped foot (the bulb candlesticks, tall and bud vases, pitchers, and sauce boats, for instance), the new ones display a raw clay that has a bit more shine and is a brighter white than the clay used to make the old line. In addition, old items were dipped in the glaze by hand, whereas the glaze on the new Fiesta is sprayed on. It is often possible to see the speckled spray pattern on new items, especially under the handles of the pitchers, etc., or under the feet of items like the candleholders, sauce boats, or bud vases.

## Specially Decorated Fiesta

You may find various decorations on Fiesta (produced not only by Homer Laughlin but by after-market decorating firms as well). Specially decorated and crested Fiesta will continue to be designed and brought to market by Homer Laughlin in dinnerware sets and specialty items, both as exclusives for retailers or for sale at its own outlet store. In addition, you may find exclusive designs done by after-market decorating firms as well as several exclusive lines done for China Specialities, including versions of Sunporch and Mexicana on white Fiesta pictured in Plates 171 and 172.

## Licensed Fiesta Accessories

Homer Laughlin licensed several companies to use the name "Genuine Fiesta Accessories." These were initially limited to the items shown in Plate 165, a rather restrained offering of table linens and a metal diner-type napkin dispenser. Since 1997, however, they have licensed many, many firms to produce a plethora of items from glass, acrylic, cloth, wood, resin, plastic, metal, enamelware, wax, and paper, as well as numerous electrical appliances — even a steam iron. (See Plate 164.) Some ceramic items (like the small hurricane lamp and picture frames) are from China; they were not made at HLC. Several items are made of a dense, heavy synthetic resin that might appear to the inexperienced collector to be ceramic (for instance, the miniature items or the picnic tablecloth weights). The variety of these items is mind boggling, and we won't even attempt to survey the scope of them all at this writing. Some were specially designed to coordinate with Fiesta's design elements (for example, the enamel cookware); some share only the colors of Fiesta (like the electric waffle iron); and some have only the Fiesta name emblazoned on the side (like the black and chrome '50s-style steam iron). Many of the accessory items have been very well received while others haven't. As of this writing, a number of them are now being discontinued by some major retailers and are available at liquidation stores. If these appeal to you, buy them — especially when they can be found at liquidations at fractions of their original prices. They will no doubt be of interest to collectors at some point in the future as curiosities. It is unlikely that some of the more unpopular or impractical items will be made again.

Editor's note: We are very grateful to Joel Wilson (China Specialties, Inc. and the *Fiesta Collector's Quarterly*) for supplying us with this up-to-date information as well as many of the photographs. Because of the lapse between the time we release our book to the publishers for printing and when the book actually hits the market, changes to the line may have occurred in the interim.

The *Fiesta Collector's Quarterly* is a newsletter published by China Specialties for collectors of old and new Fiesta, and features regular updates on color and item additions to the new Fiesta line. A sample copy and subscription form are available free upon receipt of a self-addressed, stamped, long envelope. The address for the newsletter is Fiesta Collector's Quarterly, P.O. Box 471, Valley City, OH 44280. China Specialities is an Ohio company catering to the interests of collectors of a number of locally produced dinnerware lines of the 1930s and 1940s. They also publish the *Hall China and Tea Company China Collector Club Newsletter* and commissions and distributes dated, limited edition shapes never originally produced in such patterns as Autumn Leaf, Red Poppy, Orange Poppy, Silhouette, and Blue Bouquet. The company is also the exclusive source for Hot Oven China rolling pins. In addition, several of the specially decorated Fiesta collector items shown in this section were made exclusively for China Specialties.

## Early Modifications

**Plate 124**
*Advertising Brochure.*
This is the original advertising brochure from the February 1986 introduction party at the West Virginia Cultural Center in Charleston. These line drawings were made from publicity photographs of sample items made from semi-vitreous clay. Consequently, they never made it into regular production, since a last-minute decision to go with a fully vitrified body that would meet the requirements of the food service industry was made subsequent to these photos being taken. Note the old-style teapot lid, Ironstone-style sugar bowl, casserole, and coffee server and compare them to those shown in the 1987 brochure below.

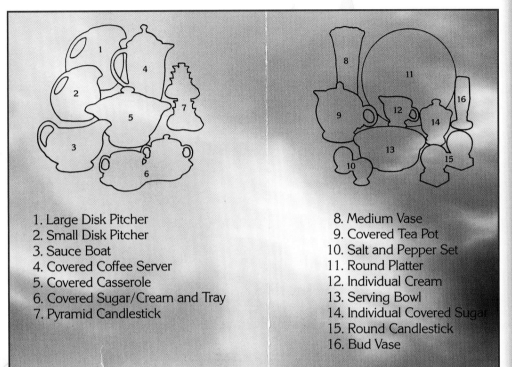

1. Large Disk Pitcher
2. Small Disk Pitcher
3. Sauce Boat
4. Covered Coffee Server
5. Covered Casserole
6. Covered Sugar/Cream and Tray
7. Pyramid Candlestick
8. Medium Vase
9. Covered Tea Pot
10. Salt and Pepper Set
11. Round Platter
12. Individual Cream
13. Serving Bowl
14. Individual Covered Sugar
15. Round Candlestick
16. Bud Vase

Reproduced by permission of the Homer Laughlin China Company.

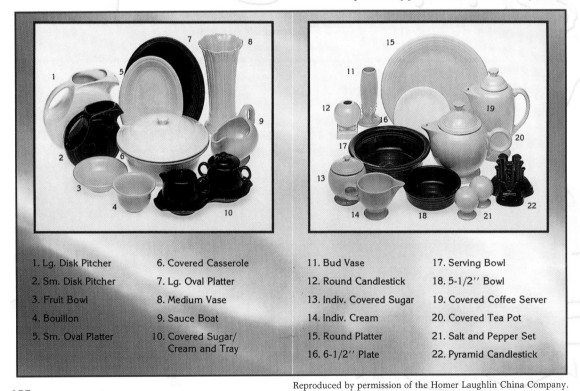

1. Lg. Disk Pitcher
2. Sm. Disk Pitcher
3. Fruit Bowl
4. Bouillon
5. Sm. Oval Platter
6. Covered Casserole
7. Lg. Oval Platter
8. Medium Vase
9. Sauce Boat
10. Covered Sugar/Cream and Tray
11. Bud Vase
12. Round Candlestick
13. Indiv. Covered Sugar
14. Indiv. Cream
15. Round Platter
16. 6-1/2″ Plate
17. Serving Bowl
18. 5-1/2″ Bowl
19. Covered Coffee Server
20. Covered Tea Pot
21. Salt and Pepper Set
22. Pyramid Candlestick

Reproduced by permission of the Homer Laughlin China Company.

**Plate 125**
*Advertising Brochure.*
This is an advertising brochure from 1987 that shows the actual items being produced from the vitreous clay. Note that the original coffeepot lid is now being used on the teapot (the dome shape deformed less during firing than the original flat lid), and the casserole and coffee server as well as the sugar bowl have been redesigned since the previous brochure.

**Plate 126**
*Coffeepots.*
The coffeepot in the background was the original design, but when the decision was made to switch to a fully vitrified body, it warped so severely, few lids would fit, resulting in an unacceptable scrap rate. This style was made through a couple of production runs in the early months of 1986 before it was changed to the one in the foreground. Collectors value the original style coffeepot at $250.00+, if the lid fits reasonably well. (Note: Our picture, though well composed and photographed, tends to make the restyled pot artificially large in comparison to the one in the background — in reality, the opposite is true.)

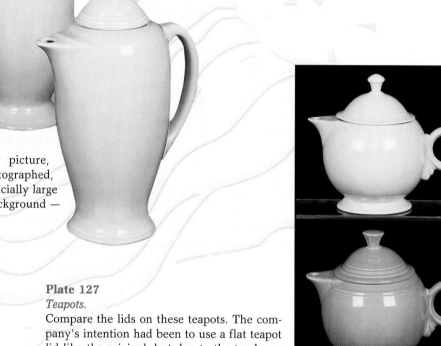

**Plate 127**
*Teapots.*
Compare the lids on these teapots. The company's intention had been to use a flat teapot lid like the original, but due to the tendency of the vitrified clay to warp, the original style coffeepot lid was substituted, as you can see on the white example. Later, once all the existing coffeepot lids were used up, a fluted finial was adapted to this lid. The teapot opening remained large until about 1989 when it was modified to a smaller opening with a flange. The teapot still looks the same as the pink one once the lid is on, but the lid now has an inner groove, and a raised flange was added to the base, resulting in a tighter and more satisfactory fit.

**Plate 128**
*Sugar Bowls.*
The sugar bowl in the 1986 brochure is shown here alongside an Amberstone example; both utilize the Ironstone shape. This was soon replaced with one made from the vintage marmalade mold (without the notch for the spoon); you'll see it behind and to the right alongside the individual sugar bowl, the only other one in the Post86 assortment. Photo courtesy Laura and Christopher Monley.

**Plate 129**
Front of company flyer, c. 1996.

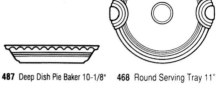

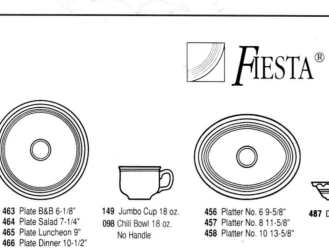

463 Plate B&B 6-1/8"
464 Plate Salad 7-1/4"
465 Plate Luncheon 9"
466 Plate Dinner 10-1/2"
467 Plate Chop 11-3/4"

149 Jumbo Cup 18 oz.
098 Chili Bowl 18 oz.
No Handle

456 Platter No. 6 9-5/8"
457 Platter No. 8 11-5/8"
458 Platter No. 10 13-5/8"

487 Deep Dish Pie Baker 10-1/8"

468 Round Serving Tray 11"

452 Cup 7-3/4 oz.

450 Bouillon 6-3/4 oz.

470 Saucer 5-7/8"
477 Saucer A.D. 4-7/8"
293 Jumbo Saucer 6-3/4"

453 Mug 10-1/4 oz.

460 Bowl Sm. 5-5/8" 14-1/4 oz.
461 Bowl Med. 6-7/8" 19 oz.
471 Bowl Veg. Lg. 39-1/4 oz.

459 Fruit 5-3/8" 6-1/4 oz.
472 Stacking Cereal
Bowl 6-1/2" 11 oz.

821 Sugar & Cream Tray Set

498 Indiv. Covd. Sugar 8-3/4 oz.

451 No. 7 Rim Soup 9" 13-1/4 oz.
462 Pasta Bowl 12" 21-3/4 oz.

492 Indiv. Cream 7 oz.

486 Sauceboat 18-1/2 oz.

494 Covd. Butter

489 Pyramid
Candlestick 3-3/8"

476 Cup A.D.
3 oz.

488 Round
Candlestick 3-5/8"

497 Salt 2-1/4"
Pepper 2-1/4"
Salt & Pepper Set

469 Napkin Rings
4-Piece Set

490 Bud Vase 6"

493 Covd. Coffee 36 oz.

496 Covd. Teapot 44 oz.

491 Medium Vase 9-5/8"

484 Disc Pitcher Lg. 67-1/4 oz.
485 Disc Pitcher Sm. 28 oz.
475 Miniature Disc Pitcher 4-3/4 oz.

495 Covd. Casserole
51-1/2 oz.

THE HOMER LAUGHLIN CHINA CO.

All products are lead free.

Volume measurements are brim-full capacities.

Reproduced by permission of the Homer Laughlin China Company.

**Plate 130**
Back of company flyer, c. 1996.

# Colors and Shapes

**Plate 131**
*Assorted Pieces.*
The new cobalt is a much darker tone than either the original 1936 cobalt or the limited edition sapphire. This photo was taken very soon after the Post86 line was introduced; notice how light the rose pieces are. Over the years, HLC has been slowly making it a deeper and richer tone; it's now almost a hot pink, which is especially obvious if you try to add to a set purchased in the earlier years of production.

**Plate 132**
*Assorted Pieces.*
A warm, sunny Southwestern atmosphere is created here by apricot, new turquoise, new yellow, and sea mist green. If you have trouble deciding whether your cobalt and turquoise tripods are old or new, take a look at their bases. If they are fully glazed underneath, they're old.

**Plate 133**
*Assorted Pieces.*
This photo features items in persimmon and the limited edition color that was produced in winter of 1996, sapphire. Unlike the limited edition lilac, which was made for two full years, sapphire was limited to 180 firing days in an extremely narrow number of items.

**Plate 134**
*Tripod Candleholders.*
Here are the infamous lilac tripod candleholders. These have attracted more interest than any other item that was ever made in lilac, since they were produced in a very limited quantity for Bloomingdale's to use as an in-store promotion. Collectors have paid dearly for a pair to call their own! The tripod candleholder shape in the regular colors was no longer available from normal retailers and became a Homer Laughlin China Retail Outlet Store exclusive in 2001.

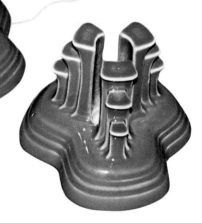

**Plate 135**
*Vases and Candleholders.*
Shown here are pearl gray, a standard color from 1999 – 2001, and the limited editon two-year color juniper that was made in only 2000 and 2001. During 1999 in anticipation of the millennium, Homer Laughlin produced three different vases. Millennium I (far right) was an exclusive for Bloomingdale's and was limited to 1,000 of each color. Millennium II, which resembles a double-spouted disk pitcher, was an exclusive for Macy's. Millennium III (which resembles the 1930s 12" red vase shown in the morgue photograph in Plate 482) was available in all colors except black and apricot, and it was available to all retailers. All three were discontinued at the end of 1999.
Photo courtesy Harvey Linn, Jr.

**Plate 136**
*Assorted Lilac Items.*

**Plate 137**
*Assorted Lilac Items.*
The bulb candleholders and bud vase were made exclusively for China Specialties, the after-dinner cup and saucer for both Bloomingdale's and China Specialties. As Homer Laughlin traditionally gives only a six-month exclusive on such items, some of these pieces may have been made for other retailers as well during the two-year production period.

**Plate 138**
Front side of brochure, April 2004.

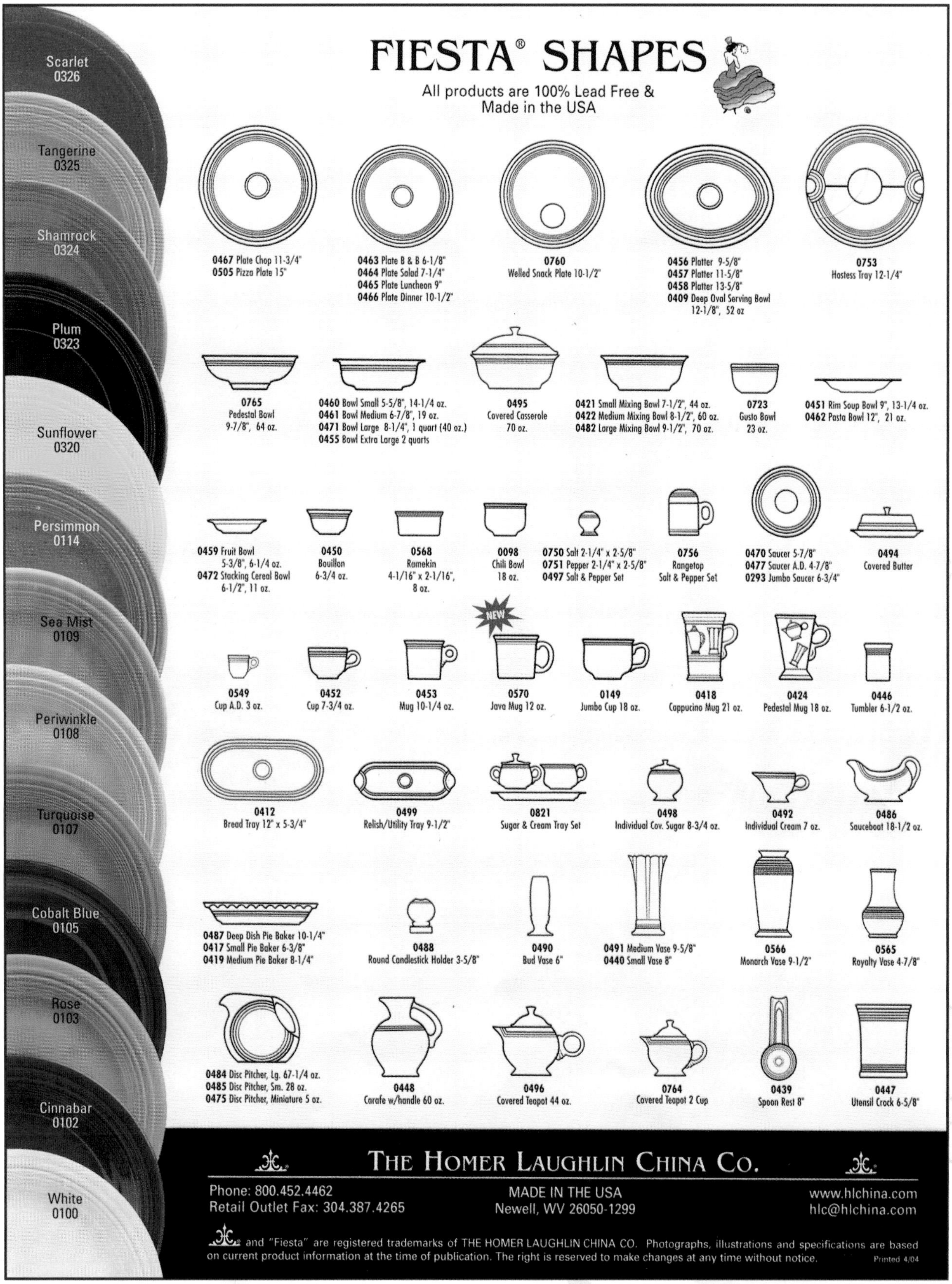

Scarlet 0326
Tangerine 0325
Shamrock 0324
Plum 0323
Sunflower 0320
Persimmon 0114
Sea Mist 0109
Periwinkle 0108
Turquoise 0107
Cobalt Blue 0105
Rose 0103
Cinnabar 0102
White 0100
FIESTA® SHAPES
All products are 100% Lead Free & Made in the USA
0467 Plate Chop 11-3/4"
0505 Pizza Plate 15"
0463 Plate B & B 6-1/8"
0464 Plate Salad 7-1/4"
0465 Plate Luncheon 9"
0466 Plate Dinner 10-1/2"
0760 Welled Snack Plate 10-1/2"
0456 Platter 9-5/8"
0457 Platter 11-5/8"
0458 Platter 13-5/8"
0409 Deep Oval Serving Bowl 12-1/8", 52 oz
0753 Hostess Tray 12-1/4"
0765 Pedestal Bowl 9-7/8", 64 oz.
0460 Bowl Small 5-5/8", 14-1/4 oz.
0461 Bowl Medium 6-7/8", 19 oz.
0471 Bowl Large 8-1/4", 1 quart (40 oz.)
0455 Bowl Extra Large 2 quarts
0495 Covered Casserole 70 oz.
0421 Small Mixing Bowl 7-1/2", 44 oz.
0422 Medium Mixing Bowl 8-1/2", 60 oz.
0482 Large Mixing Bowl 9-1/2", 70 oz.
0723 Gusto Bowl 23 oz.
0451 Rim Soup Bowl 9", 13-1/4 oz.
0462 Pasta Bowl 12", 21 oz.
0459 Fruit Bowl 5-3/8", 6-1/4 oz.
0472 Stacking Cereal Bowl 6-1/2", 11 oz.
0450 Bouillon 6-3/4 oz.
0568 Ramekin 4-1/16" x 2-1/16", 8 oz.
0098 Chili Bowl 18 oz.
0750 Salt 2-1/4" x 2-5/8"
0751 Pepper 2-1/4" x 2-5/8"
0497 Salt & Pepper Set
0756 Rangetop Salt & Pepper Set
0470 Saucer 5-7/8"
0477 Saucer A.D. 4-7/8"
0293 Jumbo Saucer 6-3/4"
0494 Covered Butter
NEW
0549 Cup A.D. 3 oz.
0452 Cup 7-3/4 oz.
0453 Mug 10-1/4 oz.
0570 Java Mug 12 oz.
0149 Jumbo Cup 18 oz.
0418 Cappucino Mug 21 oz.
0424 Pedestal Mug 18 oz.
0446 Tumbler 6-1/2 oz.
0412 Bread Tray 12" x 5-3/4"
0499 Relish/Utility Tray 9-1/2"
0821 Sugar & Cream Tray Set
0498 Individual Cov. Sugar 8-3/4 oz.
0492 Individual Cream 7 oz.
0486 Sauceboat 18-1/2 oz.
0487 Deep Dish Pie Baker 10-1/4"
0417 Small Pie Baker 6-3/8"
0419 Medium Pie Baker 8-1/4"
0488 Round Candlestick Holder 3-5/8"
0490 Bud Vase 6"
0491 Medium Vase 9-5/8"
0440 Small Vase 8"
0566 Monarch Vase 9-1/2"
0565 Royalty Vase 4-7/8"
0484 Disc Pitcher, Lg. 67-1/4 oz.
0485 Disc Pitcher, Sm. 28 oz.
0475 Disc Pitcher, Miniature 5 oz.
0448 Carafe w/handle 60 oz.
0496 Covered Teapot 44 oz.
0764 Covered Teapot 2 Cup
0439 Spoon Rest 8"
0447 Utensil Crock 6-5/8"
THE HOMER LAUGHLIN CHINA CO.
Phone: 800.452.4462
Retail Outlet Fax: 304.387.4265
MADE IN THE USA
Newell, WV 26050-1299
www.hlchina.com
hlc@hlchina.com
and "Fiesta" are registered trademarks of THE HOMER LAUGHLIN CHINA CO. Photographs, illustrations and specifications are based on current product information at the time of publication. The right is reserved to make changes at any time without notice.
Printed 4/04


Reproduced by permission of the Homer Laughlin China Company.

**Plate 139**
Back side of brochure, April 2004.

**Plate 140**
*Medium Vase and Flower Vase.*
The last limited edition color was juniper, which was only produced for the two-year period of 2000 through 2001 only. A deep teal blue-green, it is shown here in the medium vase. Next to it is a piece that will never be made in chartreuse with the exception of this sample, a 7½" vase. The small flower vase was in fact added to the line at some point in 2000, but chartreuse was discontinued in December of 1999, so this pre-production sample is quite coveted.

**Plate 141**
*Presentation Bowl.*
Raspberry presentation bowls were produced by HLC in December of 1997 to celebrate the five hundred millionth piece of Fiesta produced since 1936. Only five hundred were made, nearly all of which were presented to owners and shareholders of this private, family-held company. Fifteen of the bowls were donated to charity auctions to benefit educational scholarship funds in the Newell/East Liverpool area in June and July of 1998. They were later produced in black (exclusive to HLC's factory retail outlet), rose, yellow, turquoise, periwinkle blue, sea mist green, cobalt, persimmon, pearl gray, white, and chartreuse (exclusive to Dayton-Hudson Marshall Fields).

**Plate 142**
*Christmas Ornaments.*
Since 1997, Homer Laughlin has produced a yearly Fiesta Christmas ornament shaped like a miniature Fiesta plate. In addition to the two 1997 ornaments you see here (both fronts and backs are shown), there is also one that features the same holly and red ribbon decoration found on the Holiday Fiesta line. These are produced in solid colors adorned with the Fiesta Senorita in 24k gold. Other colors will be utilized each year.

**Plates 143 and 144**
*Gift Sets.*
Special novelty gift sets of Fiesta available in 1999 at the HLC outlet store. Right: "Cookies For Santa" welled snack plate and cup. Below: "Some Bunny's been eating out of my Fiesta," child's Easter place setting of 9" plate, 12-oz. cereal bowl, and tumbler. Photos courtesy Mick and Lorna Chase/Fiesta Plus.

## East Liverpool High School Alumni Specials

Following are examples of limited edition items made for the East Liverpool High School Alumni's yearly auction. Though HLC produced auction items before then, since the raspberry presentation bowls were sold in 1998, collector interest in these limited edition items has seriously increased.

Here is a list of each year's offering — quantity and color are noted:

*1998* – Twelve raspberry presentation bowls: Produced in black (exclusive to HLC's factory retail outlet), rose, yellow, turquoise, periwinkle blue, sea mist green, cobalt, persimmon, pearl gray, white, chartreuse (exclusive to Dayton-Hudson Marshall Fields), and the limited numbered edition of five hundred in raspberry.

*1998* – Twenty-four chartreuse coffeepots: Produced in white, black, rose, apricot, cobalt, yellow, turquoise, periwinkle blue, sea mist green, lilac, persimmon, pearl gray, juniper, cinnabar, and sunflower, as well as limited numbered editions of twenty-four in chartreuse and twenty-four in shamrock.

*1999* – Twenty-four black Millennium I vases: Produced in white, rose, cobalt, yellow, turquoise, sea mist green, persimmon, chartreuse, pearl gray, and limited numbered editions of twenty-four in black and twenty-four in tangerine.

*2000* – Twenty-four juniper Millennium III vases: Produced in white, rose, cobalt, yellow, turquoise, periwinkle blue, sea mist green, persimmon, chartreuse, and pearl gray, as well as a limited edition of twenty-four in juniper and one glazed in sunflower which was donated to HLCCA and auctioned off during the 2000 HLCCA conference in Pittsburgh.

*2001* – Twenty-one "Fiestaware 2000" Jonathan Parry pitchers. This pitcher was never put in regular production — the line was stopped in 2000, then a limited numbered edition of twenty-four was produced for auction in sunflower. (Sample prototypes have been rumored in cobalt, juniper, and persimmon.)

*2002* – Twenty-four juniper Royalty vases: Produced in white, black, rose, cobalt, yellow, turquoise, periwinkle blue, sea mist green, persimmon, cinnabar, sunflower, plum, shamrock, tangerine, scarlet, and a limited numbered edition of twenty-four in juniper.

*2003* – Twenty-four shamrock coffeepots. (See coffeepot information given for 1998).

*2004* – Twenty-four tangerine Millennium I vases. (See Millennium I vase information given for 1999.)

**Plate 145**
*Assorted Pieces.*
2003 shamrock coffeepot; tangerine Millennium I vase; 1998 chartreuse coffeepot; and 2000 juniper Millennium III vase (bottom inscription shown on the right). Photo courtesy David Schaefer.

**Plate 146**
This is the bottom inscription on the 2000 juniper Millennium III vase. Photo courtesy Harvey Linn, Jr.

**Plates 147 and 148**
*First and Second Generations of Holiday Fiesta.*
The original line (sans the ribbon, Plate 148) was produced for the 1987 Christmas season only and was not a huge success. The revised line, currently offered by Homer Laughlin, has a larger decal and features a red ribbon in addition to the holly and berry motif. (Much better!) You will also find several other Christmas-themed decorations, including Christmas trees in various Fiesta colors at the rim of white Fiesta plates, and one with snowmen, done as exclusives for various retailers.

**Plate 149**
*Dinner Plates.*
These dinner plates are currently being marketed by HLC — a theme for every holiday and some just designed with the kids in mind: Thanksgiving, Turkey Day, Stars and Stripes, Snowman (on cobalt), Scarecrow, Candy Corn, Sugar Plum Fairy, Cowboy, and Rubber Ducky. Photo courtesy Joel Wilson.

**Plates 150 and 151**
*"My First Fiesta®"*
This child-sized set called "My First Fiesta®" was introduced in 1999; the original color selection is shown. Assembled from a mixture of items from the adult line (2-cup teapot, ring-handled after-dinner cup, after-dinner saucer, 6" plate) and specially designed

items (miniature covered sugar and creamer), it comes in a specially decorated box. With the original light yellow glaze having been discontinued from the regular line in late 2002, Homer Laughlin took the opportunity to revamp the color lineup of the "My First Fiesta®" set to reflect the more popular bright colors. The new version has the assorted colors of shamrock, plum, sunflower, and tangerine. Photo courtesy Mick and Lorna Chase/Fiesta Plus.

**Plate 152**
*"Hometown Heroes®"*
"Hometown Heroes®" is the name of this darling three-piece children's set. Also currently on the market is a similar set called "Rubber Ducky" (bath bubbles and rubber ducks is the theme) and another three-piece set called "Baby's First Fiesta®" — too cute! Photo courtesy Mick and Lorna Chase/Fiesta Plus.

**Plate 153**
*Mickey Mouse Disk Pitcher.*
This disk water pitcher is one of only 2,088 made for and distributed by the Disney Channel© as an incentive program reward. Even though the production quantity seems high, it's quite collectible and difficult to locate. Photo courtesy Chuck Denlinger.

**Plate 154**

*Lamp and Clock.*

The Fiesta lamp (shown with its original shade) was produced in 1993 as a J.C. Penney exclusive. It met with little success and was offered for one season only. To the right is the clock. Introduced as a Penney's exclusive in 1993, it was discontinued for a brief period, then brought back to the general line. The clock is found in all colors produced during the period except lilac. It was discontinued a second time in 2001.

**Plates 155 and 156**

*Commemorative Items.*

For Fiesta's sixtieth birthday in 1996, Homer Laughlin produced several commemorative items: a 5-piece beverage set shown above in sapphire (the pitcher is shown again on the right in the sought-after lilac glaze), mugs, a serving tray, and a clock. Besides the two colors shown here, the beverage set was also made in turquoise, cobalt, periwinkle, persimmon, and rose. Rose sets were very limited (possibly to less than three hundred, although there is no way to be exact). These sets normally retailed for about $50.00, although sale prices were nearer $30.00. The mugs are lettered "Genuine Fiesta, 60th Anniversary, 1936 – 1996, still proudly made in the U.S.A. by the Homer Laughlin China Company." The round serving tray was a new design, but one we feel Rhead would approve. (This is the earliest version; subsequent versions of this tray feature smooth-edged handles). The anniversary clock features the special logo instead of the dancing senorita at the 12 o'clock position.

## Commemoratives and Exclusives

**Plates 157 and 158**
*Warner Brothers Exclusives.*
Homer Laughlin has also produced Fiesta place settings and serving pieces for Warner Brothers stores that feature a different Looney Tunes character for each color (very popular with collectors). White features Tweety Bird; periwinkle blue, Bugs Bunny; turquoise, Daffy Duck; yellow, Sylvester; and rose, Porky Pig.

**Plate 159**
*Quatra Pitcher.*
An exclusive design for Macy's department stores, Quatra features white Fiesta to which Homer Laughlin has added four concentric rings of periwinkle blue, sea mist green, yellow, and persimmon at the edge.

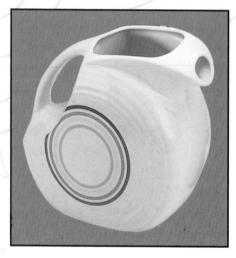

**Plates 160 and 161**
*Plates.*
These plates were produced soon after Homer Laughlin's fiftieth anniversary. The plate on the left was made by HLC for its dealers; it shows the company's new restaurant china logo. The other was made for dealers and collectors; it is the 12" white chop plate with the Fiesta logo in mango red. A relative few were produced in yellow and apricot with the Mango Red decoration.

## Plate 162
*Bloomingdale's Set.*
This was a Bloomingdale's exclusive for 2001; it features shooting stars and the words "Fiesta Celebrates the Third Millennium" on one side, and the Fiesta dancing lady on the other. There was a similar set issued for 2000. Photo courtesy Joyce and Dan Stephens/Fiesta4.us.

## Plate 163
*Flatware.*
Homer Laughlin also introduced coordinating plastic-handled flatware. The solid-color plastic handles feature a partial ring design, and each piece is marked Fiesta on the back on the stainless steel tang. Besides the place settings: dinner and salad forks, tea and soup spoons, and dinner knives, there are serving pieces, including a pie lifter, slotted and regular tablespoons, and a cold meat fork. It was made in all the colors listed for the dinnerware except sapphire. (Lilac was made in place-setting items only — no serving pieces.) In addition, true red and emerald green were made as accessories for the Holiday Fiesta. (To keep yours looking new, use the air-dry cycle on your dishwasher and avoid lemon dish soap.) Photo courtesy Joel Wilson.

## Plate 164
*Promo Card.*
An official promotion card showing Fiesta licensed accessories made by other manufacturers. (Those are HLC-produced genuine Fiesta mugs on the mug rack and a handled Fiesta serving tray.) Included are enamel cookware and colanders, resin magnets and cheese picks, picture frames, and wax candles. The plaid fabric items are by Audrey, and these (in various combinations of Fiesta colors) replaced the earlier Fiesta print by Dakota shown in Plate 165.

Reproduced by permission of the Homer Laughlin China Company.

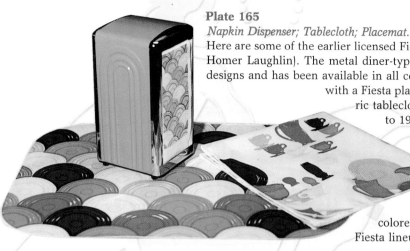

### Plate 165

*Napkin Dispenser; Tablecloth; Placemat.*

Here are some of the earlier licensed Fiesta products (made by manufacturers other than Homer Laughlin). The metal diner-type napkin dispenser is one of the more enduring designs and has been available in all colors except lilac. The paper napkins are printed with a Fiesta plate design in assorted pastels. Also shown is a fabric tablecloth produced by Dakota for a limited time, 1994 to 1995. Fabric accessories were available in a scatter print as well as an all-over plate design. In addition to tablecloths, you may find chair pads, curtains, placemats, and napkins by the same company. All items were available in the "original color" version (eagerly sought by collectors) as well as a pastel-colored print that coordinates well with the Post86 Fiesta lineup.

### Plate 166

*Magnets.*

These Fiesta magnets are in the vintage colors. They were put out by General Housewares Corp. under licensure from HLC and were limited to a two-year production in these colors. You'll also find magnets in Post86 colors. Photo courtesy Philip Gray.

### Plate 167

*Assortment of Items from the Fiesta Mates Line.*

This line lacks the typical Fiesta styling; these pieces were taken from the regular restaurant line and dipped in Fiesta glazes. From left: sugar packet holder, fry pan server, 18-oz. jumbo cup and saucer, 4-oz. ramekin, 18-oz. jumbo bowl, 5-oz. creamer, Tower and Denver mugs, and 10" oval baker. Photo courtesy Joel Wilson.

**Plate 168**
*Fiesta 2000.*
In 2000 Homer Laughlin added this shape to its retail dinnerware line. Designed by Jonathan Parry prior to his death, this line has a contemporary, vaguely Oriental feel, with abstract embossed designs reminiscent of bamboo leaves in a 1¼" band at the outer rim. It was dipped in a number of the more popular Fiesta glazes, including cobalt, persimmon, pearl gray, and juniper. Only because retail store buyers felt it would be more easily marketed to the public if it carried the Fiesta name, it was dubbed "Fiesta 2000." But it is not part of the Fiesta line. Fiesta 2000 is totally separate and is related to contemporary Fiesta in the same tangential way Tango was to the Fiesta ware of the 1930s or Rhythm in the 1950s, and in the future will no doubt be viewed in much the same way as those lines are by today's Fiesta collectors. Only brought out in a very basic line, it was not a real success and was withdrawn from the marketplace by the end of 2000. Photo courtesy Joel Wilson.

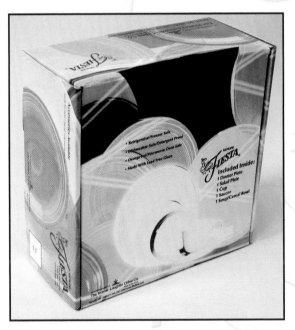

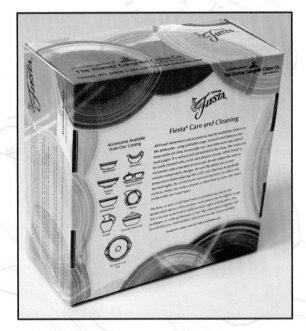

**Plates 169 and 170**
*Prototype Box.*
This prototype die-cut cardboard box designed to hold a place setting of Post86 Fiesta was never put in production. It was more cost effective to print labels and glue them onto white boxes, which is the current choice of packaging. Photos courtesy David Schaefer.

**Plate 171**
*Sunporch Grouping.*
The Sunporch decoration on white Fiesta was made in 1998. The decal was modified somewhat from the original Sunporch line to leave no doubt in anyone's mind that the dinnerware pictured on the table actually is Fiesta! All the items in this line were limited to five hundred pieces and were available only to *Fiesta Collector's Quarterly* subscribers and through an antique mall near the HLC plant in East Liverpool.

**Plate 172**
*Mexican Grouping.*
This is the new version of Mexicana, available for the first time in 2000. The decal is fired on white Fiesta and features cobalt lines and accents. This line duplicates a concept from an original '30s set featuring Mexicana-decorated, Century-shaped cups with blue lining and cobalt Fiesta saucers and undertrays. Like Sunporch, all items in this line were also limited to five hundred pieces and were available only to club members/subscribers and at the antique mall near the HLC plant.

**Plate 173**
*Sunporch Tea Set.*
I couldn't resist showing you my very own personalized Sunporch tea set and tray. Thanks, Joel.

**Plate 174**
*50th Anniversary Mugs.*
To commemorate Fiesta's fiftieth anniversary, HLC made these mugs for China Specialties. Less than six hundred sets were produced, each consisting of ten white mugs decorated with the Dancing Senorita trademark in a different Fiesta color (red, yellow, dark blue, turquoise, light green, forest green, rose, chartreuse, gray, and medium green.)

**Plate 175**
*60th Anniversary Pitcher.*
This pitcher is an example of the 60th anniversary Fiesta commemorative (limited to six hundred pieces) that was made for China Specialties in 1996. The decal was created from original artwork done for a vintage advertising brochure and is permanently fired on. These may be found with a subscriber's name and a serial number inscribed in gold under the base.

**Plate 176**
*Moon Over Miami.*
Moon Over Miami is the name of this terrific design; this disk pitcher is only one of several pieces in the line. It features a pink flamingo fired onto black Fiesta. You may also find a calendar plate (the 13" chop plate) with 1993 in a Deco reserve centering the twelve months of the year depicted as calendar pages, also a China Specialties special order.

**Plate 177**
*Shelf Display Signs.*
Also exclusive to *Fiesta Collector's Quarterly* (and distributed only to their subscribers), Homer Laughlin designed a special shelf display sign, similar to department store advertising pieces you often see in other china lines. They were made in persimmon in 1995, turquoise in 1996, apricot in 1997, chartreuse in 1998, rose in 1999, and the retired yellow in 2002. According to China Specialties, juniper-glazed sign blanks were in fact made and have been warehoused for a number of years. Plans are that they will be decorated and released to FCQ subscribers concurrent with the release of this, the tenth edition of our book — what a nice tribute!

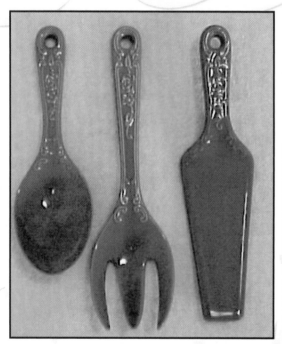

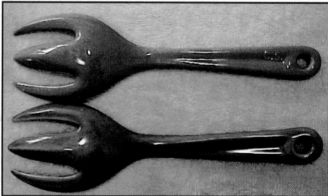

**Plates 178 and 179**
*China Specialties OvenServe Spoon, Fork, and Cake Server.*
Shown here in the coveted lilac, these recreations are imported; they are not Homer Laughlin products. All the new utensils are marked on the back with a small "c.s." embossed in the mold as can be seen on the back of the turquoise fork handle (shown next to a vintage green Kitchen Kraft fork) in Plate 179. In addition to the lilac and turquoise shown here, they were as made in forest green, rose, and ivory vellum.

**Plate 180**
*Maverick Menagerie.*
These molds were recreated by China Specialties. Unlike most mavericks (non-HLC made), they were modeled from "scratch" rather than from a mold that was made from an original, so they're the same size as the genuine Harlequin animals and incredibly detailed. Five animals were produced: the cat, the donkey, the duck, the lamb, and the fish, shown here in lilac alongside the original maroon fish of the Harlequin line. These animals are not glazed inside, however, which makes them seem lighter in weight than the old ones. They are being custom glazed in various new colors and are marked on the underside with the "Maverick Menagerie" oval backstamp on the partially closed-in base shown above. (Animals from the original animal line have a completely open bottom.) The duck was also used as inspiration for a pie bird, which was never part of the original animal line.

*Exclusives for the Homer Laughlin China Collector's Association:* The HLCCA is a nonprofit 501(c) (3) volunteer association bringing together collectors of Homer Laughlin china company dinnerware. HLCCA was formed in July 1998, for the purpose of sharing information about HLC's nineteenth, twentieth, and now twenty-first century dinnerware with collectors, authors, researchers, museums, and libraries. The HLCCA holds an annual conference, alternating biennially between Pittsburgh, Pennsylvania, and other major U.S. cities. The conference activities span four days and include a pre-conference show and sale, exhibits, a banquet with keynote speaker, conference HLCCA exclusives, and local tourism opportunities. For more information call toll-free, 1-877-847-5222, or visit online, www.hlca.org. For membership information, see page 6. Shown on these pages is only a sampling of the items made exclusively for the club.

**Plate 181**
*Juice Pitcher Exclusives.*
HLCCA is celebrating Art Deco styling and the 1930s with a series of limited edition Fiesta juice pitcher exclusives. Released in 1999, the pearl gray pitcher celebrates the 1930 opening of the Chrysler Building, a landmark in Art Deco style. Two were released in 2000. The juice pitcher celebrating 1931 features a decal of the stylized Dick Tracy, and the 1932 yellow pitcher exclusive commemorates the Golden Age of Radio. Released in

2001, the 1933 pitcher, decaled in six metallic glazes on black, features the 1933 Chicago World's Fair "Century of Progress." A 2002 release, the 1934 juice pitcher commemorates transoceanic voyage and was produced on juniper and periwinkle. In 2003 the sixth juice pitcher, for 1935, glazed in plum, commemorates "Dish Night at the Movies," and features a movie marquee in metallic glazes. The seventh, released in 2004, celebrating 1936, commemorates Fredrick H. Rhead and the introduction of Fiesta. It was produced in tangerine and features Rhead's personal bookplate on the reverse side, courtesy of the Homer Laughlin China Company. Each year the pitchers are unveiled to members at the HLCCA conference.

### Plate 182
*Dick Tracy Pitchers.*

Here's the Dick Tracy juice pitcher again alongside a full-size disk water pitcher that is extremely rare. The decals were sent to HLC for the purpose of making samples. HLC misunderstood and put the decal on the large pitcher by mistake. This is one of only two that were made. Note the HLC sticker on the bottom. The other one is in a museum; they're truly unique and virtually priceless. Photo courtesy Chuck Denlinger.

### Plate 183
*2001 & 2002 Conference Giveaways.*

The sunflower Geo bowl centered with the HLCCA logo was made exclusively as a giveaway for the club's 2001 conference in Pittsburgh, Pennsylvania. The other two items, the pie baker (limited edition of 144) and the utensil crock (limited edition of 35) are from the 2002 conference in New Orleans, Louisiana. Photo courtesy David Schaefer.

### Plate 184
*2003 Conference Giveaways.*

Baseball was the theme of the fifth anniversary conference in 2003 that was held in Pittsburgh. The teapots were used as centerpieces, and the sugar bowls were giveaways for each member attending the conference. A limited edition of only 40 teapots was produced, and the sugar bowls were limited to an edition of 144. Both the candleholders and the salt and pepper shakers are currently in production and may be purchased from www.hlcca.org. Each piece includes an HLCCA baseball collector card featuring all four baseball-decaled Fiesta items. Photo courtesy David Schaefer.

**Plate 185**
*2004 Conference Giveaways.*
Here are examples of some of the 2004 conference exclusives in Post86 turquoise with a Phoenix metallic decal: the carafe (limited edition of 40) and the bread tray (limited edition of 144). Photo courtesy David Schaefer.

**Plate 186**
*Scarlet Java Mug.*
The newest Fiesta color, scarlet, was released to the public in August/September 2004. HLC also introduced the new Java 12-oz. mug, bigger than the normal Fiesta mug, with a larger "C" handle. Dave Conley, national sales and marketing director of HLC, produced a limited edition of 144 new scarlet Java mugs like the one shown here for the HLCCA and presented them to attendees at the 2004 conference held in Phoenix, Arizona. Photo courtesy David Schaefer.

**Plate 187**
*Conference Poster.*
Collectors are now adding posters like this one from the 2004 HLCCA conference in Phoenix to their Post86 collections. Paper ephemera such as these posters are a good way to chronicle the club's history. Inspired by HLC's Mexican-decaled lines and accented with Fiesta, this poster was designed by David Schaefer. At the conference auction, when autographed by club officers and/or Dave Conley, the HLC representative, examples such as this one often bring from $60.00 to $150.00. Photo courtesy David Schaefer.

*Exclusives for the Betty Crocker Catalog:* In these photos are a few examples of Fiesta offered through the Betty Crocker catalogs. Some lines, especially Black Cat, Happy Pumpkin, Watermelon, and Doughboy are already piquing the interest of collectors. Photos used by permission of General Mills.

**Plate 188**
*Betty Bowl.*
Fall 2002.

**Plate 189**
*Canisters.*
Currently available.

**Plate 190**
*Diner Collection.*
January 2003.

**Plate 191**
*Kiwi.* January 2004; *Watermelon.* Spring 2003.

**Plate 192**
*Doughboy.*
January 2004.

**Plate 193**
*Halloween Night.*
Fall 2004.

**Plate 194**
*Collectible Pitcher.*
Several colors made, Fall 2004.

**Plate 195**
*Happy Pumpkin.* Fall 2002; *Black Cat.* Fall 2003.

**Plate 196**
*Pillsbury Bake-Off Pitcher.*
January 2004.

*Other Exclusives:* Mega China is currently marketing a few lines of decorated Fiesta that are starting to show up on eBay; and though right now interest in them is limited, we wanted to at least acquaint you with them. They have three other Fiesta-based offerings: Baby's First Christmas, Trio of Hearts, and Easter Egg.

**Plate 198**
*Moonshine Mug.* Photo courtesy Mick and Lorna Chase/Fiesta Plus.

**Plate 197**
*Mystique Pitcher.* Photo courtesy Janet Shower/New Collections.

**Plate 199**
*Champagne Tumbler.* Photo courtesy Mick and Lorna Chase/Fiesta Plus.

**Plate 200**
*Space-Decorated Set.*
This line, reflecting a retro space pattern, was made for the American Museum of Natural History in New York City to commemorate the opening of the Rose Center for Earth and Space. It features colorful Deco planets on cobalt. These items were produced: Tom and Jerry mug, 9" salad plate, bud vase, serving tray, disk pitcher, and clock. Photo courtesy Harvey Linn, Jr.

Harlequin was produced by Homer Laughlin in an effort to serve all markets and to fit every budget. It was a less expensive dinnerware and was sold without trademark through the F. W. Woolworth Company exclusively. The following is an excerpt from one of the company's original illustrated brochures:

> The new Harlequin Pottery offers a gift to table gaiety. It brings the magic of bright, exciting color to the table, dresses the festive board with pleasantness and personality, makes of every meal a cheerful and companionable occasion.
>
> The new ware comes in four lovely colors . . . Yellow, Green, Red, and Blue . . . and offers the hostess endless possibilities for creating interesting and appealing color effects on her table. All the colors are brilliant and eye-catching . . . designed to go together effectively in any combination the hostess may desire. To set a table with Harlequin is an adventure in decoration. Plates are of one color, cups of another, saucers and platters of another . . . you can give free range to your artistic instincts.
>
> And it is very easy to build up a comprehensive set of Harlequin in whatever items and colors you desire, because it may be bought by the piece at extremely reasonable prices.
>
> Sold Exclusively by
> F. W. WOOLWORTH CO. STORES

Although it was first listed on company records as early as 1936, Harlequin was not actively introduced to the public until 1938.

It was designed by Fredrick Rhead, and like Fiesta the style was pure Art Deco. Rhead again used the band of rings device as its only ornamentation, but this time chose to space the rings well away from the rim. Flat pieces were round and concave with the center areas left plain. Hollow ware pieces were cone-shaped; bowls were flared. Handles were applied with small ornaments at their bases and, with few exceptions, were extremely angular.

Over the years the color assortment grew to include all of Fiesta's lovely colors with the exceptions of ivory and dark blue. The original colors (those mentioned in the brochure we just quoted), however, were developed just for Harlequin. Harlequin yellow was a lighter and brighter tint than Fiesta yellow; the green was a spruce green, and the blue tended toward a mauve shade. It is interesting to note that the color the company referred to as "red" is actually maroon. To avoid confusion, today's collectors reserve "red" for the orange-red color of Fiesta red.

It seems logical here to conclude that because Harlequin was not extensively promoted until 1938 that it would have been then or soon after that the line was expanded and new colors added. The new colors of the '40s were red (orange-red like Fiesta's — called tangerine by the company), rose (though records show a color called salmon that preceded rose, if indeed these are two individual shades, the difference is so slight it is of no significance to today's collectors), turquoise, and light green. (There are some pieces whose production dates we can't pinpoint beyond the fact that they were not part of the original line but were listed as discontinued by 1952. Many of these are rarely, if ever, found in light green. This leads us to believe that light green may not have been added until the mid-1940s.)

Gray, chartreuse, and forest (dark) green were new in the '50s. Harlequin yellow, turquoise, and rose continued to be produced. By 1959 the color assortment was reduced to four colors again — red (coinciding with the resumed production of Fiesta red), turquoise, Harlequin yellow, and the last new color, medium green.

The original line consisted of these items: 10", 9", 7", and 6" plates; 8" soup plate; 9" nappy; salt and pepper shakers; covered casserole; teacup and saucer; creamer, regular; sugar bowl; 11" platter; 5½" fruit; double egg cup; and 4½" tumbler.

These pieces were soon added to the original line: cream soup cup, sauce boat, after-dinner cup and saucer, novelty creamer, 13" platter, teapot, syrup*, service water jug, 36s bowl, basketweave ashtray, regular ashtray, 36s oatmeal, individual salad bowl, 22-oz. jug, 4½" tumbler, ashtray saucer*, basketweave nut dish, relish tray with inserts*, individual egg cup*, individual creamer*, candleholders*, marmalade*, butter dish, large cup (tankard), and 9" baker. Of the assortment, those items marked with an asterisk (indicating them to be rare or non-existent in light green) were probably the first to be discontinued. Knowing that the Fiesta line suffered a severe pruning during 1944 – 1945, it would certainly follow that the same fate would befall Harlequin.

The material available to us for study dated May 1952 indicates that even more pieces had by then been dropped: the 9" baker, the covered butter dish, the individual creamer, and the tankard.

Harlequin proved to be quite popular and sold very well into the late 1950s when sales began to diminish. Records show that the final piece was actually manufactured in 1964.

In 1939 the Hamilton Ross Co. offered a Harlequin look-alike which they called Sevilla. It came in assorted solid colors, eight in all, with the same angular handles, and similar style and decoration. The round platter was distinctive. It featured closed handles formed by the band of rings device which was allowed to sweep gradually outward to just past mid-point; no doubt you have seen an occasional piece.

In 1979 Homer Laughlin announced that they had been approached and would comply with a request from the F.W. Woolworth Company to reissue the Harlequin line, one of that company's all-time bestsellers, as part of their 100th anniversary celebration. The Harlequin Ironstone dinnerware HLC produced was a very limited line and is easily recognized. It was made in two original colors: yellow and turquoise; a medium green that was slightly different than the original; and a new shade, coral. The sugar bowl was restyled with closed handles and a solid finial. A round platter (the original was oval) in coral was included in the 45-piece set which was comprised of only plates, salad plates, cereal/soups, cups and saucers, yellow sugar, turquoise creamer, and a round green vegetable bowl. The plates were backstamped Homer Laughlin (the old ones are not marked), and even the pieces made from authentic molds are easy to distinguish from the old Harlequin. Because many of the lovely colors of the original line and virtually none of its unique accessory pieces were reproduced, this late line has never been a threat to the investments of the many collectors who love Harlequin dinnerware. We have talked with several dealers who actually felt the reissue stimulated interest in the old line.

A letter from the company dated April 1983 advised that Woolworth's as well as a few other dealers throughout the country were carrying the new Harlequin. It stated that a few round platters and vegetable bowls had been made in yellow by mistake, and that some of these were backstamped "through error in the Dipping Department." (These are shown in Plate 201 along with a white, a nonstandard color, plate backstamped 1980 and a coral saucer, which should have been unmarked, backstamped 1982.) Production continued for no more than a couple of years; and compared to the old line, sales were much more limited.

**Plate 201**
*Items Glazed/Backstamped in Error.*

**Plate 202**
*Ashtray Saucer.*
Though very rare, a few of the ashtray saucers have been reported in ivory — not a standard Harlequin color, though we know of an ivory tumbler and sugar bowl base as well.

**Plate 203**

*Basketweave Ashtray (left front).*
None of the ashtrays were in the original assortment, but all were added very early — possibly even before 1940. The basketweave version may be found in all twelve colors, including medium green.

*Ashtray Saucer (top).*
This is an unusual item, made to serve a dual purpose. These are hard to find; and because none have been reported in the '50s colors (gray, chartreuse, and forest green for this line), medium green, or light green, they were probably discontinued in the mid-'40s. Advanced collectors question the existence of rose — let us know if you have one.

*Regular Ashtray (right).*
So dubbed by collectors to make a distinction between the three styles, this one comes in the first eight colors only; it's scarce in light green.

**Plate 204**

*Two Unusual Harlequin Ashtrays.*
The red one on the left has advertising for a tavern in East Liverpool. The design is done in gold. The spruce green regular ashtray is marked on the back, with "HLCo USA." That mark is either silver or platinum.
Photo courtesy Becky Turner.

Note: In the early 1980s, HLC produced a line called Table Fair in ivory with rusty brown speckles. The salad and dinner plates were made from Harlequin molds. A second line utilizing the speckled glaze was decorated with a textured rim band and a blooming strawberry plant in the center well.

**Plate 205**

*36s Oatmeal Bowl (far left).*
Shown here in light green, the 36s oatmeal measures 6½" in diameter. They're scarce in spruce green and very rare in maroon. See the chapter entitled "Dating Codes and English Measurements" for an explanation of the term "36s."

*Nappy (center back).*
The nappy, shown in spruce green, was part of the original line and can be found in all colors, although it is rare in medium green. It's 9" in diameter.

*Individual Salad Bowl (right back).*
The individual salad is not so hard to find in the '50s colors; it's scarce in red, maroon, spruce green, and medium green.

*36s Bowl (far right).*
Shown in a very rare color, medium green, the 36s bowl was evidently made not much later than 1959 when this color was added to the line. It's scarce in maroon and spruce.

*Fruit Bowl, 5½" (center front).*
This bowl has also been found in a slightly larger version (6" diameter) in maroon, blue, spruce green, and yellow.

**Plate 206**
*Cream Soup Bowl.*
This piece can be found in all colors; like its Fiesta counterpart, it's very rare in medium green and commands a hefty price when one comes up for sale.

**Plate 207**
*Oval Baker.*
Discontinued before the '50s colors were introduced, the oval baker is found in the first eight colors only. (Remember, though rose was a '50s color in Fiesta, it was introduced to the Harlequin line soon after 1938.) This bowl measures 9" in length.

**Plate 208**
*Mixing Bowls.*
These are the Kitchen Kraft bowls. The original owner bought them from the factory by mail order for $2.05 plus postage ($1.00 for the 10", 65¢ for the 8", and 40¢ for the 6"). They are unmarked. The set was also available with the smallest bowl in red for an additional 20¢.

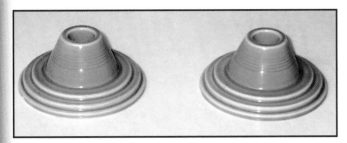

**Plate 209**
*Candleholders.*
These are not at all easy to find in any color; in fact, we once thought they were non-existent in light green. At latest count, we can verify two pairs that are in permanent collections.

**Plate 210**
*Butter Dish, ½-lb.*
Originally a Jade piece, this butter dish was later glazed in Harlequin and Riviera colors and sold with both lines. They have been found in these colors: cobalt blue, rose, mauve blue, spruce green, light green, maroon, turquoise, red, and ivory. Three have been reported in Fiesta yellow as well.

**Plate 211**
*Casserole.*
These are scarce in the '50s colors — especially dark green — and they're extremely rare in medium green (shown here, one of two known).

**Plate 212**
*High-Lip Creamer (top row).*
The "high-lip" creamer is found in the four original colors only. Note the difference in the length of the lips on the two shown. The fact that they were trimmed by hand doesn't wholly explain the difference, since only these two variations have been reported. Evidently the style was deliberately changed at some point.
*Individual Creamer (top right).*
You'll find this tiny pitcher only in the first eight colors. They're really not at all difficult to find, but they are scarce in light green.
*Regular Creamer (bottom row).*
This item is available in all twelve colors.
*Sugar Bowl (center bottom row).*
One collector reports that upon comparing several sugar bowls in his collection, he suspects those with the inside rings were earlier

and that these rings were eliminated sometime during the '40s. Just the base has been reported in ivory.
*Novelty Creamer (bottom right).*
As far as we know, only one of these exists in medium green, but you can expect to find them in all the other colors.

**Plate 213**
*Novelty Creamer.*
Until the eighth edition we always reported that the novelty creamer was non-existent in medium green, but this photo shows there's at least one — and collectors believe this is the only one! It's shown alongside another very rare item, a medium green service water pitcher.

**Plate 214**
*Demitasse Coffee Cup and Saucer.*
These have become rare in the '50s colors gray, chartreuse, and forest green, and they're extremely scarce in medium green. They don't appear on the 1959 listing when medium green was introduced, so they couldn't have been made in any large quantity in that color.

**Plate 215**
*Large Cup.*
This may be the tankard found listed in company material as being discontinued before 1952. As close as we can pinpoint the introduction of the '50s colors is fall 1951, which would leave this in production for only a few months and explain why it is so rare. But there are two factors that seem to discredit the tankard theory: for years, I had one in medium green, a '50s color, in my own collection, and the body of this cup is the same shape as the Epicure cups from the mid-'50s. Only recently have the saucers been found; they're the same as the Rhythm saucers, but old store stock discovered in original cartons confirmed that they did double duty as saucers for these Harlequin cups.

**Plate 216**
*Double Egg Cup.*
This egg cup will hold an egg in both the top and bottom (not all at once!). The small end was to accommodate a boiled egg; the larger end was for a poached egg, the custom at that time being to dunk toast points into the soft poached egg yolk. They're found in all twelve colors, but only four have been reported in medium green.

*Nut Dish.*
The small basketweave nut dishes are found in the first eight colors; they're scarce in light green, though not as rare as we once believed.

*Individual Egg Cup.*
Though fairly common in yellow, spruce green, mauve blue, maroon, turquoise, rose, and red, they're very rare in light green.

*Perfume Bottle.*
These are not a standard part of the Harlequin line but are of interest to Harlequin collectors since they were

dipped in Harlequin glazes. They're hard to find; most of them are yellow, but light green has also been reported. (See photo below).

*Marmalade.*
Found in the first eight colors only, they're scarce in rose, and light green marmalades are very rare.

**Plate 217**
*Perfume Bottles.*
These come in the two sizes shown here. The tall yellow example is in Harlequin yellow, the shorter one is Fiesta yellow. Green is rare. The only one I've ever had was the shorter version. It measures 2⅛", which will help you judge the height of the taller one. Photo courtesy Becky Turner.

**Plate 218**
*Nut Cups.*
A complete set of Harlequin nut cups in all eight colors. Photo courtesy Craig Macaluso, Metairie, LA.

**Plate 219**
*Japanese Imports.*
The basketweave ashtray and nut dish were copied from these Japanese imports. We thought you'd enjoy seeing the originals. They carry the mark "Marutomo Ware Made in Japan."

**Plate 220**
*Tumblers.*
These were discontinued before the '50s colors were introduced, so they're found in only the first eight colors. Remember, though rose was strictly a '50s color in the Fiesta line, it was made in Harlequin from the late '30s until late in the '50s, so don't be surprised to find a rose example, even though we don't show one here. One has been reported in ivory, a non-standard Harlequin color.
*Service Water Pitcher.*
Look for the Fiesta-like band of rings near the base of this pitcher. This will help you identify the Harlequin pitcher from several look-alikes by other companies. These were produced in all twelve colors; they're very rare in medium green and scarce in gray and dark green. Several have now been reported in Fiesta yellow; we once saw one of these etched "Treasure Island, 1939."

**Plate 221**
*Service Water Pitcher.*

The owner of the service water pitcher on the left has done research and has learned that this was a design model originally intended for Fiesta (instead, the disk style was selected.) Eventually a decision was made to include it in the Harlequin line; but not before certain modifications were implemented. These changes were made so that it would better resemble Hall's successful line of service jugs that had a more pronounced ball-shaped body (notice how the front of the prototype has a more gentle "S" curve). The handle was altered as well. Originally the handle flowed from the upper edge of the rim; on the standard issue (Plate 222) the handle attaches just above the body, which probably made it stronger. Photo courtesy Richard and Dianna Megyese.

**Plate 222**

**Plate 223**

*Salt and Pepper Shakers.*

These were made in all of Harlequin's colors; they're all easy to find except medium green.

*Jug, 22-oz.*

These are commonly found in the first eleven colors; they're extremely rare in medium green — only three have been reported.

*Deep Plate.*

These can be found in all twelve colors; they're 8" in diameter.

*Sauce Boat.*

These are fairly easy to find in any of the twelve Harlequin colors, though they're scarce in medium green.

**Plate 224**

*Plates, 10", 9", 7", 6".*

The 10" dinner plate is becoming very hard to find; the 9" and 7" have been reported in ivory, and a 9" has been found in cobalt — neither are standard colors.

*Platters, 10", 13".*

These are generally easy to find in all twelve colors, though they're both rare in medium green.

**Plate 225**

*"Harlequin Pie Plate."*

This piece has long been a mystery that finally may have been solved with this edition. We've always thought the rings looked like Harlequin, and since many collectors refer to it as the "Harlequin pie plate," we'll put it in this section. Collectors have long believed that it was an HLC product, but company representatives wouldn't verify that for us when we questioned them about it years ago. Through further research, however, information has come to light that strongly suggests that it is. You can recognize this plate by the three rings on the outside of the wall and the four on the inside. (Collectors report a similar plate by another company that has four rings on both the outside and the inside walls and makes a dull flat sound when tapped rather than the ring made by the Homer Laughlin plate.) These have been found in cobalt, Fiesta green, and yellow. My source tells me that this plate as well as a second style was mentioned in Rhead's journal. The second style is a custard pie plate that is 9" in diameter, has no rings, and a rounded flange. It has a larger wet foot than the ringed pie plate or the Kitchen Kraft pie plates, and it's not as deep as other pie plates produced by Homer Laughlin. When the pie server is placed in this one (and only this one), it rests perfectly flat on the flange as well as the bottom of the plate. Of the latter, two are known to exist in private collections, one cobalt and the other yellow. Neither of these pie plates has ever been found on company price lists.

### Plate 226
*Relish Tray.*

These are rare! As strange as it seems...bases are actually Fiesta. The color combination as shown is the most common. Rose, turquoise, and spruce have been reported as well, but they are extremely hard to find; and as far as we know, none have been found in light green. As strange as it may seem, two trays with all four inserts done in rose have been located.

### Plate 227
*Syrup.*

Syrups are scarce and have been reported in only red, yellow, mauve blue, spruce green, turquoise, light green, and ivory (and just one in each of the last three colors — let us hear from you if you have one in these colors.) A veteran collector of twenty-two years doubts they even exist. It's been years since these were reported to us, so we have no idea from whom the reports originate — but we had doubters that light green candleholders existed, too, now we know of five pairs.

### Plate 228
*Teacups and Saucers.*

These are relatively easy to find in all twelve colors. One has been found in a non-standard shade, Skytone blue.

*Teapot.*

Teapots were made in all twelve colors but are very rare in medium green. One has been reported in cobalt.

**Plate 229**
*Medium Green Harlequin.*
Medium green Harlequin is even rarer than medium green Fiesta. The water pitcher is extremely rare; so is the teapot. No more than four or five of either are accounted for at this time. Only one novelty creamer is known to exist. (See Plate 213.)

**Plate 230**
*Harlequin Souvenirs.*
Left to right: Engraved individual creamer, front side, "World's Fair," back side, "Annie"; engraved individual creamer, San Francisco 1941; engraved demitasse cup, "Hollywood 1940;" cold-painted individual creamer, "Washington, D.C."; (it also has a black line painted on the handle); gold decal on individual creamer, "Souvenir Barbara Fritche." Other souvenir pieces not pictured: cold-painted donkey and shakers with water slide decals that have names of various places. One donkey was from as far away from HLC as Kellogg, Idaho. Photo courtesy Becky Turner.

**Plate 231**
*Boxed Set.*
Here's a very rare boxed set of Harlequin from the '50s. Colors are rose, dark green, yellow, and turquoise. This is the starter set that was advertised in Woolworth's catalogs. The cost was $3.49 in 1955 and $3.98 in 1957. Photo courtesy Becky Turner.

**Plate 232**
*Company Brochure.*
This is the outside of the brochure that came with the '50s boxed set of Harlequin. This was folded, so you are seeing the back and the front. Photo courtesy Becky Turner.

THE HOMER LAUGHLIN CHINA CO.
NEWELL, W. VA.

Harlequin Pottery offers a gift to table gayety. It brings the magic of bright exciting color to the table, dresses the festive board with pleasantness and personality, makes of every meal a cheerful and companionable occasion.

This ware comes in six lovely colors - Yellow, Green, Chartreuse, Turquoise, Gray and Salmon - and offers the hostess endless possibilities for creating interesting and appealing color effects on her table. All the colors are brilliant and eye-catching - designed to go together effectively in any combination the hostess may desire. To set a table with Harlequin is an adventure in decoration. Plates may be of one color, cups of another, saucers and platters of another - you can give free range to your artistic instincts.

It is very easy to build up a comprehensive set of Harlequin in whatever items and colors you desire, because it may be bought by the piece at extremely reasonable prices.

•

*Sold Exclusively by*
**F. W. WOOLWORTH CO. STORES**

HARLEQUIN

*Harlequin*
by
HOMER LAUGHLIN

**Plate 233**
*Catalog Page.*
The Woolworth catalog from Christmas
1957. Photo courtesy Becky Turner.

28

By *HOMER LAUGHLIN CHINA CO.*

"Harlequin" dinnerware. 16-piece starter set includes
four each of 7″ plates, fruit dishes, cups, saucers. Lustrous
yellow, turquoise, salmon, green.    Complete set, **3.98**\*
Open stock pieces, each **19c** to **89c**

**Plate 234**
*Company Brochure, 1979.*
See the introduction to the Harlequin
section for information on the reissue.

## Animals

During the late '30s and early '40s when miniatures such as these were enjoying a heyday, HLC produced this menagerie as a part of the Harlequin line. There are six, and each was made in four colors: maroon, spruce green, mauve blue, and yellow. They were marketed primarily through Woolworth Company stores.

There are no original Harlequin Animals other than those pictured below, although you may find some that are very similar. The duck has a twin, a perpetually hungry little gander, his head bent into a permanent feeding position; but he was made by the Brush Pottery Company. Although several collectors were almost sure their 2½" elephant belonged in the group, HLC disowned him. A donkey look-alike pulling a cart may make you wonder at first, but a closer examination will reveal an uncharacteristic lack of sharp detail, and some of these have been found to bear a "California" mark.

"Mavericks" is a term adopted by collectors to indicate animals that have been glazed by someone outside the Homer Laughlin China Company. In rare cases, you may find one in a standard Harlequin color that has been completely covered with gold, or it may be simply gold trimmed. One company involved in decorating the animals was Kaulware of Chicago, who utilized an iridescent glaze and gold hand-painted trim. You will find salt and pepper shakers in a slightly smaller size, indicating that they were cast from molds made from the original animals (see Plate 236). The Maverick "guard" cats in Plate 238 are in white with colored trim.

Another company responsible for producing some of the Mavericks was founded by John Kass, who operated in the East Liverpool, Ohio, area. During the Depression after his retail business failed, Kass built a small pottery, employed members of his family, and began to make novelty items — salt and pepper shakers, small animal figures (Mavericks among them), and cups and saucers. A descendant of Kass's explained that it was a common practice in those days for area potters to "make each other's items, and no one took offense." All Kass's work was done painstakingly by hand from the casting to the final decoration. Business increased in the '40s; the old buildings were replaced with modern structures, and more people were employed. "We made the Harlequin animals from the very beginning," she continues. "For some reason the ducks and penguins were made right up into the '50s." The letter goes on to say that there were other companies in the area who also made these animals. You will find that some of these are considerably smaller than the Harlequin animals and made of a finer, more porcelain-like material. Though most will be white with gold trim, some may be in colors. We have a gold-trimmed cobalt cat; and, until you compare it with the genuine article, you can't be sure that it isn't authentic. It measures 2½" long compared to the one I have in maroon that is a good ¼" longer. These smaller animals are worth considerably less than Mavericks that are full size, or nearly so.

**Plate 235**
*Harlequin Animals.*
Original Harlequin animals in authentic glazes.

**Plate 236**
*Salt and Pepper Shakers.*
These penguins are a slightly smaller size, indicating that they were cast from molds made from the original animals.

**Plate 237**
*"Maverick Animals."*
See page 91 for information on Maverick Menagerie by China Specialties, Inc.

**Plate 238**
*"Maverick Guard Cats."*

**Plate 239**
*Red Animals.*
Though probably not a production run, there are a few red cats being found; a red duck and penguin have been reported as well as a penguin in black. Be alert for painted frauds. Collectors tell us of finding red animals whose color, feel, and weight were perfect but the paint was chipping off.

**Plate 240**
*Harlequin Animals.*
Shown are turquoise, light green, and cobalt blue animals borrowed from HLC for their portrait photo. These are from HLC's archives; don't expect to find them on the market, though a rare few have made it to the outside. We know of one lucky man who has a turquoise duck in his collection. Note the difference in the penguins. The one in Plate 235 has a wider head than the one here. The green example was the original style, but collectors tell us the difference often goes undetected today.

# RIVIERA AND IVORY CENTURY

Riviera was introduced in 1938 and until sometime prior to 1950 was sold exclusively by the Murphy Company. In contrast to Fiesta and Harlequin, the line was quite limited. It was unmarked, lighter in weight, and therefore less expensive. Only rarely will you find a piece with the Homer Laughlin gold stamp. Of the three colored dinnerware lines, it has the rather dubious distinction of being the only one which was not originally created as such. Its forerunner was a line called Century — an ivory line with a vellum glaze. Century shapes were also decorated with a wide variety of decals and were the basis of many lines such as Mexicana and Hacienda. An enterprising designer (Rhead, no doubt) applied the popular colored glazes to these shapes, and Riviera was born. Even the shakers were from another line. They were originally designed as Tango, which accounts for the six-section design in contrast to the square Riviera shape.

Though all the company literature we've seen never included ivory as a standard Riviera color, it must have been, since it was the company itself who marketed a 16-piece set of mauve blue, yellow, light green, and ivory during the war when red had been temporarily withdrawn. Collectors appreciate the effect of the ivory with the other colors and find there are several interesting items that are available to them only in the ivory glaze.

Records for this line are especially scanty; but as accurately and completely as possible, here is a listing of the items in the line as it was first introduced. Sizes have been translated from the English measurements listed by the company to actual sizes to the nearest inch.

| | | | |
|---|---|---|---|
| 11" Dish (Platter) | 13" Dish (Platter) | 10" Plate | 9" Plate |
| 6" Plate | Teacup and Saucer | Fruit | 9" Baker (Oval Vegetable Bowl) |
| Salt and Pepper Shakers | Covered Casserole | 8" Deep Plate | 8" Nappy |
| 6" Oatmeal | Tumbler (with Handle) | Open Jug | Teapot |
| Sauce Boat | Creamer | (also found with lid) | Covered Sugar |

We have also found 12" and 16" platters, a covered syrup pitcher, a juice pitcher, juice tumblers, and butter dishes in two sizes: a half-pound and a quarter-pound.

**Plate 241**
*Batter Set.*
Photo courtesy Harvey Linn, Jr.

**Plate 242**
*Batter Set.*

**Plate 243**
*Batter Set.*
The color combination of the set above on the left was standard issue. Notice that it utilizes one of the rare cobalt pieces as well as the lid for the jug. These lids had been reported only in green and ivory until we received the photo of an all red set, shown in Plate 242. The set shown here is a very unusual set. Not only is the tray square (virtually all are rectangular), but it includes a covered sugar bowl as well — a seldom seen component. All four pieces carry the Wells peacock mark and Warranted 18k gold.

**Plate 244**
*Bowls: Baker, Nappy, Fruit, Oatmeal.*
Left to right: baker, oval with straight sides, 9" long; nappy, 7¼" diameter; baker, oval with curved sides, 9" long. In front: fruit, 5½"; oatmeal, 6". The oatmeal is slightly deeper than the fruit bowl and is rather scarce.

**Plate 246**
*Unusual Sugar Bowl and Creamer.*
This is the green glaze trimmed in gold; these have also been reported in an unusual lime green (not chartreuse).

**Plate 245**
*Cream Soup Bowl with Liner.*
Don't expect to find these in the colored glazes; they're technically Century, but collectors enjoy adding them to their Riviera for contrast. Here the 8" plate (actual measurement 7¾") does double duty as the underliner.

**Plate 247**
*Unusual Sugar Bowl and Creamer.*
Very unusual sugar bowl and creamer with the HLC USA stamp mark in platinum. Photo courtesy Pat Bunetta.

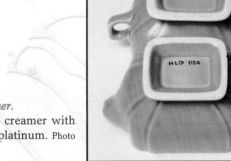

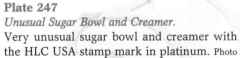

**Plate 248**
*Butter Dishes in Ivory.*
These three ivory butter dishes were utilized with the Century Vellum line as well as Riviera. None are marked.
Photo courtesy Harvey Linn, Jr.

**Plates 249 and 250**
*Butter Dishes.*
This green example still has the original Riviera sticker and price tag; for an example in such wonderful condition and with the very seldom-seen labels, you should expect to pay about double book price. These are rarely found in the cobalt and turquoise glazes. Both are shown above.

**Plate 251**
*Butter Dishes; Sugar Bowl and Creamer; Covered Jug.*
Occasionally, the green jug, though still very hard to find, turns up complete with lid; red examples are scarce and very seldom are they found with a lid. Lids have never been found on mauve blue and yellow examples. The larger ½-lb. butter dish is more readily found than the smaller and is available in mauve blue, rose, spruce green, light green, turquoise, maroon, cobalt blue, red, ivory, and in both Fiesta and Harlequin yellow.

**Plate 252**
*Covered Jugs.*
All are hard to find and the mauve blue and yellow jugs that have been reported have all been without lids.

**Plate 254**
*Casserole.*
A very nice piece and one that may prove difficult to find; the large size of these casseroles along with their distinctive styling and wonderful colors make them spectacular additions to any Riviera collection.

**Plate 253**
*Juice Pitcher.*
Shown here in the very rare red color.

**Plate 255**
*Juice Pitcher; Juice Tumblers.*
The pitcher is scarce in any color but is standard in yellow. It's very rare in mauve blue, shown here, and red (see Plate 253). In the original sets, the tumblers were turquoise, mauve blue, red, yellow, light green, and ivory.

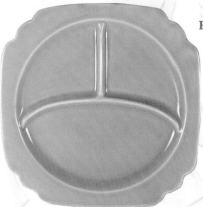

**Plate 256**
*Compartment Plate, 9¾".*
This unique item was reported to us just as we went to press with the seventh edition, and to date, we've never heard of a second one. It was a gift to a collector given by a friend with the comment, "This looks like that stuff you collect."

**Plate 257**
*Deep Plate; Salt and Pepper Shakers; Syrup Pitcher; Handled Tumblers.*
As you can see, there are six orange-like segments that make up the design of the salt and pepper shakers. These were borrowed from the Tango line, so you may find them in Tango's color too. Two pairs have been found in a true primary red glaze — origin unconfirmed. Here's the covered syrup in red again; it's a darling piece and very hard to find. Ivory tumblers are scarce and command high prices. Though not Homer Laughlin products, you may find sets of glass tumblers (one style with a smooth surface, another with vertically paneled sides), each with a solid band of one of the Riviera colors at the rim. One set was bought at auction still in the original box marked "Juanita Beverage Set, Rosenthal and Ruben, Inc., Binghampton, NY, 1938." There were two each of the four colors (light green, mauve blue, yellow, and red) in four sizes: 3", 3½", 4", and 5¼". Matching swizzle sticks completed the 40-piece set. See Plates 380 and 381 for an illustration of the glassware.

**Plate 258**
*Plates, 10", 9", 7", 6".*
The 10" plates are very hard to find. The 7" plate is sometimes found in cobalt blue, and collectors also report this size in Fiesta yellow. (See Plate 436 for a Fiesta Ensemble ad showing both cobalt and Fiesta yellow 7" plates.) An 8" plate (7¾" actual measurement) has been reported in ivory.

**Plate 259**
*Platters.*
11½", no handles, oval well; 11¼" with closed handles, oval well. You'll also find 13½" and 12" platters with the closed handles. A collector has reported finding a 13½" platter with closed handles and a rectangular well (possibly like the one in the Fiesta Ensemble, Plate 441) and an ivory 16" example has been reported as well. There is a square platter with handles that measures 11½"; it's shown with the batter set in Plate 243. All cobalt Riviera platters are hard to find; a few in the 13" size with the oval well have been noted over the years, but recently one with a rectangular well was found.

**Plate 260**
*Sauce Boat.*
These have never been considered at all hard to find, but since sending out our last survey, we have received many comments indicating that Riviera in general is becoming scarce.

**Plate 261**
*Teapot; Teacups; Saucers.*
Teapots have been scarce for several years. Now that Riviera is getting harder to find, good serving pieces are all in short supply. Even the once-common cups and saucers are difficult to acquire in mint condition.

**Plate 262**
*Covered Syrup Pitcher; Fast-Stand Sauce Dish; Demitasse Cup and Saucer.*
The syrup pitcher is extremely rare in ivory. The other two pieces are from the Century line; none have ever been reported in the other four Riviera colors and both are hard to find. Photo courtesy Harvey Linn, Jr.

**Plate 263**
*Tidbit Tray; 4½" Jug; Utility Bowl; Salt and Pepper Shakers.*
Here are more Century items. You will find the shakers in Riviera colors, and one two-tier tidbit tray has been reported in mauve blue. But the jug (a size between the batter pitcher and the syrup) and the utility bowl were never part of the Riviera line. One collector reports the earliest back-stamp she has in her Century collection indicates a 1933 production date.

**Plate 264**
*Riviera with Decals.*
Here's the batter set — a lovely floral decal and gold trim. Never plentiful, decorated sets like this one have almost disappeared from the market.

**Plate 265**
*Wells Peacock Trademark.*
The Wells family became involved with the company as early as 1889 when William Edwin Wells became Homer Laughlin's partner. Succeeding generations continued as leaders of the firm.

**Plate 266**
*Riviera with Red Stripes.*
As difficult as red-striped Fiesta is to find, these pieces are even more unique. Judging from the size of the teapot, the platter must be 16". It is dated 1933/1934, probably made well before the striped Fiesta line. Besides the platter and teapot shown, the partial set contained plates and bowls in three sizes. Most items were marked with the Wells peacock in silver. I also have photos (forgive me, I don't remember who sent them) of a 9" nappy and two styles of oval bakers; a butter dish has been reported as well.

# OTHER COLORED DINNERWARE LINES

## Carnival

Carnival was made exclusively for the Quaker Oats Company who gave it away to its customers, one piece packed in each box of Mother's Carnival Oats. While no records exist to verify the year in which it was first produced, we must assume it was in the late 1930s or early '40s by reason of the color assortment. Harlequin yellow, turquoise (both of which were first used by HLC in 1938), light green, and Fiesta red were evidently the original colors. The only mention of Carnival in company files was dated 1952; it lists these glazes: dark green, turquoise, gray, and Harlequin yellow. You'll also occasionally find examples in cobalt, Fiesta yellow, and ivory. (Notice the cups on the front of the boxes shown below — all are different versions of the Mother's Oats boxes that featured Carnival, each with cups that vary in color.) The 1952 record also itemized the pieces in production at that time; these are listed with suggested values in the back of the book. A company representative recalled that coupons were included in the boxes, redeemable for the larger pieces. Perhaps there were plates, bowls, and platters — to date, however, none have been found, leading collectors to believe it was a breakfast set shown in its entirety on the box.

**Plates 267 to 269**
*Examples of Mother's Oats boxes featuring Carnival.*

# *Epicure*

Epicure is a '50s line — with the '50s streamline styling and bright pastel colors. Anyone who remembers what a great era that was for growing up can tell you about pink and gray. Argyle socks were pink and gray! If your sweater was pink, your skirt or corduroys were gray. Turquoise was popular in home decorating — even down to appliances. And these were the colors of Epicure: dawn pink, charcoal gray, turquoise blue, and snow white.

The designer was Don Schreckengost, who also designed Rhythm. We can find no information pinpointing production dates, but collectors tell us that virtually all of their Epicure is stamped 1955. The only exception ever reported was a set of plates in pink that were marked 1960. For a complete listing of available items, see the "Suggested Values" section in the back of the book.

The nut dish could pass for a butter pat, and the ashtray is so rare some even doubt its existence. But one is shown in *Homer Laughlin China*, by Jo Cunningham and Darlene Nossaman (Schiffer Publishing). It's shaped like a shallow bowl with long, wide extensions on two sides, one of which has rests for four cigarettes. A long-time Epicure collector tells us to beware of the tidbits — not all are original. He says only a very few were factory made; most were simply home craft projects. (The giveaway is the scratch marks from where the drill walks around the plate before digging in.) The factory-made tidbits have white plastic inserts with brass rings on top that do not fold down.

Epicure is not easy to find, but many collectors view it as an exciting challenge. Its appeal is due to the influence of its famous designer and today's strong interest in the styles and colors of the '50s.

**Plate 270**
*Tidbit; Creamer; Cereal/Soup Bowl; Sugar Bowl; Salt Shaker; Cup and Saucer; Individual Casserole.*
Very nearly the same size as the sugar bowl, the individual casserole (shown in charcoal gray) is very hard to find. Collectors tell us the cups and saucers are also very scarce, and one says he has a Fiesta cup in Epicure charcoal gray.

**Plate 271**
*Coffeepot; Plates; Nappy; Gravy Bowl; Ladle; Covered Vegetable Casserole.*
The pink nappy is the 9" size (it actually measures 8¾"); plates are 10" and 6½". The turquoise gravy boat holds a charcoal gray ladle.

**Plate 272**
*Coffepots.*
You'll probably never see examples of all four colors together in one place again. These are very hard to find and command a high price when one is offered for sale. Photo courtesy www.moodindigonewyork.com

## Jubilee

Jubilee was presented by Homer Laughlin in 1948 in celebration of its 75th year of ceramic leadership. Shapes were simple and contemporary. It was offered in four colors: celadon green (blue-gray), shell pink, mist gray, and cream beige. Very soon after its introduction, HLC began to market many other lines of dinnerware employing its basic shapes.

**Plate 273**
*Double Egg Cup; Coupe Soup, 8"; Demitasse Cup and Saucer; Plates, 6", 7", 9", 10"; Teacup and Saucer; Cereal/Soup Bowl, 6"; Fruit Bowl, 5½".*

**Plate 274**
*Platters, 11", 13"; Teapot; Coffeepot; Creamer and Sugar; Casserole; Nappy, 8½"; Salt and Pepper Shakers; Fast-Stand Sauce Boat; Chop Plate, 15".*

**Plate 275**
*Kitchen Kraft Bowl Set.*
This set was glazed in the Jubilee colors and, along with the Fiesta juice set shown in Plate 40, was part of a promotion to stimulate sales. All of these items are very rare, and because of that, it's taken us what seems like an unbelievably long time to arrive at correct conclusions. Fact: only one of these three bowls was ever produced in gray, and that is the 10" size. Colors do not vary from size to size; they are as shown — shell pink, 6"; celadon green, 8"; and mist gray — an exact match to Fiesta gray — 10". Because of the fact that Jubilee's mist gray and Fiesta's gray were one and the same, the 10" bowl has always been a very desirable piece to own and has always stirred up much interest. They're not as rare as we once thought — several have surfaced since the eighth edition; though I haven't kept records, I have heard from at least a dozen collectors who have one.

*Kenilworth*

The Kenilworth Buffet Ware line was designed in 1955 by Homer Laughlin's art director, Don Schreckengost. Homer Laughlin produced this line for a very short time during the mid-1950s for Jack Kleinman, a metals manufacturer who owned plants in Brooklyn, New York, and New Jersey. (An original box with carafe inside has been found marked "A KENILWORTH Product, Jack Kleinman, Inc., Fifth Avenue, N.Y.") Although the exact origin of the Kenilworth name is not known for sure, it is believed Mr. Kleinman named the line. Various department stores in the country, such as Marshall Fields in Chicago, sold Kenilworth.

Four colors were selected for this line with three of the colors being borrowed from Epicure, a dinnerware line that was also designed by Don Schreckengost and produced by Homer Laughlin. You'll find the Kenilworth shapes in white, turquoise, pink, and a rich deep black. On very rare occasions a piece was glazed with two colors; five chowder/cereal bowls have been found in white with pink interiors.

**Plate 276**
*Kenilworth Stamp.*
This is the stamp mark most frequently found.

Some of the Kenilworth shapes carry a blue stamp mark: "Kenilworth U.S.A." A 10¼" black bowl has been found with the words "Made in U.S.A." raised in the mold. Not all Kenilworth items are marked.

At this time, twenty-three shapes have been identified, with eighteen of them being designed solely for the Kenilworth line. The Rhythm spoon rest, sauce boat, 9" salad nappy, and 5½" chowder/cereal bowl, along with Charm House salt and pepper shakers, are used to complete the line. Charm House teacups and Epicure plates are used to complement Kenilworth. Serving spoons and forks in Kenilworth colors have been found; some are plastic while others are made of plastic and brass. Only one metal ladle used with the covered soup tureen has been reported. To date no literature or price list identifying all the shapes produced for the line has ever been located.

All of the Kenilworth shapes can be found in white, the most common color. Turquoise is the second most encountered color, while pink is very hard to find. Black is considered rare and is highly valued by collectors. One lucky collector has found a Kenilworth coffeepot in turquoise, which is also a rarity. Very few Kenilworth shapes were decal decorated; most likely these were

**Plate 277**
*Fancy Kenilworth Stamp.*
This mark is seldom found.

**Plate 278**
*Extremely Rare OvenServe Mark.*
OvenServe was produced in very limited numbers. This stamp mark was found on an 11" covered casserole with a pottery lid.

manufactured in the early months of production. Rectangular 15" platters have been found with a turkey decal and an "Eames"-era style atomic starburst decal. A few pieces were decorated with decals designed from actual poker chips so that they were accurate down to the last detail. A coffeepot with decals of flowers and 22k gold trim has been reported, marked with the Homer Laughlin Kenilworth blue ink stamp mark and a gold stamp mark stating "Kass China Co., E. Liverpool, Ohio, 22 Karat Gold." (Kass China did a considerable amount of decorating for HLC as well as other local pottery companies during the 1950s.)

Some of the Kenilworth shapes were designed with metal or plastic lids and handles and a supporting brass foot or stand. One of the handles used for the Kenilworth carafe is made of a black material; it's neither metal nor plastic, but possibly hard rubber. The brass stands were designed to hold a clear glass candleholder, allowing for food or beverages to be kept warm. Examples in our color plates are complete as issued.

Collectors report Kenilworth is proving to be very difficult to find, which is very likely due to the relatively short period of time Kenilworth was produced. The collector who likes the '50s shapes and colored dinnerware will find the Kenilworth buffet ware very appealing. This buffet ware is currently the only line we are aware of that incorporates the use of color. We are looking forward to hearing from anyone who has additional information to share regarding this exciting line.

For a complete listing of available items along with their measurements, see the "Suggested Values" section of this book.

(This information was provided by Pat Bunetta and J.T. Vaughn who have researched Kenilworth for several years and have been so kind and willing to share their knowledge of the line with us. Photography throughout this chapter is by J.T. Vaughn.)

**Plate 279**
*Bowl, Salad, 10¼", with Fork and Spoon.*
The base ring must be present for this bowl to be considered complete.

**Plate 280**
*Bowl, Salad, 10¼", with Five 5½" Cereal/Chowder Bowls in White with Pink Interiors.*
The two-color glaze treatment is very rare.

**Plate 281**
*Bowl, Salad, 10¼", with Eight 5½" Cereal/Chowder Bowls in Black (Rare).*

**Plate 282**
*Bowl, Oval Nappy, 2¾" x 10" x 9¾"; with Brass Wire Foot.*
No lid. Hard to find. Designed to match the ice bucket and soup tureen.

**Plate 283**
*Bowl, Salad Nappy; 3¾" x 9¼".*
Also marketed as part of the Rhythm line and in those colors.

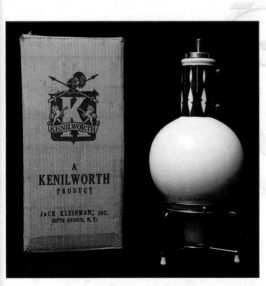

**Plate 284**
*Carafe in Original Box.*
Carafes were made either with brass or plastic lids; both had cork seals. (See reference in narrative page 124.)

**Plate 285**
*Carafes, 10".*
Note the reticulated brass neck bands, the plastic lids, and the black hard rubber handles. Two carafes in Fiesta light green, not a stardard Kenilworth color, are known to exist. One sold on eBay several years ago, and the other is in a private collection.

**Plate 286**
*Carafes.*
Three types of handles are utilized here, and there are two styles of wire bases shown; two have plastic lids while the one in the middle is brass. Notice that the brass neck bands are not reticulated.

**Plate 287**
*Casserole, 8"; with Brass Lid and Warmer Base.*
These virtually always have a brass lid, but just before going to press, an example in turquoise with a pottery lid was found.

**Plate 288**
*Casseroles, 8", with Brass Lids and Double Warmer Base.*

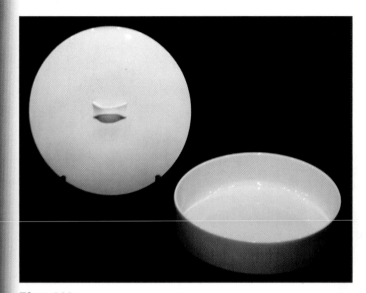

**Plate 289**
*Casserole, OvenServe, 11".*
Only one complete example of this very rare casserole has been reported. See the mark this item carries in Plate 278.

**Plate 290**
*Casserole, 10".*
The lid to this casserole has a brass collar, brass finial, and a ceramic center. The lid is very rare.

**Plate 291**
*Chip and Dip Set, 10".*
A brass metal double candleholder changes this 10" salad bowl and the 5½" cereal/chowder into a great chip and dip set.

**Plate 292**
*Chip and Dip Set, 11".*
This set is comprised of the 11" comport (see Plate 295), a 5½" cereal/chowder bowl, and a brass candleholder that holds three candles.

**Plate 293**
*Coffeepot, 10½"; Sugar Bowl; Creamer.*
Each piece is accented with a brass band at its base; both the coffeepot and the sugar bowl must have their lids to be considered complete.

**Plate 295**
*Comport, 11".*
This elegant piece utilizes the brass base and is shown in the most commonly found Kenilworth color, white.

**Plate 294**
*Coffeepot with Decal and 22k Gold.*
This example and one in turquoise are both one-of-a-kind and are in private collections.

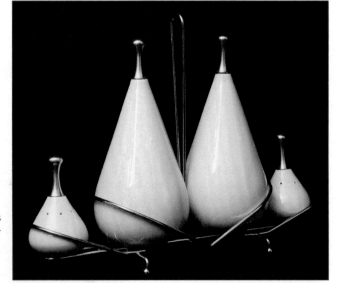

**Plate 296**
*Cruet Set.*
Although right at home with Kenilworth, this set is actually a Go-Along made by Loomiswear, not HLC.

**Plate 297**
*Ice Bucket, 8" x 8½".*
Complete with a brass lid, brass stand, and a glass liner. Its design matches the oval nappy and the soup tureen.

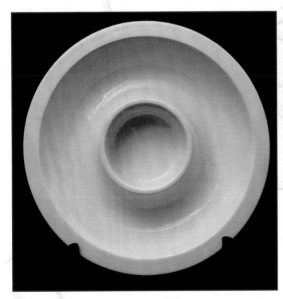

**Plate 298**
*Pie Plate, 10".*

**Plate 299**
*Platter, 15".*
Shown here with the now-familiar turkey decal (decaled Kenilworth is rare), this platter can also be found with a brass stand designed to hold two clear glass candle cups.

**Plate 300**
*Relish Tray, 10½".*
This one-piece relish is rare indeed; only one is known to exist in a private collection. There is also a round relish that has six pie-shaped sections; it's also extremely rare.

**Plate 301**
*Sauce Boat; Bowl, Cereal/Chowder, 5½"; Spoon Rest; Salt and Pepper Shakers.*
All but the latter utilize shapes from the Rhythm line; the shakers are Charm House. A spoon rest in white with ½" turquoise dots has been found.

**Plate 302**
*Soup Tureen, 8" x 8½", with Slotted Brass Lid; Brass Candle-Warmer Stand; Brass Ladle.*
This was designed to match the oval nappy and the ice bucket. Only one complete example exists that we know of.

**Plate 303**
*Tray, Serving, 15", with Brass Collar.*
These are very hard to find.

## Pastel Nautilus

HLC's Nautilus was made from the '30s into the '50s. It was often decaled; it was fancy-trimmed without decals; it was combined with Fiesta's first four colors to make the four Harmony sets; and in 1940 (no other date marks have been reported) it was dipped in the pastel glazes of Serenade — pink, yellow, green, and blue — and offered to the public as Pastel Nautilus.

The line is scarce, to be sure, but very attractive; and if you have the patience to work at it, collecting a complete set would represent quite an accomplishment. For a complete listing of available items, see "Suggested Values" in the back of the book.

**Plate 304**
*Casserole.*

**Plate 305**
*Bowls.*
Clockwise: tab-handled soup, 6"
cereal, 5" fruit, and cream soup.

**Plate 306**
*9", 7", and 6" Plates; Teacup; Double Egg Cup; Creamer.*

## Rhythm

Rhythm is a '50s line designed by Don Schreckengost, a designer whose streamline styling is attracting more and more attention as interest in dinnerware from this era continues to increase. Though we found very little information on this line at HLC, those with large collections report backstamps with dates indicating a span of production from 1950 to 1960. It was made in Harlequin yellow, chartreuse, gray, forest green, and burgundy (collectors call it maroon).

Though the spoon rest has been found in the colors of Harlequin and bearing a Harlequin paper label, Mr. Schreckengost confirmed the fact that he had originally designed it for Rhythm. It was a piece that HLC used in several lines including Kenilworth. You'll sometimes find it with decals — Rhythm Rose and American Provincial are the most common.

For a complete listing of available items, see "Suggested Values" in the back of the book.

**Plate 307**
*Casserole; Nappy; Soup; Fruit; Footed Cereal/Chowder.*
The 5½" fruit is shown center front; to the right is the 5½" footed cereal. The nappy (forest green) measures 9"; the soup is 8¼". The casserole is very hard to find.

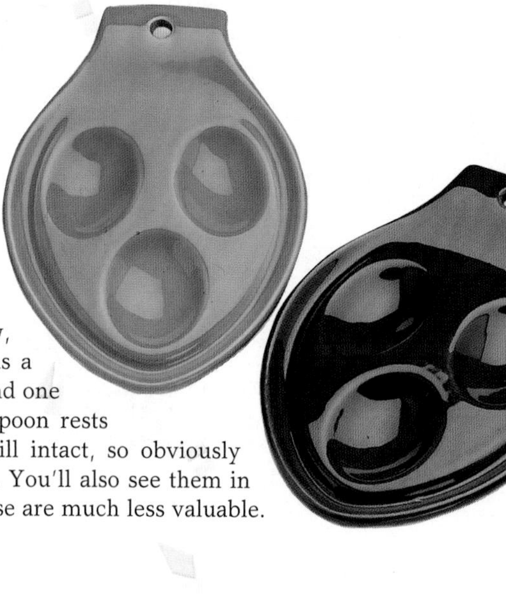

**Plate 308**
*Spoon Rests.*
These have been reported in yellow, turquoise, and forest green, as well as a very rare example in medium green and one in Fiesta red. One of the turquoise spoon rests was found with a Harlequin label still intact, so obviously these were sold with that line as well. You'll also see them in white with a decal decoration, but those are much less valuable.

**Plate 309**
*Three-tier Tidbit; Platters; Cup and Saucer; Teapot.*
These platters measure 13½" and 11½" long. We've had a report that a Rhythm platter has been found with the turkey decal. (See Plate 111.)

**Plate 310**
*Demitasse Cups and Saucers.*
A new and very exciting find are these demitasse cups and saucers shown in three of the five colors of Rhythm. Needless to say, these are very rare!
Photo courtesy Chuck Denlinger.

**Plate 311**
*Marked Demitasse Cup and Saucer.*
Very rare indeed! Photo courtesy Becky Turner.

**Plate 312**
*Plates; Sauce Boat and Stand; Sugar Bowl; Snack Plate; Salt and Pepper Shakers.*
Plates measure 10", 9", 7", and 6". There is also an 8" plate — both it and the 7" plate are scarce. Though once considered nonexistent, we have had reports of a few divided plates in maroon. They're very hard to find in any color.

**Plate 313**
*Footed Cereal/Chowder Bowl; Salad Bowl; Teapot.*
The focus of this grouping is the salad bowl; it measures 3¾" x 9¼". They're very hard to find and have been reported in only turquoise and green from the Rhythm color assortment; but they are also shown in the Kenilworth chapter in the turquoise as well as pink, and one has been found in white, another standard Kenilworth color. A mint-in-box set has been reported in forest green — the salad bowl, six matching cereal/chowder bowls, and a dark green plastic salad spoon and fork.

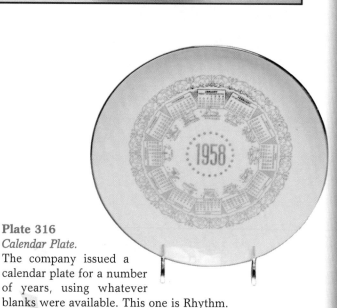

**Plate 314**
*Soup Bowls.*
These flat soup bowls are Brittany shapes glazed in all the Rhythm colors. They're marked HLC and carry dates coinciding with Rhythm's production period.

**Plate 315**
*Disney Plates.*
These 7" plates are decorated with decals of popular Disney characters. Photo courtesy Mick and Lorna Chase/Fiesta Plus.

**Plate 316**
*Calendar Plate.*
The company issued a calendar plate for a number of years, using whatever blanks were available. This one is Rhythm.

**Plate 317**
*Mixing Bowls.*

These are the Kitchen Kraft bowls; this particular combination of color identifies them as Rhythm. They measure 10" (always chartreuse), 8" (yellow), and 6" (forest green), and they have a dry (wiped free of glaze) foot. They were part of a sales campaign, a ploy the company also used to promote Fiesta and Jubilee. Our eighth edition shared the discovery of a maroon Fiesta juice tumbler, which seems to indicate that the theory held by collectors for many years was fact: the gray juice pitcher and tumblers in chartreuse, forest green, gray, and finally maroon were a Rhythm promotion.

## Seller's Line

In the eighth edition, we included a photo of a Seller's cup, not really knowing much about it. Since then we've heard from two collectors who were willing to share the information their research has revealed. These cups and saucers were produced for the M. Seller Co., a distributing firm with locations in the West. They may have just been salesmen's giveaways. Note the cross between Carnival (the body of the cup) and Harlequin (colors, saucer rings). Since this photo, one of the researchers has reported finding one in Harlequin yellow. Fiesta yellow is shown here. These are very rare.

**Plate 318**
*Seller's Cups.*

## *Serenade*

Serenade was a pastel dinnerware line that was produced for only three or four years, from about 1939 (it was mentioned in the American Potter's brochure from the World's Fair) until the early '40s. It was offered in four lovely pastel shades: yellow, green, pink, and blue. Although not well accepted by the public when it was introduced, today's collectors find its soft delicate hues and dainty contours appealing. There is growing interest in this elusive pattern, but prices are still relatively moderate.

Lug soups and teapots are rare; so are 10" plates. You may also find deep plates, 7" plates, 5" fruits, and 9" nappies to be scarce. Sugar bowls are harder to find than creamers, and the lid for the casserole (the only Kitchen Kraft piece dipped in Serenade colors) is very rare.

**Plate 319**
*Chop Plate, 13"; Teapot; Creamer and Sugar Bowl; Cup and Saucer.* Photo courtesy Shel Izen.

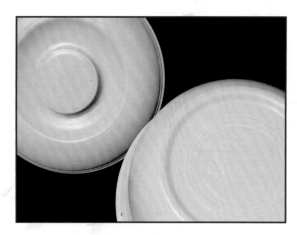

**Plate 320**
*Casserole, Kitchen Kraft.*
These continue to be very hard to find. This photo shows you the unique use of the embossed Serenade logo. Photo courtesy Pat Bunetta.

**Plate 321**
*Casseroles, Kitchen Kraft, in Two Styles of Metal Holders.*
Photo courtesy Pat Bunetta.

**Plate 323**
*Casserole.*
This is the standard Serenade casserole. Photo courtesy Shel Izen.

**Plate 322**
*Deep Plate; Nappy, 9"; Sauce Boat; Fruit Bowl, 6"; Lug (Tab-Handled) Soup Bowl.* Photo courtesy Shel Izen.

**Plate 324**
*Plates, 10", 9", and 6"; Platter, 12½"; Pickle Dish; Salt and Pepper Shakers.* Photo courtesy Shel Izen.

## Skytone

This is a seldom-seen but very attractive line of dinnerware utilizing the shapes of Jubilee. It was sold through the '50s in both the plain blue and white seen here and with decals. What makes this line unusual is that the beautiful blue hue comes not from the glaze but from the clay used in its production. In addition to the pieces shown with the Jubilee line, you may also find a butter dish in the Amberstone shape with a blue lid and a white base.

**Plate 325**
*Examples of Skytone.*

## Suntone

Here's another colored line of dinnerware — the shapes are Jubilee, and it is from the same time period as Skytone. The clay used in its production was terra-cotta brown, the glaze itself was clear. According to company records, decaled Suntone was marketed as well. The Jubilee shapes proved very popular through the '50s, and the company utilized them for many attractive patterns, changing the name of the shape to Debutante when the lines were white-glazed.

**Plate 326**
*Cup and Saucer.*
A very interesting, very small cup and saucer, shown with the teacup and Jubilee demitasse cup for comparison. Was it from a child's set? We don't know. Does anyone?

**Plate 327**
*Suntone Grouping.*

# Tango

Tango was introduced in the late '30s, made for promotion through Newberry's and the McLellan Stores Company, New York City. For some reason, it was not a good seller — perhaps its rather Colonial design seemed a bit out of step alongside other styles of colored dinnerware. Standard colors were spruce green, mauve blue, yellow, and maroon; but, as you can see, a few pieces may also be found in Fiesta red.

The line was rather limited; all available items are shown below, although unconfirmed rumors occasionally circulate concerning the existence of an egg cup. Until the egg cup can be verified, we assume that the line consisted of a fruit bowl; deep plate; oval vegetable bowl; round nappy; casserole with lid; creamer and sugar bowl; cup and saucer; plates, 10", 9", 7", and 6"; platter; and salt and pepper shakers. The shakers should look very familiar to Riviera collectors. They were original with this line; but since their shape was compatible, they were borrowed for use with Riviera.

Though many collectors like the shapes and colors of the line, dealers tell us that because it's so hard to find, few actually attempt to collect it. Proving once again that value is a relative thing, those that collect recommended much higher prices in our survey than those who sell, because to them, the fact that it is so scarce makes it worth much more than suggested book prices — no doubt a sentiment shared by collectors of other minor lines as well.

Demitasse cups and saucers are available in all of Tango's colors (including red), on HLC's Republic shape.

The W.S. George Company made a line very similar to Tango, but its glazes are rather dull and the definition of the "petals" somewhat indistinct in comparison. You'll be able to recognize Tango by the raised line just inside the shaped rim.

**Plate 328**
*Tango Grouping.*

## Wells Art Glaze

This line was produced from 1930 until at least 1935 in the colors shown: rust, peach, green, and yellow. A burnt orange matt similar to Fiesta red has also been reported as well as turquoise matt and an unusual gray-blue matte (examples in Plate 331). It's a lovely design, and records list an extensive assortment. It's very scarce and to reassemble a set is a challenge to be sure, but one collectors don't mind rising to meet, and values continue to appreciate. Dealers tell us Arts and Crafts enthusiasts have discovered this line, accounting for some of the price increases.

**Plate 329**
*Chop Plate; Covered Jug; Baker; Sugar Bowl with Lid; Teacup and Saucer; Demitasse Cup and Saucer; Handled Coffee Cup.*
The handled chop plate is 10", the covered jug is 9", and the oval baker is 9" long. The cup on the far right is inscribed "Coffee" and is 4¾" tall. You can see it with more detail in Plate 333.

**Plate 330**
*Teapots.*
Both teapots are scarce, and though we once thought the one on the left was very rare, several more have been found. The shape is from a standard HLC line called Empress. Most seem to be in yellow, though one was reported in turquoise, one in green (both marked "Wells"), and one in the celadon green of the Jubilee line. On the right is the traditional Wells Art Glaze teapot; you'll see it again in Plate 334.

**Plate 331**
*Unusual Gray-Blue Matte Examples.*

**Plate 332**
*Cream Soup Bowl with Underliner.*
These are seldom seen items; the underliner has a recessed ring.

**Plate 333**
*Coffee Mug.*
Here's a better view of the 4¾" coffee mug, a seldom seen piece.

**Plate 334**
*Plates; Teapot; Teacup and Saucer; Creamer and Sugar.*
Shown are the 9", 8", and 6" plates, and a square one that measures 8".

**Plate 335**
*Covered Muffin.*
This is a wonderful item and very rare.
It fits on the 8" plate.

**Plate 336**
*Batter Set.*
The covered jug, covered syrup pitcher, and oval tray comprise this very rare set. You may also find these in white with floral decals.

**Plate 337**
*Demitasse Pot; Individual Sugar; Creamer.*
Note the differences in the handles on the sugar bowl shown here and the one in Plate 334.

# MEXICAN DECALED LINES

When first introduced in the late '30s, Homer Laughlin's Mexican-style dinnerware lines were met with great enthusiasm. Speaking of Mexicana, which would prove to be one of their bestsellers, a tradepaper from May 1938, had this to say:

> When this Homer Laughlin pattern was first exhibited last (1937) July at the House Furnishing Show, it was an immediate smash hit. Its popularity has grown steadily ever since, and retailers have found it a constant and dependable source of profit. It started the vogue for the Mexican motif in crockery decoration which has since swept the country.
>
> And small wonder! For this Mexicana pattern is smart, colorful, and attractive. It embodies the old-world atmosphere of Mexico with the modern verve and personality which is so appealing to American housewives. Applied to the pleasing, beautifully designed Homer Laughlin shapes, it presents a bestseller of the first order.

Several other companies produced similarly decorated lines with a decided Mexican flavor — Paden City, Vernon Kilns, Crown, and Stetson, to name but a few. Besides the Mexican lines we're more familiar with, HLC also made several others, some of which you'll see farther back in this section. However, most of them are very hard to find.

HLC's three principal Mexican decals are Mexicana (occasionally marked "Mexicana" with a gold backstamp), Hacienda, and Conchita. With rare exception, these lines are virtually always found on two shapes: Century and Swing. Century, based on the number of pieces that have turned up, was the much more successful line. (There are, however, rare items in Swing that may be nonexistent in Century.)

Neither Hacienda nor Conchita has been found with trim lines other than red, but Mexicana turns up comparatively often with blue trim — especially in Kitchen Kraft, Eggshell Nautilus, and Swing. In its first year of Century production, green and yellow trim lines were used as well. Yet here's an anomaly: the non-red trim can be found on Century Mexicana 10" plates, 7" plates, cups, fruits, flat soups, and serving nappies, but on no other items — not even saucers, which seems especially strange. One collector found a mixed set of cobalt Fiesta (saucers, 6" plates, sugar bowl, and original creamer) with blue-line Mexicana (cups, 10" plates, and flat soups). The Mexicana cup looks great on the Fiesta saucer. Could it be this was another Harmony set that HLC didn't advertise in a national medium? Besides the primary-color trims we've mentioned, we've had a single report of pieces with brown trim (see Plate 363) and some with no trim at all.

## Conchita

Conchita is a line that utilizes Century shapes. A fairly extensive line of Kitchen Kraft was offered as well, though collectors tell us that it's not as plentiful as Kitchen Kraft with the Mexicana decal. Virtually all Conchita is trimmed in red.

**Plate 338**
*Platter, 11½"; Creamer and Sugar Bowl; Cup and Saucer.*
These tumblers were featured in the Fiesta Ensembles (see Plate 379). They look especially good with the Mexican lines. There were two sets — one comprised of the three directly in front of the platter. A second set consisted of the one to the far left, a larger tumbler with the Fiesta dancing girl (see Plate 375) and a small juice glass with a guitar. These fired-on designs can be found on both plain and lightly paneled glasses. Still another style has been reported: paneled tumblers in two sizes with no top ring of color but two tiers of fired-on designs in the four primary colors, a bull and cactus scene on the front and pottery jars and a burro on the back. They're very rare and were likely made by the same company during the same time period.

143

**Plate 339**
*Kitchen Kraft Server; Underplate; Individual Casserole.*
Notice the original label on the underplate. This is the Nautilus shape, which is the shape collectors tell us was used with virtually every Kitchen Kraft line.

**Plate 340**
*OvenServe Casserole; Kitchen Kraft Underplate; Cake Plate; Covered Jar; Covered Jug.*
The casserole is marked "Handy Andy" on the base; and although it's hard to see in the photo, there is an embossed design at the rim of the lid as well as around the outside of the underplate above it. These two pieces were found together, complete with the metal base — a rare find. You'll find this casserole with other decals, one a wheat and flower motif.

**Plate 341**
*Kitchen Kraft Jars, Small, Medium, and Large; Salt and Pepper Shakers.*
The shakers are turned to show the decals on both sides.

# Hacienda

This is a rather extensive line and is probably second only to Mexicana in availability. Both patterns are on Century shapes with few exceptions. Unlike Mexicana, however, you'll find no matching Kitchen Kraft line for Hacienda. The only exceptions ever reported were nested mixing bowls (6½" x 3¾", 8¼" x 4½", and 10¾" x 5¾"); the only one we've actually ever seen was a special order made for R. B. Broyles Furniture Co., Birmingham, Alabama, who also gave away Mexicana bowls. See Plates 342 and 343.

**Plates 342 and 343**
*Mixing Bowl and Stamp.*
Photos courtesy Michael Bailey.

**Plate 344**
*Butter Dish, ½-lb.; Teapot; Cream Soup Bowl.*
All of these items are relatively hard to find. Because of the consistency with which these butter dishes have been used in Century-based lines, we originally assumed their shape to be Century. The butter bottom even looks like Century because of its striped tab-like extensions; but it's actually Jade instead (See Plate 362). The Hacienda teapot turns up more often than its matching casserole. The reverse is true of Century Mexicana, and only the casserole has been reported in Century Conchita.

**Plate 345**
*Covered Jug.*
Because this piece is complete with the lid, it's twice as nice. This is a rare item.

### Plate 346
*Butter Dish.*
The round Century butter dish in the Mexican decaled lines is hard to find. Photo courtesy Jack and Sandra Bond.

### Plate 347
*Plate, 10"; Fruit Bowl, 5"; Cup and Saucer; Creamer and Sugar Bowl.*

### Plate 348
*Casserole.*
This is the regular Century casserole. It's a large, very attractive item, and extremely hard to find.

### Plate 349
*Casserole.*
This is a better view of the lovely and very elusive Nautilus casserole shown in Plate 351.

**Plate 350**
*Swing Demitasse Cups and Saucers; Teacup and Saucer.*
These are the only demitasse cups and saucers we've ever heard of with Mexican decals. Here are two, Mexicana and Hacienda, shown for size comparison on either side of a Swing Conchita teacup and saucer.

**Plate 351**
*Nautilus Deep Plate; Platter, 13"; Plate, 9"; Casserole; Creamer and Sugar Bowl; Sauce Boat; Teacup and Saucer.*
Hacienda on the Nautilus shape is rare, and the line is doubly unusual in that the color is white, not ivory.

**Plate 352**
*Swing Creamer and Sugar Bowl; Utility Tray; Casserole with Lid; Luncheon and Bread and Butter Plates; Fruit Bowl; Cup and Saucer; Platter, 11½"; Covered Sauce Bowl with Saucer; Salt and Pepper Shakers.*
These items feature the Hacienda decal applied to an HLC shape other than Century. This is Swing, and again the background color is white. Mexicana and Conchita also appear on Swing.

## *Mexicana*

Of the three major patterns, this one is the most extensive. Trim lines may be red or blue (to a lesser extent), but green, yellow, and even brown trims are also found, though rarely. Mexicana on shapes other than Century is very unusual.

**Plate 353**
*Liberty Mexicana.*
Here's a very rare item — Mexicana on the Liberty shape.

**Plate 354**
*Platter, 13½"; Sugar Bowl and Creamer; Baker, 9"; Lug Soup Bowl.*
The same square platter as shown with the ivory batter set in Plate 243 has also been found in this pattern.

**Plate 355**
*Kitchen Kraft Cake Plate; Covered Jug; Stacking Refrigerator Units and Lid; Salt and Pepper Shakers.*

**Plate 356**
*Fast-stand Gravy Boat; Teapot; Cream Soup Bowl; 1-Pint Bowl.*
Photo courtesy Jack and Sandra Bond.

**Plate 357**
*Covered Casserole.*

**Plate 358**
*Batter Set.*
Decaled Century lines from the early '30s (such as English Garden or Columbine) often include batter sets, but here's one from a mid- to late-'30s line, Mexicana. Adding to the intrigue is the fact that the larger jug is dated "D-35" (April 1935), a full two years before HLC put this decal into general use! The smaller syrup jug is not dated but we assume from the creamier color of its glaze that it's a later production.

**Plate 359**
*Virginia Rose — This time as a very rare variation of the Mexicana line.*
Shown are the 9½" and 6" plates, teacup and saucer, and the 5" fruit bowl.

**Plate 360**
*Nautilus Eggshell.*
Pieces shown here are dated 1937. Note the blue-line trim and the stark white background. This line is very, very rare. Shown are the 13" platter, 9" and 7" plates, 5" fruit, creamer and sugar bowl, and teacup and saucer.

## Max-i-cana

We've never found an official name for this pattern anywhere in the company's files, but it's been dubbed "Max-i-cana" by collectors. The siesta-taking Mexican snoozing under his sombrero amid jugs, jars, and cacti is shown in Plate 361 on Fiesta shapes and in Plate 362 on Yellowstone (the butter dish is Jade). The cup and saucer in Plate 363 is unusual in that not only does it combine shapes from two different lines (the saucer is Century; the cup is Carnival), but it is also trimmed in brown, which is the first time this trim has been reported to us.

**Plate 361**
*Fiesta Max-i-cana Platter; Cup and Saucer; 4¾" Fruit.*

**Plate 362**
*Yellowstone Platter, 13½"; Sauce Boat Liner, 8½"; Sauce Boat; Egg Cup; Rolled-Edge Egg Cup; Casserole; Creamer and Sugar Bowl; and Jade Butter Dish.*
(As of this edition, a Yellowstone Max-i-cana teapot has yet to be reported.)

**Plate 363**
*Cup and Saucer.*
Here's that very rare cup and saucer — note that the saucer is Century while the cup is Carnival. The brown trim has never been reported to us. Photo courtesy Jack and Sandra Bond.

**Plate 364**
*Butter Dish.*
This is a great shot of the Jade Max-i-cana butter dish, showing great detail. Photo courtesy Jack and Sandra Bond.

## Mexicali

**Plate 365**
*Yellow Harlequin Mexicali.*
Until the seventh edition, Virginia Rose was the only shape we knew that was decorated with the Mexicali decal. This picture shows a set of yellow Harlequin Mexicali. This must have been a very exciting acquisition. Not a single other piece has ever surfaced that we know of, but the owner was lucky enough to buy the set intact. Century has also been found with this decal.

**Plate 366**
*Gravy Boat.*
In addition to Harlequin, Virginia Rose, Swing, and Century, the Mexicali decal has also been discovered on Nautilus, Eggshell Nautilus, Republic, Theme, and this example on a Marigold gravy boat. A variant of the larger decal was used on pieces such as cups, gravy boats, creamers, and sugar bowls. See the Harlequin gravy boat in Plate 365 — it has this decal variation. Photo courtesy Melicety Deatherage.

**Plate 367**
*11½" Platter; Creamer and Sugar.*
Swing is the shape shown here with the 11½" platter decorated in the Mexicali pattern. The creamer and sugar bowl are in the Conchita design. All pieces are marked "Eggshell," a term used to indicate HLC's lightweight semiporcelain.

**Plate 368**
*Century.*
Examples of Mexicali on the Century shape have been found with a dark red trim around the inner well; some have no trim at all. Photo courtesy Melicety Deatherage.

**Plate 369**
*Virginia Rose.*
Shown here with the Mexicali decal. You'll have to look long and hard for an example of this line! They are extremely rare.

## Ranchera

**Plate 370**
*Nautilus Shape.*
This south-of-the-border dinnerware line utilizes the Nautilus shape again, this time with a decal we've never seen before. We have no knowledge of its official name, but the collector who shared this find with us suggests we call it "Ranchera."

## Other Mexican Decals

**Plate 371**
*Plate, 10".*
This pattern is similar to Mexicali; the shape again is Century.

**Plate 372**
*Century Arizona.*
Cup and saucer with red trim.
Photo courtesy Melicety Deatherage.

**Plate 373**
*Century Arizona.*
Although all the Mexican decaled lines are scarce, Arizona is considered one of the most difficult to acquire. This decal has been seen on Century and Nautilus. Photo courtesy Geri and Dan Tucker.

**Plate 374**
Here's another interesting design, again on Century. The decal name "Pueblo" is stamped on the bottom in gold. From the backstamps of known examples, it can be gathered that the decal was used as early as 1933 and as late as 1940. Besides the sugar bowl pictured, cups, saucers, and a creamer have been found on the Century shape and on Nautilus plates. This pattern is seen with even less regularity than Arizona. Photo courtesy Melicety Deatherage.

# GO-ALONGS

With the unprecedented popularity of the brightly colored dinnerware lines made by Homer Laughlin and its contemporaries, many types of housewares were designed to enhance the festive look they evoked, and today's collectors search for these wonderful items to extend the scopes of their interests. They've coined the term "Go-Alongs" to refer to the metal parts (frames, handles, etc.), woodenware, flatware, and linens made during the years when this type of home décor was in vogue. It is not uncommon to find items that carry the name "Fiesta." We've seen a Fiesta-labeled tablecloth (a damask plaid that we've shown in past editions), a Fiesta Ware Mohawk Brandy bottle (simply a black jug, not made by HLC), and a Fiesta Outing Kit (two plastic aqua and pink Thermos bottles and accessories in a thermal carrying case). Recently a dish towel with a border design of Fiesta colors was reported with "Fiestaline Dish Towel, Los Angeles 48, California 15¢," on the label. Just remember that HLC's patent was for dinnerware production only — the company made nothing else.

## Glassware and Place Accessories

Many Go-Alongs have a strong South-of-the-Border look. Colors are vivid, primary tones, and the dancing senorita or the guitar-strumming Mexican gent are prevalent motifs. The tumblers in Plate 375 have a fired-on depiction of the Fiesta dancing girl logo. They measure 4¾" high, and they're in the original colors. (See Plate 338 for more information.) The water set in Plate 376 is decorated with both — the pitcher is 9½" tall, the tumblers range from 4¾" (8-oz.) to 3¾" (the center one holds 8 ounces while the one on the right holds only 4 ounces). Collectors report that the larger tumbler is most common, and shot glasses in this pattern have been found as well. In Plate 377 are tumblers with a similar theme, and in Plate 378 you'll see wooden napkin rings, placecard holders, cord-wrapped enameled tumblers, and a set of coasters in a wire ware frame. Plate 379 displays a wonderful set of glassware in the original box that is stamped "40-Pc Genuine Fiesta Ensemble." It contains twenty-four tumblers in three sizes and four colors, eight clear glass ashtrays, and eight swizzle sticks, each tipped in the four colors. These were included in one of the Fiesta Ensembles (see Plate 437) that were boxed and shipped at the factory along with a service of matching cutlery with Catalin handles in matching colors. Examples of these Go-Alongs are shown in Plate 380. Note also the salt and pepper shakers that accompanied some of the ensemble sets. The tumblers in Plate 381 illustrate another style of coordinating glassware. This style was paired up with

**Plate 375**
*Tumblers.*
Photo courtesy Diane Petipas/Mood Indigo

**Plate 376**
*Pitcher and Tumblers.*

155

the "Juanita Ensemble," which consisted of a service for eight in the Riviera pattern, matching cutlery, these tumblers in four sizes, glass ashtrays, and swizzle sticks. While the glassware pictured here is paneled, there is another style that is not. Shown are red (5¼"), light green (4"), yellow (3½"), and mauve blue (3"). There are other lines of glassware that are compatible with the '50s colors of both Fiesta and Rhythm: water and juice tumblers with narrow bands of color in gray, dark green, chartreuse, and burgundy. In Plate 382 you'll see the glassware from a dessert service for eight that contained 7" Fiesta plates, two each in red, cobalt, yellow, and green, and these tumblers and sherbets. Though the glass is of good quality, the red is only fired on. The current owner was able to trace this set back to the '40s when an HLC employee gave it to a friend as a wedding gift. Rattan holders have been dyed to match genuine Fiesta tumblers in Plate 383.

**Plate 377**
*Tumblers.*

**Plate 378**
*Wooden Napkin Rings; Placecard Holders; Tumblers; Coasters.*

**Plate 379**
*Very Rare Boxed "Fiesta Ensemble" Set.*
Photo courtesy Thomas G. Schafer.

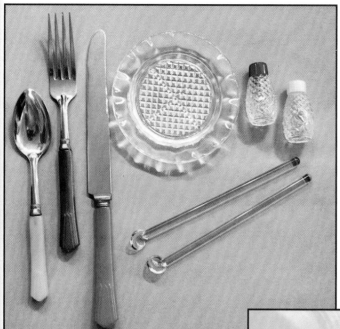

**Plate 380**
*Accessory Pieces from the "Fiesta Ensemble."*
Photo courtesy Fred Mutchler.

**Plate 381**
*Tumblers from the "Juanita Ensemble."*

**Plate 382**
*Glassware from Desert Service.*
These came with coordinating 7" Fiesta plates.

**Plate 383**
*Rattan Holders Dyed to Match Fiesta Tumblers.*

157

## Quikut Cutlery

The "Fiesta Ensemble" (see Plates 437, 439, and 441) offered by the company in the early years of production included a set of flatware with Catalin (plastic) handles, color coordinated to match the dinnerware. Several other patterns of Catalin-handled cutlery were on the market during this period — an especially intriguing set is shown here (note the name on the box). Collectors love to use this type of flatware to re-create the ensemble look. Prices vary greatly — if you find it a piece at a time, you should be able to buy at much lower prices per piece than if you purchase a place setting, especially if salad forks or tablespoons are included. Boxed sets that contain service for eight or more with several extra serving pieces go at a premium. The matching Chef's Set is extremely rare — this boxed, unused set is the only one known in such wonderful, original condition.

**Plate 385**
*Chef's Set.*
Photo courtesy Desert Productions.

**Plate 384**
*Flatware Set.*

## Metal Fittings

The "#614 sweetmeat dish" (actually the cream soup bowl), "#606 marmalade jar," the cake plate with metal fittings (Plate 386), the "#609 double tidbit with folding stand" (Plate 387), the "#610 salad service set" (Plate 389), the "#608 8" casserole and frame" (Plate 388), and the condiment set (Plate 390) were part of Homer Laughlin's "#600 Gift Assortment of Colored Ware." Because the colors listed on the company order sheet that shows this assortment are red, green, blue, and yellow, we assume that it was offered in the early days of production. A similar assortment was marketed under the name "Royal Chrome." There is another frame that will hold both the marmalade and the mustard, and you may find a metal rotating base that turns the six-part Fiesta relish tray into a lazy Susan. Note that in Plate 390 the frame is shown finished in both chrome and enamel. It's very rare to find any shakers or mustards that are marked; but all three pieces in the enameled frame are marked "HLC USA" with an ink stamp, as you can see in Plate 391.

You'll find rattan-wrapped handles similar to the one on the mixing bowl (now ice bucket) in Plate 392 in sizes to fit the 7", 9", and 10" plates (this size also fits the relish tray), as well as both of the chop plates. All are exact matches to the metal handle offered in combination with the chop plate in the 1939 – 1943 selling campaign, so we'd almost bet these were routed through HLC! The ash stand in Plate 395 is a fantastic futuristic style right out of the '50s — so is the Fiesta deep plate in chartreuse.

The beverage carrier in Plate 396 is wire-ware. Was it marketed by HLC? Not that we know of. But there were evidently promotions offered by the company for which there are no documentation, so who is to say!

Riviera and Harlequin with metal enhancements are shown in Plates 394 through 399. Notice that the fittings on the two nut bowls and the two-tier tidbit are obviously the work of the same company. The tidbit is usually found only in ivory, but one has been reported in green, complete with a green glass knob. The decaled Harlequin tumbler has been outfitted with a footed base and handle for a soda-fountain look. (Other metal enhancements are shown in Plate 401 as well — a 5½" dripolator insert converts the teapot to a coffeepot, and the reticulat-

**Plate 386**
*#614 Sweetmeat Dish; #606 Marmalade Jar; Cake Plate.*

ed casserole frame was shown on company literature along with matching frames for the Kitchen Kraft platter and 10" pie plate, the 8½" and 9½" Fiesta nappies, and the promotional casserole.)

**Plate 387**
*#609 Double Tidbit with Folding Stand.*

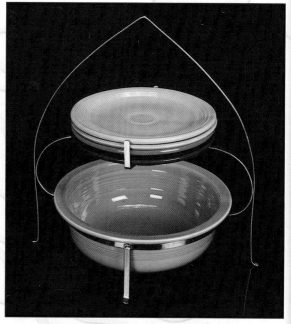

**Plate 388**
*#608 Casserole, 8".*
(See Plate 19.)

**Plate 389**
*#610 Salad Service Set.*

**Plate 390**
*Condiment Frames.*
Shown in two finishes — chrome and enameled. Photo courtesy Pat Bunetta.

**Plate 391**
*HLC USA Mark.*
All three pieces in the enameled frame (above left) have this mark. It's very rare to find marked shakers or mustards. Photo courtesy Pat Bunetta.

**Plate 393**
*Three-Tiered Tidbit Tray.*
Note that this tidbit tray has a ring handle; you'll also find examples with the triangular terminal that was used on the Amberstone tray. Both are generally accepted as original.

**Plate 392**
*Ice Bucket.*

**Plate 394**
*Riviera Nut Bowl.*

**Plate 395**
*'50s Ash Stand.*

**Plate 396**
*Wireware Holder for Beverage Set.*

**Plate 399**
*Soda Fountain Holder.*
Containing Harlequin tumbler with antique car decal.

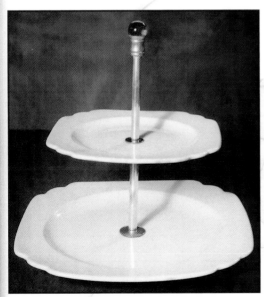

**Plate 397**
*Riviera Two-Tiered Tidbit.*

**Plate 398**
*Harlequin Nut Bowl.*

## Woodenware

The woodenware items in Plates 399 through 402 are all examples of Fiesta-Wood. It was made by the G.H. Specialty Co., Milwaukee, Wisconsin. Note its characteristic band of rings. The 10" glass insert for the large server in Plate 401 is from a line called Intaglio, made by Indiana Glass during the '30s. The mushroom-shaped center section in the party tray is for hors d'oeuvres; it's pierced to hold toothpicks and can be removed. You'll find other Fiesta-Wood items as well. Plates 403 and 404 illustrate woodenware by other companies — another hors d'oeuvres tray with a snoozing Mexican punctuating the banded border and a fruit-decorated lazy Susan base that holds a 15" Fiesta chop plate. We've also seen nappies in holders very similar to this one. (See page 159 for description of the metal items in Plate 401.)

**Plate 400**
*Salad Bowl.*

**Plate 401**
*Large Serving Tray.*

**Plate 402**
*Hors d'oeuvres Party Tray.*

**Plate 403**
*Lazy Susan.*

**Plate 404**
*Hors d'oeuvres Tray.*

## Decaled Tin Kitchenware

Notice the Fiesta-like dinnerware shown in the decals on the items in Plates 405 through 407. Collectors tell us that these pieces are sometimes found on yellow in addition to the white background shown here, and a matching three-tier vegetable bin and a kitchen stool have been found as well. The bread box in Plate 408 has a Mexicana-like decal — the only piece with this design that we know of. Owens-Illinois Can Co. made a line of tinware called Fiesta (what else) that was decorated in "Roman stripes in red, blue, and green on yellow." This set consisted of canisters, a bread box, a dustpan, a garbage pan, a 14½" wastebasket, and a kitchen stool. Yet another line is shown in Plate 414 with the Fiesta cabinet. In our files we have a photo of a 12" turquoise chop plate to which has been added a tinware cake-safe top. The lid is enameled in a matching turquoise, and it's topped with a wooden knob.

Plate 405

Plate 406

163

**Plate 407**
*Wastebasket.*

**Plate 408**
*Bread Box.*

## Enameled Tinware

Below is the Fiesta popcorn set marketed during the '40s. This set was bought at an Arizona auction still in the original carton marked "Snack Set #90, US Mfg Corp, Decatur, IL." Note the genuine Fiesta salt shaker and creamer, no doubt for the melted butter. The auctioneer said there had been a wooden spoon that had disappeared from the box. Though we have no way of knowing for sure, the presence of the two pieces of Fiesta suggests this set may have been marketed by HLC. The bowls turn up every once in awhile, but this set — complete, unused, and in the original box — may well be the only one around. You may find a very similar set made for Jolly Time Popcorn — without the Fiesta-like rings. The bowls in the cloverleaf wireware stand below are the same as the popcorn bowls in Plate 409.

**Plate 409**
*Popcorn Set with Box.*
Photo courtesy Desert Productions.

**Plate 410**
*Popcorn Bowls.*

## Miscellaneous

**Plate 411**
*Hankscraft Egg Cooker.*
In the early 1940s, the Hankscraft Company marketed its electric egg cooker in service sets that included the cooker as shown, "four vari-colored Fiesta egg cups (red, yellow, blue, and green), ivory (pottery) poaching dish, Fiesta salt and pepper shakers, and maple plywood tray." This set was called the "Fiesta Egg Service" and sold for $9.50 to $13.70, depending upon whose catalog you happened to be using. The set as shown has not been listed in any of these catalogs but is the one more often found. Obviously, these egg cups are not Fiesta. They're made of the same vitrified material as the cooker itself (which is identical to the one pictured with the Fiesta set mentioned above) and are smaller than genuine Fiesta egg cups. The colors are fired on, and in addition to the red example shown here, the cooker has also been found in green and yellow. Remember, this was a Hankscraft product — not made by Homer Laughlin, not genuine Fiesta! A similar idea found in a gift-giving ad from a Christmas 1937 *American Home* magazine featured a Westinghouse sandwich grill on a tray large enough to accommodate it, a small cutting board, and several pieces of Fiesta: the utility tray with what appears in the photograph to be the center relish tray insert nestled in one end, a stack of small plates, salt and pepper shakers, a mustard, and a marmalade.

**Plate 412**
*Buzza Cardozo Fiestacraft Paper.*
Fiesta colors and a Mexican theme make this wrapping paper a fun Go-Along. It's copyrighted 1938.

**Plate 413**
*Serviset by Sutherland.*
Found in its original cellophane wrap, this set contains a paper table cover and four paper napkins. It was made in Kalamazoo, Michigan, and copyrighted 1949.

**Plate 414**

*Kitchen Cabinet and Accessories.*

We've heard of some strange things, but none has ever topped the kitchen cabinet shown here. Note the red, green, cobalt, and yellow trim. The Hoosier-type cabinet has a porcelain work surface, flour sifter, and utensil

NO-U-28-F-FIESTA

**Plate 415**

and bread drawers. Attached side cabinets house storage shelves. Each piece is marked with code numbers and "Fiesta." Detective work by the current owner located the manufacturer, the Marsh Furniture Company of High Point, North Carolina, who is still in business today. Their sales manager said it was common at the time for Marsh to special order a variation of their cabinets for large customers such as Montgomery Ward or J.C. Penney. With the introduction of Fiesta by HLC in 1936, he assumed the special order may have been a marketing tie-in by one of its retailers or even possibly for a store display. All tinware accessory items pictured are stamped "Tindeco," once a major tin products company in Baltimore. Plate 415 shows the code numbers stenciled on the back of the cabinet.

**Plate 416**
*Do-it-yourself Decals.*
These were readily available in 5- and 10¢ stores, and collectors have reported finding sheets of them such as the one shown here. The back of the sheet reads "Designs by Betty Best, Festivalware, Set #5001." They were produced in 1945 by the American Decalcomania Co. of Chicago and New York. You may find tiles that have been commercially decorated with these decals, and shelf paper by Betty Brite that also features Fiesta dishes.

**Plate 417**
*Japan Tea Set.*
This set will be as close as you'll get to a vintage Fiesta children's tea set, but this one never saw the light of day at HLC. It's marked "Made in Japan." We show the teapot, creamer, and sugar bowl, but also included in the service for six were plates, cups, and saucers.

# COMMERCIAL ADAPTATIONS AND EPHEMERA

The commercial use of Fiesta in advertising and television has become so commonplace that we've become almost blaisè about it. You see it alongside featured recipes, in store ads, and on product containers, cookbook covers, greeting cards, etc. It's always fun to recognize Homer Laughlin dinnerware in the kitchens of many TV sitcom homes, and though more often than not, it's Fiesta you see; occasionally the other HLC lines show up as well.

If you enjoy collecting vintage ephemera, try to find the October 10, 1936, issue of *The Saturday Evening Post*. Inside is a beautiful two-page Armstrong floor covering ad with a vintage kitchen-dining room fairly blooming with Fiesta. Another ad featuring Fiesta appeared in *Better Homes and Gardens*, December 1936. *Household Magazine*, September 1937, has a full page of quick and easy luncheon recipes. The picture shows an uncovered Fiesta casserole full of onion soup and three uncovered onion soup bowls sitting around it.

## Company Price Lists

Plate 418

Plate 419

Advertising materials — especially HLC's own — make interesting and desirable additions to our collections, and they're certainly worthwhile investments as well! The company's price lists contain a wealth of information. They've been our main source of study, and as new ones are found to fill in the gaps, we may yet learn more. Because most of them are dated, we have been able to learn when items were introduced or dropped, what colors were in production during a given year, and occasionally we would pick up a tidbit of information that would help in answering one of our many questions. Fiesta price lists, though by no means easy to find, come up for sale much more often than those that represent the company's other lines.

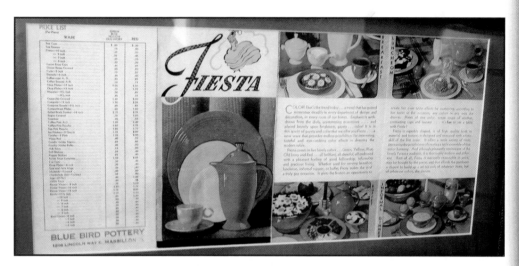

Plate 420

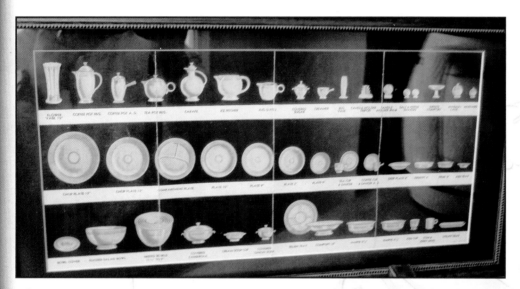

Plate 421

| | | |
|---|---|---|
| — 9 inch ........................ | .50 | .75 |
| — 8 inch ........................ | .40 | .60 |
| — 7 inch ........................ | .35 | .50 |
| — 6 inch ........................ | .25 | .40 |
| — 5 inch ........................ | .20 | .35 |
| Bowl Covers—8 inch .................. | .30 | .40 |
| —7 inch .................. | .30 | .40 |
| —6 inch .................. | .20 | .30 |
| —5 inch .................. | .20 | .30 |

Plate 422

**Plates 420 – 422**

*Price List.*

Views of the super rare early price list that shows the covers for the nested bowls. Only four sizes are listed, 8", 7", 6", and 5", and as you can see in Plate 422, they sold for a mere 20¢ – 40¢. In Plate 421, you'll see a lid in the bottom row on the far left. Photos courtesy Fred Mutchler.

Plate 423

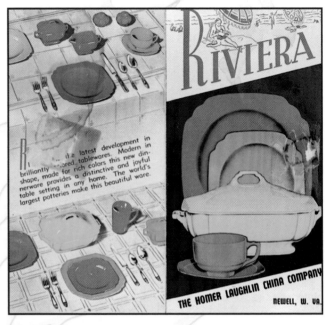

Plate 424

Plate 425

This beautiful new chinaware, EPICURE, is proudly produced by the skilled craftsmen of The Homer Laughlin China Company, the world's largest pottery. It is the result of American women's demand for an oven-to-table service, casual enough for the terrace and yet gracious enough for the candle-light dinner. Carefully styled to blend beauty with function—this lovely dinnerware lends itself to either traditional or contemporary decor and forms a table setting of incomparable charm.

**FILL OUT FORM ON OTHER SIDE AND PRESENT TO YOUR FAVORITE STORE**

NAME _____

STREET AND NO. _____

CITY _____ STATE _____

(TEAR OFF HERE)

HOMER *Epicure* LAUGHLIN

OMAHA CROCKERY CO.
1118 Harney St., OMAHA 2, NEBRASKA

*Epicure*
**AMERICA'S SMARTEST CASUAL DINNERWARE**

**Plate 426**

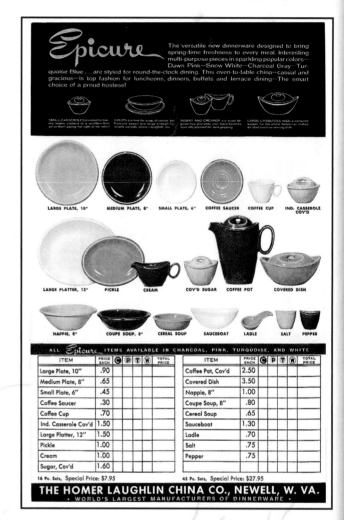

*Epicure* The versatile new dinnerware designed to bring spring-time freshness to every meal. Interesting multi-purpose pieces in sparkling popular colors— Dawn Pink—Snow White—Charcoal Gray—Turquoise Blue ... are styled for round-the-clock dining. This oven-to-table china—casual and gracious—is top fashion for luncheons, dinners, buffets and terrace dining—The smart choice of a proud hostess!

LARGE PLATE, 10"  MEDIUM PLATE, 8"  SMALL PLATE, 6"  COFFEE SAUCER  COFFEE CUP  IND. CASSEROLE COV'D

LARGE PLATTER, 12"  PICKLE  CREAM  COV'D SUGAR  COFFEE POT  COVERED DISH

NAPPIE, 8"  COUPE SOUP, 8"  CEREAL SOUP  SAUCEBOAT  LADLE  SALT  PEPPER

ALL *Epicure* ITEMS AVAILABLE IN CHARCOAL, PINK, TURQUOISE, AND WHITE

| ITEM | PRICE EACH | C | P | T | W | TOTAL PRICE | ITEM | PRICE EACH | C | P | T | W | TOTAL PRICE |
|------|-----------|---|---|---|---|-------------|------|-----------|---|---|---|---|-------------|
| Large Plate, 10" | .90 | | | | | | Coffee Pot, Cov'd | 2.50 | | | | | |
| Medium Plate, 8" | .65 | | | | | | Covered Dish | 3.50 | | | | | |
| Small Plate, 6" | .45 | | | | | | Nappie, 8" | 1.00 | | | | | |
| Coffee Saucer | .30 | | | | | | Coupe Soup, 8" | .80 | | | | | |
| Coffee Cup | .70 | | | | | | Cereal Soup | .65 | | | | | |
| Ind. Casserole Cov'd | 1.50 | | | | | | Sauceboat | 1.30 | | | | | |
| Large Platter, 12" | 1.50 | | | | | | Ladle | .70 | | | | | |
| Pickle | 1.00 | | | | | | Salt | .75 | | | | | |
| Cream | 1.00 | | | | | | Pepper | .75 | | | | | |
| Sugar, Cov'd | 1.60 | | | | | | | | | | | | |

16 Pc. Sets, Special Price: $7.95  45 Pc. Sets, Special Price: $27.95

**THE HOMER LAUGHLIN CHINA CO., NEWELL, W. VA.**
• WORLD'S LARGEST MANUFACTURERS OF DINNERWARE •

**Plate 427**

## Fiesta Store Display

**Plate 428**
*Store Display.*
This cardboard store display captures and conveys the festive appeal of Fiesta dinnerware. This particular one never left the HLC pottery, but a few collectors report being lucky enough to have found one elsewhere. There were actually two of the small side sections; one is missing from this example. You can judge its size from the mixing bowls on either side. One of these complete and still in its original box, setup instructions included, has been found! The box is embossed "1 Set Fiesta Display, Omaha Grocery Co., Omaha Nebr. To Breeding Hdwe Co. Winterset Iowa."

## *Original Packaging Material*

**Plate 429**

*Boxes.*

Examples such as these vintage packing boxes make great additions to our collections. Especially popular are those depicting the dancing girl logo. Imagine finding the four-place dinner service still mint in the box! The Fiesta sugar bowl and lid in Plate 431 are in the medium green glaze; the second box holds cups in turf green.

**Plate 430**
Photo courtesy David Schaefer.

**Plate 431**
Photo courtesy David Schaefer.

Plate 433

**Plate 432**
*Boxes.*

The photo on the left contains the box for the "45 Piece Service for Eight" that the 1978 reissue of Harlequin dinnerware came in as well as a carton for a "16 pc. Set" of Riviera in green, mauve blue, yellow, and ivory. The box is stamped "Recycle for the War" which is probably the reason red was not included! Amberstone items in their original wrappers are shown in Plate 433. Many of these pieces were accompanied by a "Bonus Certificate" good for a "Free Sheffield Deluxe Amberstone Tray with attractive golden handle" (redeemable for 10 bonus certificates). Photos courtesy Harvey Linn, Jr.

## Catalog and Newspaper Ads

**Plate 434**
With eye-popping color, this ad appeared in the December 1938 Christmas Gifts for the Home catalog issued by J. L. Hudson, Detroit, Michigan, with "as many ideas as the toys in Santa's Pack." The mixing bowl set is called "Rainbow Mixing Bowl Set," and is described as containing a 7" bowl in yellow, the 8" in green, the 9" in blue, and the 9" in red. In the box at the bottom, a 20-pc. Fiesta set is offered for $4.80; it is referred to as the "Rainbow" set as well. Photo courtesy David Schaefer.

**Plate 435**

In this ad there's quite a variety offered — not only Fiesta but Riviera as well. It's from Continental Production Inc., Chicago, Illinois, its 1943 catalog titled "Practical Holiday Gifts for a Merry Christmas." It's interesting in that in the Fiesta Specials section at the bottom (nearly all of the promotional items), the description is given for the four-piece sugar and creamer set with a turquoise tray (however, cobalt is shown), and the stack set colors are listed as turquoise, yellow, and blue, with a red cover. The "turquoise" piece is obviously the original green, and since no turquoise stack units have ever been found, more than likely the person writing the ad copy was just unfamiliar with the product line. Photo courtesy David Schaefer.

**Plate 436**

A color copy of this ad (McClurg's 1942 Holiday Season Fiesta) wasn't available, but I think you'll still find it very interesting. Note item #44 — Salad (it's next to the big salad bowl if you have trouble reading the small numbers), it's further described in the Open Stock Price List as "Salad, Handled and Footed, 8" — obviously the base of the standard casserole (which is #12 in the upper right-hand corner). Though I haven't seen one myself, the owner of this unusual ephemera tells me he has seen several magazine ads where the casserole bottom had been used to hold salad components such as tomatoes, boiled eggs, etc., rather than the greens themselves. Photo courtesy Pat Bunetta.

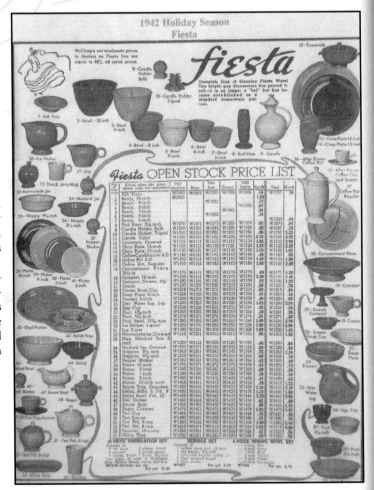

Described in an earlier chapter, these ensembles were offered in combinations of only four basic colors along with coordinating glassware tumblers and accessories. Those with the fired-on Mexican decorations came with Fiesta ensembles, while the Juanita ensemble contained tumblers with a band of color at the rim, either with paneled or plain sides. You'll see both in these ads and again in the "Go-Alongs" chapter. The cobalt 7" Riviera plates pictured in the ensemble in Plate 437 affirm our suspicions that they were indeed dipped to go with an ensemble set. Note the terms: $2.00 down and $2.00 per month — how's that for an easy payment plan! This particular Fiesta ensemble ad ran in a Sear's Christmas catalog (Special Edition, Dec. 1939). Also shown (Plates 438 – 440) are three full-page newspaper ads — one for the Juanita ensemble (all Riviera, though the name is mentioned nowhere in the ad), one that is a pleasant mix of both Fiesta and Riviera, and one from 1952 showing the new "'50s" colors. Newspaper ads are very rare (as one collector observed: "even harder to find than a turquoise onion soup bowl"), and they're valued very highly. Both sides are shown (Plates 441 and 442) of an insert flyer that was probably included in a box of Fiesta to introduce merchants to the ensemble promotions. Its colors are pristine, the folds are original, and the sepia-tone graphics and copy on the back have never been seen before. Its owner believes this to be the only example of an ad of this type found thus far. One other ensemble reported to us included ninety pieces of Fiesta (no Riviera at all) that was given away by a lumber store to the winner of a 25-word essay contest. Photos courtesy Fred Mutchler.

Plate 438

Plate 437

Plate 439

Plate 440

Plate 441

Plate 442

## Commercialized Fiesta Ware

The ashtray (Plate 443) seems to have been a popular item for advertising use. This one reads "Compliments of Sears, Roebuck & Co." In the center left photo you'll see an ivory 9" Kitchen Kraft pie plate that was a grocery store giveaway more than fifty years ago. (Alongside it is an example in a non-standard Kitchen Kraft glaze — Harlequin spruce green.) For several years, the Lazarus department store issued Fiesta items to commemorate its anniversaries — mugs for the eighty-sixth year, a fruit bowl for its eighty-seventh, a plate for its eighty-eighth, an egg cup for its eighty-ninth, and a tumbler for its ninetieth. The turquoise syrup bottom (Plate 449) is still full of the Dutchess brand tea that was sold in it many years ago; these have been reported in ivory, red, and cobalt as well. One was found with the original top and this label: "SS Pierce Co., Boston, Epicure, Cal., Orange Blossom Honey."

**Plate 443**
*Ashtray.*

**Plate 445**
*Lazarus Anniversary Fruit Bowl.*

**Plate 444**
*Plates.*

**Plate 448**
*Lazarus Anniversary Tumbler.*

**Plate 446**
*Lazarus Anniversary Egg Cup.*

**Plate 447**
*Lazarus Anniversary Items.*
Photo courtesy Crag Macaluso, Metairie, LA.

**Plate 449**
*Syrup.*

## Can Labels, Oats Boxes, and Seed Packets

As more and more collectors begin searching for related material to add to their ever-growing collections, paper items like these are becoming very popular.

**Plate 450**
*Can Label.*

Photo courtesy Harvey Linn, Jr.

**Plate 451**
*Seed Packet.*

Photo courtesy Harvey Linn, Jr.

**Plate 452**
*Can Label.*

Photo courtesy Harvey Linn, Jr.

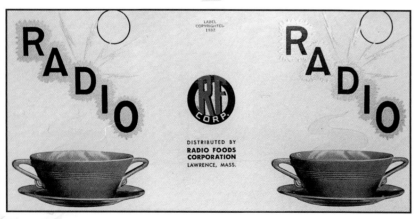

**Plate 453**
*Soup Can Label.*

Photo courtesy Harvey Linn, Jr.

**Plate 454**
*Rolled Oats Box.*

Photo courtesy Harvey Linn, Jr.

## Punch-Outs

**Plate 455**
These were distributed by the National Dairy Council during the '50s. Originally there were eight in the series, but they were reissued in the '60s, and four more were added, for a total of twelve.

## Miscellaneous

**Plate 456**
*Flour Sack.*
This is no doubt the strangest item ever reported to us — a Fiesta flour sack, made of printed cotton — the type that housewives used to make aprons and dresses out of in the '40s. The dancing girl is identical to HLC's, down to the wavy lines that surround her, and (talk about spooky) the style of print in "Fiesta" matches the new Fiesta mark — and even better, matches the title of this book! It was bought at a farm sale in Nebraska in 1998, and I've never heard of another one, so passing it off as a hoax seems premature. HLC had no information on it. Does anyone?

**Plate 457**
*Ice Cream Parlor Decoration.*
This heavy cardboard wall decoration piled high with cake and an ice cream sundae measures 8½" x 6". Photo courtesy Harvey Linn, Jr.

**Plate 458**
*Restaurant Soup Menu.*
Genuine Turtle soup? How exotic is that! Here's a great Heinz metal and cardboard advertising piece with double appeal due to the great Fiesta graphics. It measures 25" x 12", and it's from the early '40s. Photo courtesy Desert Productions.

## Advertising Mugs

Collectors have reported a variety of advertising mugs — one decorated with a caricature of Lucille Ball signed "Love, Lucy," from the Desilu Studios sounds especially unique. The Jackson Custom China Co. of Falls Creek, Pennsylvania, once made mugs similar to the Tom and Jerry. We've heard of them in brown with a cream interior and (hold on to your hats) maroon! How'd you like a set of those for your morning coffee! These were evidently not made on any large scale, but in case you should see some of them around, don't be taken in. The same company also produced a child's set consisting of a divided plate, a 6" bowl, and the Tom and Jerry, all in white decorated with a blue stenciled Donald Duck and friends.

Tom and Jerry mugs in Fiesta colors with advertising are rare, though it isn't uncommon to find examples with color on the inside only (and some will be found without the advertising). These were produced during the late '60s into the early '70s.

**Plate 459**
*Tom and Jerry Mugs.*
The exteriors are white, not ivory. Interior colors may be turquoise, yellow, rose, amberstone, or turf green.

**Plate 460**
*Sit 'n Sip Set.*
Pictured here with its original carton, the Sit 'n Sip set was marketed during the late '60s into the early '70s. Most, though not all, carry advertising messages. You'll often see a similar type of mug set in gift stores today, containing instructions to use the coaster as a lid to keep your coffee hot longer, as may have been the practice then.

**Plate 461**
*Mug.*
This mug has the vintage-style handle, though the sides are straighter. It was presented by the state of West Virginia to commemorate the introduction of the newly reintroduced Fiesta ware line in 1986.

## Buick Mugs, Ashtrays, and Coasters

**Plate 462**
*Ashtray.*
Inscription reads: "1963 Buick Management Meeting, December 11-12." It is 8¾" in diameter and has six cigarette rests. The design on the coasters in Plate 463 is identical to this piece.

**Plate 463**
*Series of Six Mugs and Coasters.*
All of these items were distributed at annual meetings of Buick Management and its Retirement Club members from 1964 through 1969. Represented on the mugs are a 1924 Model 48 Buick, a 1904 Model B Buick, a 1936 Buick Special, a 1941 Buick Roadmaster, a 1908 Model 10 Buick, and a 1916 Model D Buick. Also illustrated are the coasters that accompanied them; these have the same graphics as the ashtray in the previous photo and are hard to find. Photo courtesy Michael and Carol Wowk.

181

# HLC Calendar Trade Cards

These trade cards were given out at sales conventions and pottery shows to dinnerware buyers. Prior to the mid-'30s, various pictures of the factory were used on one side with the calendar on the other, but then HLC began the practice of picturing whatever dinnerware line they were spotlighting that year to promote sales. These are made of plastic or celluloid, and are about 4¾" x 2½".

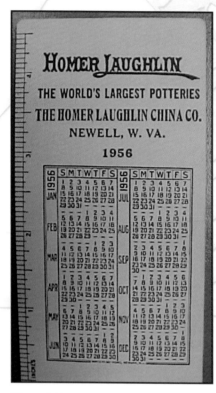

**Plate 464**
*Backside of 1956 Calendar.*
Photo courtesy Joel Wilson.

**Plate 465**
*OvenServe, 1935.*
Photo courtesy Joel Wilson.

**Plate 466**
*Fiesta, 1938.*
Photo courtesy Joel Wilson.

**Plate 467**
*Harlequin, 1939.*
Photo courtesy Joel Wilson.

**Plate 468**
*Serenade, 1940.*
Photo courtesy Joel Wilson.

**Plate 469**
*Georgian Eggshell, 1941.*
Photo courtesy Joel Wilson.

**Plate 470**
*Jubilee, 1949.*
Photo courtesy Joel Wilson.

**Plate 471**
*Bali Flower, 1952.*
Photo courtesy Joel Wilson.

**Plate 472**
*Highland Plaid, 1953.*
Photo courtesy Joel Wilson.

**Plate 473**
*Blue Willow, 1956.*
Photo courtesy Joel Wilson.

# A WORD TO THE WISE

As any collector of colored dinnerware knows, there are many lines with characteristics very similar to Homer Laughlin's. Not just Fiesta, but in fact nearly any of HLC's solid-color patterns has a look-alike. Potteries made a practice of reproducing each other's colors and designs, especially those that had proven to be successful on the market. For instance, Bauer's Monterey (1934) is very similar to Fiesta in both color and design. The cake stand shown in Plate 477 is a good example of that line. The band of rings, weight, and feel of this piece might cause even a seasoned collector to have second thoughts. In addition to the turquoise shown, Monterey also came in maroon, yellow, green, orange-red, medium blue, and ivory. Bauer's earlier line called Ring (1932), though with chunkier, heavier lines, was also produced in the bright solid glazes.

Serenade's counterpart was Lu-Ray by Taylor, Smith & Taylor. Pastel colors and simple lines were characteristic of both. Rhythm had a twin in Universal's Ballerina line. W.S. George made Rainbow, which is very easily confused with HLC's Tango line. And many other companies, among them Vernon Kilns, Franciscan, Metlox, Coors, and French Saxon China, produced solid-color dinnerware as well.

Even the Mexican decaled lines had competition. Stetson made Mexicalis, Paden City had Patio, Mt. Clemens produced Old Mexico, and Tia Juana was a line by the Knowles Company. So it is obvious that it takes a certain amount of study and caution to become a knowledgeable collector. To become familiar with the lines mentioned above, we recommend the *Collector's Encyclopedia of American Dinnerware, Second Edition,* by Jo Cunningham. If you are a beginning collector intending to limit your buying to a particular line of Homer Laughlin's colored dinnerware, use this book as your guideline. It would be rare (though not entirely impossible) to

**Plate 474**
*Teapots.*
This photo contains a wonderful array of shapes and colors. These teapots represent lines that were Fiesta's contemporaries; they were produced by various manufacturers, all located in Ohio. The green pot is Taylor, Smith & Taylor's Vistosa, a line styled with pastry-crimped rims and handles trimmed with tiny blossoms. Vistosa was made in Fiesta-like red, cobalt blue, yellow, and light green. Caliente (the cobalt teapot) was made by Paden City; its streamlined styling featured hollow ware which had bases designed with four petal-like feet and colors identical to Vistosa's. The large red teapot (top right) is Valencia by Shawnee, and the smaller red pot (bottom right) is part of Knowles' Yorktown line.

find an authentic, previously undiscovered item that by now we have not shown, thanks to the faithfulness of our readers in reporting such finds; so be extremely suspicious!

Marks can be confusing as well. In the late '70s, Franciscan marketed a line called Kaleidoscope, but according to Deleen Enge in the book *Franciscan: Plain and Fancy*, the serving pieces that went with the line were called Fiesta. Pitchers with a "Fiesta" ink stamp and the familiar large "F" (Franciscan) trademark have been found in white, yellow, cobalt, and gray-blue, but according to Enge, the color assortment also included cocoa, tangerine, dark green, and a color they called Sandman.

In Plate 475 is a line by Mikasa called Moderna, designed by Larry Laslo. This line was carried by some of the larger mail-order firms in 1985 and 1986. It was available in several colors; each piece is marked "Mikasa." White "Fiesta" has been featured in restaurants located in Rockefeller Center by Restaurant Associates, who commissioned Rego China of Whitestone, Queens, to make the ware for them. Nineteen pieces were designed; although none of the original molds were used, the style is unmistakable.

In the fall of 1998, Wal-Mart carried a knock-off line very similar to Fiesta — plates, bowls, and mugs — using the graduated concentric ring design. The mugs were larger than genuine Fiesta and had a "C" handle, rather than the ring. This line came in turquoise, yellow, periwinkle, and persimmon. By summer 2000 lilac and seamist green had been added, along with a line of "Mates" in two different patterns. Differences are obvious, though, and it isn't hard to distinguish between it and genuine Fiesta. Much of it is marked "Gibson, Thailand." And that seems to have been only one of many lines produced in recent years that draw either from the colors of the new Fiesta or the styling; some copy both. Nearly any housewares catalog or discount department store offers at least one copycat line.

**Plate 475**
*Moderna.*
Designed by Larry Laslo for Mikasa.

**Plate 476**
*Fiesta-like Cup.*
The collector who reported this Fiesta fraud chose this cup from among several that were probably genuine, because it seemed to be in better shape than some of the others. When he got home with it, he noticed that it was slightly smaller and lighter and that there were abnormalities in the shape of the bowl and the handle. On closer examination he found that it was faintly marked "England."

**Plate 477**
*Other HLC Look-alikes.*
The bud vase, with an obviously inferior glaze, is just enough smaller to indicate that it has been cast from a mold made from an original. The little disk pitcher really is not from a child's set of Fiesta, even though its color and design suggest that it might well be. The cobalt pitcher looks very much like the Harlequin novelty creamer, but it has no band of rings. The donkey may look like its Harlequin counterpart but sometimes pulls a cart marked "California." In the background is the Bauer cake stand mentioned earlier.

**Plate 478**

**Plate 479**

**Plates 478, 479, and 480**
*Bowls.*

These are still "mystery bowls," even though we know a little more about them than we have in past editions. A set of these bowls came up for sale on eBay last year; the remarkable thing was that three of the bowls still carried paper labels: "Hall China Radiant Ware – Gaco." In the last edition, we tended toward Hall as the manufacturer, since they were very similar to Hall's Five-Band bowls. We know that in the 1930s, possibly into the '40s, Jewel Tea offered a set of Radiant Ware bowls marked "Hall" on the bottom, as well as this unmarked set (like the Gaco bowls on eBay) as premiums. The colors of both the Hall-marked Jewel Tea bowl set and the "Gaco" bowls match, as do the sizes at the rim, and they were more than likely made by the same company. But both sets have wet feet with saggar pin marks, a manufacturing process not typical of Hall. Our "mystery bowl" sleuth is still on the case and has let us know that side-by-side comparison shows that the "Gaco" bowls are slightly smaller in size than the Five-Band Hall bowls, the sides taper a bit more, and the band of rings don't quite match. So seemingly for now at least, Hall and HLC are both out of the running!

**Plate 480**

# THE MORGUE

Many years ago on one of our visits to HLC, we were allowed a rare treat — a visit to the dark secretive room hidden behind a locked and barred door in the uppermost niche of the office building that somehow down through the years earned the name "the morgue." Dark and dingy it might have been, but to a collector of HLC dinnerware, it was filled with excitement! We were allowed to dig through boxes and shelves where we found fantastic experimentals, beautiful trial glazes, and unfamiliar modifications of standard forms. On our second visit some years later, we returned with a professional photographer through whose photos we are able to share the fun with all of you.

One item we especially liked on our first trip through the morgue was a vase that was out on loan when we made our return visit. We've yet to have the opportunity to photograph it ourselves, but we'll try to describe it for you. It was glazed in ivory with a 6" upright disk body that looked like the joined front halves of two juice pitchers without their ice guards — actually much like the new Millennium II vase but with more pronounced spouts. There was a stack of Fiesta plates in unbelievable trial glazes — a pink beige, a spatter effect in dark brown on orange, a smoky delphinium blue, a dark red grape that might possibly be the rose ebony referred to in Rhead's article (see Plate 502), a dark russet, a deep mustard yellow, and our favorite — black with four chromium bands.

Other goodies that were out on loan during our second visit were two different styles of Harlequin candleholders that we had cataloged before. One pair was large and flat, 5½" in diameter with a 2½" tall candle cup in the center. The others were shaped like the large half of an inverted cone, 4¼" across the bottom, and 3" tall. Both styles were lovely but not quite as nice as our regular Harlequin candleholders. Some of the most exciting Harlequin pieces we saw were a demitasse cup and saucer in a beautiful high-gloss black. Trial glaze plates included light chocolate, deep gray, delphinium blue, vanilla, caramel, black, and a luscious lavender.

We hope you find this peek inside the morgue to be as much fun as it was for us to bring it to you. If you have the opportunity to visit Newell, be sure to stop at the company's museum. Many of the treasures are now on display there.

The morgue as it appeared on our first visit.

**Plate 481**
*Footed Console Bowl; ¼-lb. Butter Dish.*

The tall 6" Riviera candleholders we had fallen in love with on our first visit to the morgue were on loan, but the footed console bowl was there for our photography session. It's huge — 3½" x 8½" x 13½" long! Although the butter dish on the right is just the size to hold a ¼-lb. stick of today's butter, this style was passed up in favor of the shorter quarter-pound version and the ½-lb. size. This one was never marketed; it's 7½" long.

**Plate 482**

*Divided Relish; Carafe; Vase; Syrup; 5" Tray; Divided Relish Section; Coffee Mug;*

The divided relish is molded in one piece; it measures 11" and was a prototype that was never put into production, though two or three have made it into the hands of collectors. The carafe, 10" tall and glazed in Fiesta green, was actually produced for a buffet ware line called Kenilworth (see our new Kenilworth chapter). In the center of the photo is a magnificent red 12" Fiesta-like vase over which wars would certainly be waged if it ever escaped HLC's walls (not likely). Notice the similarity to the Post86 Fiesta Millennium III vase! The piece to the right of the vase looks very familiar except for its size. It's 6½" tall, and its proportions exactly match the Fiesta syrup's. Directly in front of it is the 5" tray, the only marked piece we saw in the morgue. Most experimentals were merely marked with a number or not at all. This one, however, was embossed "Fiesta" in the mold. It has the band of rings on the flange. The green relish section on the right was designed so that four would fit a large oval wooden tray. The coffee mug in yellow is 3" high and except for the short tapered base is exactly like the standard mug.

**Plate 483**

*Harlequin Experimentals: Nappy; Sauce Cup; Deep Dish; Bowl.*

The nappy is 4" across and is shaped like the small Fiesta fruit. Next is a sauce cup, perhaps, made from the demitasse cup mold. The deep dish in mauve blue is 2½" x 7" — it has the Harlequin rings inside. On the far right, the yellow bowl measures 2½" x 5½" in diameter.

# EXPERIMENTALS

In addition to the experimentals from the morgue, a few more rare or one-of-a-kind items have been found outside the factory. Those that were made from a specifically designed mold we'll call experimentals. Occasionally the experimental molds were used to produce a very short sample run; generally those pieces were unmarked and more often than not glazed in ivory. A few of these have escaped the confines of the factory and have been snatched up by a sprinkling of collectors richly blessed by the Fiesta gods!

**Plate 484**
*10" Comport.*
This is a scaled-down model of the standard 12" fruit comport. There are at least three collectors who have been lucky enough to find one of these.

**Plate 485**
*Individual Teapot.*
This teapot is 6" high, and the lid is interchangeable with the standard demitasse pot. Only three have been reported.

**Plate 486**
*Footed Mixing Bowl.*
This measures 9¾" tall by 6" in diameter; the high foot that has been added nicely transforms a utilitarian mixing bowl into an elegant serving piece.

**Plate 487**
*Spaghetti Bowl.*
This piece has all the earmarks of being a sample item; it's become known as the "spaghetti bowl," but we really don't know what it was specifically designed for. It's shown in a relish base for size comparison. Under the flange on the outside is the familiar band of rings. It's 1⅜" deep and 10⅞" in diameter. It's unmarked, but almost certainly Fiesta.

**Plate 488**
*French Casserole Variation.*
This is a footed version of the more familiar yellow one, and one of a kind, as far as we know.

**Plate 489**
*Unusual Bowl.*
This bowl is marked "Fiesta" in the mold. It measures 2½" x 11½", and is more shallow than the standard fruit bowl by ½".

**Plate 490**
*Creamer and Sugar Bowl on Figure-8 Tray.*
No doubt early sample items (most of them are ivory), this set rests on a standard figure-8 tray. These were never produced.

**Plate 491**
*Sugar Bowl in Brown Glaze.*
Photo courtesy Adam Anik.

**Plate 492**

*Turquoise Tumbler.*

Shown next to the vintage cobalt example on its left, a Post86 tumbler on its right, and finally, a vintage juice tumbler, this turquoise example is marked in the mold: "Fiesta!" More than likely it was a model/prototype for the juice tumbler for the '40s promotion, since turquoise wasn't introduced until 1937, and any prototype for the water tumbler would have been done well prior to 1936. The color is an exact match to vintage turquoise; it measures 3⅛" across the top, 2¼" across the bottom, and 4¼" high. It has a "wet foot," while all other Fiesta tumblers have a "dry (wiped) foot." Photo courtesy Chuck Denlinger.

**Plate 493**

*6" Tray/Underplate.*

This item was never put into production; somehow it found its way into Newell, West Virginia, where a collector found it several years ago. There's a very similar tray measuring 5" in diameter in Plate 482; both are marked "Fiesta" as shown in Plate 495 below. The original owner had used this one under the syrup pitcher, saying that it fit perfectly.

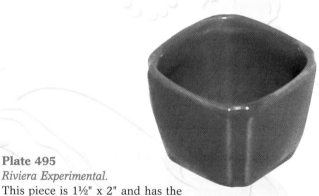

**Plate 495**

*Riviera Experimental.*

This piece is 1½" x 2" and has the typical lines of Riviera as well as the standard mauve blue glaze. A toothpick holder? A salt dip? Photo courtesy Harvey Linn, Jr.

**Plate 494**

Note the "wet foot" on this experimental.

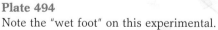

**Plate 496**

*Jugs.*

Shown is our regular two-pint jug alongside another that holds just one pint. This is the only one we've heard of and we really have no information on it.

## Inventions

**Plate 497**
*Harlequin Tumbler.*
This has been fitted with a Riviera handle
— a one-of-a-kind employee's invention.

**Plate 498**
*Chamberstick.*
The imagination of the employee who created this unique chamberstick was really on overtime! It's made from the stem of a sweets compote, a demitasse saucer, and, of course, you recognize the familiar Fiesta ring handle.

**Plate 499**
*Sherbets.*
Unproduced, though clearly marked in the mold, this pair of sherbets was made in swirling pastels. Was someone trying to imitate Niloak's Mission, using the blue Skytone clay, terra cotta from the Suntone line, and its standard white?

## Trial Glazes

**Plate 500**
*Cup and Saucer.*
This is a very early test cup and saucer; in fact the cup is the first version with the flat interior bottom. Both have code numbers in black with the numbers 820 and 821, possibly indicating the tack body number (clay body type), and the C4 may be the cone firing. The teacup and saucer came from an antique dealer who said she got them from the family of one of Rhead's maids. The story goes that Rhead had the teacup made, tested, then handed it to the maid and said "Okay, take this home and see how it holds up...see if you like it..." Well, here it is, nearly seventy some years later, still looking as new as the day it was made. Photo courtesy David Schaefer.

**Plate 501**
*Plate and Tumbler.*
Here is a 9" plate in an early turquoise test glaze numbered #017. You can easily compare the color to the standard turquoise in the tumbler. Photo courtesy David Schaefer.

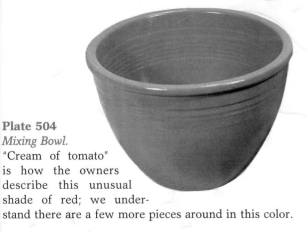

**Plate 502**
*Plates.*
Rare, early test plates, both numbered 3403 underglaze. They are made of a frail, more porous type of clay, and the glaze may be a variant of the rose ebony glaze. Photo courtesy Craig Macaluso, Metairie, LA.

**Plate 503**
*9" Plates.*
These plates are in a dark persimmon and a rich golden caramel.

**Plate 504**
*Mixing Bowl.*
"Cream of tomato" is how the owners describe this unusual shade of red; we understand there are a few more pieces around in this color.

**Plate 505**
*Ice Pitcher.*
Several pieces of this brown-mottled Fiesta red glaze have been found over the years — enough to suggest that HLC may have been at least toying with the idea of putting it into production, perhaps as competition for a line of dinnerware Stangl made that had a very similar glaze. Stangl's utilized solid turquoise on the insides of the bowls and cups as well on the top of the plates — a look HLC could have approximated by pairing the rusty red glaze with turquoise Fiesta.

**Plate 506**
*Harlequin 9" Plates.*
The owners describe the blue as being very similar to Skytone and the beige a good match for Jubilee.

**Plate 507**
*Speckled Glaze Test Plate.*
Here is an '80s Fiesta blank used to test the speckled glaze. This may have been a sample test when determining the Table Fair product line, which was produced using Harlequin plates with this type of glaze. It's numbered 12-888 on the reverse side. Photo courtesy David Schaefer.

**Plate 508**
*Fiesta Grouping.*
These trial pieces, 16 in all, were probably made during the reintroduction of Fiesta red in the late '50s, since the teacups have no interior rings and the feet are not flared. A five-digit numbering system has been used, and this seems to affirm our assumption, since most earlier trial pieces have four-digit codes under the glaze. It's very rare to find such a large number of test pieces in one grouping with code numbers that fall as closely together as these do. Photo courtesy Craig Macaluso, Metairie, LA.

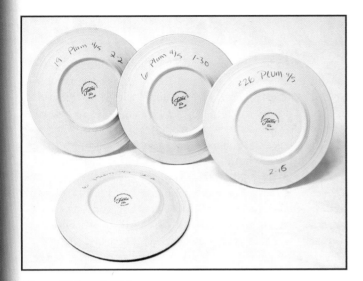

**Plates 509 and 510**
*7" Plates.*
These four plates have been sprayed with plum and tested with metallic decals for durability and proper temperature needed to keep the decals from burning. Note the Post86 marks. Photos courtesy David Schaefer.

**Plate 511**
*Riviera Syrup in Unusual Glaze.*

**Plate 512**
*Green Bowl.*
The collector who acquired this green bowl on the bottom left calls it "mystery green." It's certainly a different hue than the forest green, original green, and medium green 5½" bowls surrounding it, but with none of the blue of spruce green. Photo courtesy Gary Crafton.

# *L*AMPS

All of these lamps are made with Fiesta and Harlequin components. The red lamps (Plates 513 and 514) are both strictly Fiesta. The first one was made from the spherical section and foot of the carafe with the stem of the sweets comport added for the neck. The hole the cord goes through on the bottom is factory glazed. The other one is made of casseroles, a sweets comport stem, and a small fruit bowl as the base. The large lamp in Plate 513 was fabricated from two Harlequin casseroles; once again the neck is a Fiesta sweets comport stem, and the base may be a Harlequin cream soup bowl minus the handles. All are excellent examples of what HLC's inventive employees could do given a little time and access to the needed materials! Boudoir lamps in Plates 515, 516, and 517 were all made from either Fiesta or Harlequin syrup bottoms, more than likely assembled by another company and sold commercially, since there are several in existence and bases are nearly always identical (the marble base is unusual). In Plate 518 is a more elegantly-styled syrup lamp; this one has a wheel-cut "font" and a bobeche that is pierced to accommodate crystal prisms (now missing). The wiring is original and appears to be typical of the '30s and '40s. The socket is Canadian, but since Canadian General Electric exported these to many places including the USA, that may not indicate that this lamp was assembled there. Lastly, in Plate 519 is the syrup lamp with its original shade.

**Plate 513**
*Carafe Lamp.*

**Plate 514**
*Red Lamp.*

**Plate 515**
*Boudoir Lamp.*

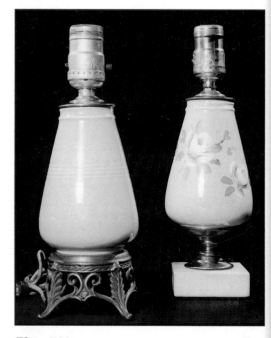

**Plate 516**
*Boudoir Lamps.*

**Plate 517**
*Boudoir Lamps.*
Photo courtesy J. T. Vaughn.

**Plate 518**
*Syrup Lamp.*

**Plate 519**
*Syrup Lamp with Original Shade.*

**Plate 520**
*Lamp Made From Saucers.*
A few years ago, these lamps were almost commonplace at outdoor shows and flea markets here in the Midwest. Here's a good way to make something both unique and useful from those stacks of saucers every collector seems to accumulate, proving that Fiesta collectors can be just as creative as HLC's employees were when inspired by Fiesta's wonderful colors and shapes. Try inverting a tumbler, adding a small vase cap or wooden piece and topping it off with a tulip-type glass shade for a darling bedside table lamp. Just remember to use a masonry bit in your drill.

# APPLE TREE BOWLS

We've always referred to these as the orange tree bowls because of their resemblance to Fenton's carnival glass pattern of the same name, and over the years some collectors have called them "peach tree." But according to Jo Cunningham's recently published book, *Homer Laughlin, A Giant Among Dishes* (Schiffer, 1998) they're correctly named Apple Tree. The design is obviously by Rhead, as it is very similar to the stylized tree motif he used to decorate Ohio art pottery very early in his career. There are six sizes, ranging from 5" to 10". Actual measurements vary a little, as is normal with HLC products, but these bowl sets may exist in two styles. One collector has pointed out that his 10" bowl (which he says is actually 9¾") is much wider than normal at the bottom, heavier, and marked with an ink stamp rather than the standard embossed mark. He has a 7½" bowl with the same characteristics.

Another collector (the owner of nine of these bowls) measured capacity as well as dimension on each example in her collection. She has two 10" bowls with the ink stamp with minor variations (9¹⁵⁄₁₆", holding 100 fluid ounces and 9¹³⁄₁₆", holding 104 fluid ounces — the increase evidently due to thinner, slightly more flaring sides). Statistics for the other sizes (for you who enjoy statistics) are 9" (9¼", holding 80 fluid ounces), 8" (8⅛", holding 48 fluid ounces), 7" (7⅛", holding 32 fluid ounces), 6" (20 fluid ounces), and 5" (12 fluid ounces). All of the latter have the standard in-mold mark. The fact that the 7½" bowl we mentioned in the previous paragraph has the unusual ink stamp and obviously would not nest with the bowls having the embossed mark supports the theory that there is probably a complete set of the ink-stamped bowls as well. Apple Tree bowls are most often glazed in turquoise, but they've also been found in ivory, yellow, and pumpkin. On rare occasions the ivory is decorated with stripes, as is the 5" bowl in Plate 521. It has three green stripes — one inside the rim, one outside the rim, and one on top.

**Plate 521**
*Set of Six Apple Tree Bowls.*
Photo courtesy Jim Carpenter.

**Plate 522**
*Ivory with Red Stripe.*

**Plate 523**
*Pumpkin Apple Tree Bowl.*

# CHILDREN'S DISHES

Children's dishes were not made in any great amount; they're hard to find, and most collectors are avid in their searches for them. You'll find some of these marked with an ink-stamped series of letters and numbers. For help in deciphering these codes, see the section called "Dating Codes and English Measurements."

**Plate 524**
*Bowl.*
"Lunch time for teddy" is the theme of this unidentified decal. The bowl is marked "Homer Laughlin, Made in USA-L36N6." Photo courtesy Chuck Denlinger.

**Plate 525**
*Baby's Plate.*
This baby's plate is marked "My Own Plate, Made For International Deepsilver, Division of the International Silver Co. by the Homer Laughlin China Co." Photo courtesy Chuck Denlinger.

**Plate 526**
*Plate and Mug.*
We've seen this comic animal decal before with variations. You'll also find it in ivory with a red stripe decoration, and in the last edition we showed it personalized with the child's name in gold lettering. It is sometimes marked "Homer Laughlin, Made in USA," and was probably produced during the first half of the '40s. This set is on white trimmed in gold. A few pieces have been found on Fiesta shapes. Photo courtesy Chuck Denlinger.

**Plate 527**
*Eggshell Nautilus.*
This is a sampling of a 15-piece set consisting of four small plates, four demitasse cups and saucers, a creamer, a sugar bowl, and a small demitasse teapot with the same comic animals on ivory with a red stripe. The teapot is marked "Homer Laughlin Eggshell, Made in USA, G 42, N5." In past editions we've also shown this decal on Fiesta shapes; values are given in the Children's Dishes section of Suggested Values. Photo courtesy Harvey Linn, Jr.

**Plate 528**
*Tom and Jerry Mug; Divided Plate.*
This set is decorated with mama rabbit and her family on a white background. Note that the Fiesta Tom and Jerry is used again. The divided plate is the first of its kind we've seen.

**Plate 529**
*Tom and the Butterfly Plate, Bowl, and Mug.*

**Plate 530**
*Restaurant Plate.*
Cowboys, branding irons, and hats decorate this plate marked "Homer Laughlin Best China," indicating that this is a piece of restaurant ware.

**Plate 531**
*Dick Tracy Plate, Mug, and Bowl.*
Borrowing a plate from the Century line, this set is rare and very collectible because of the crossover interest in the character collectible field. These are especially sought after, collectors tell us, in California, due to the popularity of collectibles pertaining to the movie industry in that area.

**Plates 532 and 533**
*Bowl and Mug.*
This is a seldom seen decal, very Art Deco in style. On the 6½" bowl is a little girl with a black doll in a wagon being pulled by an Oriental child. There are three more decals on the outside — a cat, a squirrel, and a red shoe, It's marked with the dinnerware HLC logo, "Homer Laughlin, Made in USA, K39 N8"; the mug is marked "W1353." A three-piece set with this decal on ivory vellum has also been reported. Photo on the left courtesy Chuck Denlinger.

Plate 534

Plate 535

**Plates 534, 535, and 536**
*Unknown Line.*
What a shame we've never learned the official name of the line represented here. It's decorated with various scenes of children engaged in outdoor activities, and its shapes are Genesee and Empress. From the provenance provided by the owner, whose mother used these dishes when she was a child, and because we know these two shapes were standard during those years, we date this line to 1910 – 1920. Other area companies produced lines with these decals, among them Edwin Knowles and the East Liverpool Pottery (ELPCO).

Plate 536

**Plate 537**

**Plates 537 and 538**
*Nursery Rhymes Line.*
Nursery Rhymes are the theme for this line. The shape is Yellowstone, and these pieces have a family provenance as well. They were given to the owner's mother by her grandfather, a glassblower who worked in many of the glass and pottery houses in the area. The stamp on the back dates this line to 1926. Shown are only two pieces from a nearly complete set.

**Plate 538**

**Plates 539 and 540**
*Advertising Dishes.*
Advertising children's dishes by Homer Laughlin. The bowl is decorated with the familiar green and white checks of the Ralston Purina Company; these were made as premiums for Ralston customers. The Little Orphan Annie mug was produced in the vellum glaze as a premium for the Ovaltine company. It's marked "Manufactured exclusively for the Wander Co., Chicago, Makers of Ovaltine."

# KITCHEN KRAFT AND OVENSERVE

As early as the '30s, Homer Laughlin China was the leading manufacturer of a very successful type of oven-to-table kitchenware. These lines were called OvenServe and Kitchen Kraft. Offered in an extensive assortment of items, patterns, and decals, today's collectors find them most interesting to research and reassemble into matching sets.

The label on the right was found on a floral-embossed spoon and fork set in the rust glaze; examples of this line are shown on page 204.

Guaranteed
To Withstand Changes of

## Oven-Dinner Ware
"THE OVEN WARE FOR TABLE SERVICE"

The Homer Laughlin China Co.
Newell, W. Va.

**Plate 541**
*Casserole in Metal Holder; Cake Plate; Medium Covered Jar; Stacking Refrigerator Set; Salt and Pepper Shakers; Pie Server.*
This tulip-decaled line is marked "Kitchen Kraft, OvenServe." Shown here is only a sampling of items that are available in these decaled lines.

**Plate 542**
*Examples of Floral-Decaled Kitchen Kraft.*

Plates 543 through 546 contain examples of the OvenServe line embossed with the same floral pattern that decorates the handles of the Fiesta Kitchen Kraft spoon, fork, and server. The line was offered with seven different glazes and treatments: plain ivory, ivory with green or blue flowers, pumpkin, melon yellow, polychromed (blue, pink, and green flowers), and with the Wells Art Glaze mark and colors. Two casseroles have been found in Wells Art Glaze, one green, the other rust; and two ashtrays, one green and the other peach. These are very rare.

**Plate 543**
*Gravy Boat/Sauce Boat.*
This very rare item measures 3½" x 5½" long and it holds 12 ounces. Don't confuse it with the more common creamer.

**Plate 544**
*2½-Quart Casserole and Underplate.*
This very attractive style is decorated with decals over the embossed flowers.

**Plate 545**
*Batter Pitcher.*
This piece is rare; it's shown in a very hard-to-find color, white.

**Plate 546**
*Decaled Mixing Bowl, 12".*
Photo courtesy Dan and Geri Tucker.

**Plate 547**
*Mixing Bowl, 11".*
In the curdled green of the Wells Art Glaze line.

**Plate 548**
*Custard Set in Wire Rack.*

**Plate 549**
*Covered Bean Pot, 4½".*
Photo courtesy Bob Shriner/ABC Antiques.

**Plate 550**
*Kitchen Kraft: Kitchen Bouquet Pie Plate and Platter.*

**Plate 551**
*Kitchen Kraft Ashtray.*
Hard to find in any color, the ashtray is shown here in pumpkin and ivory. These two are from a set of four purchased together back in the '80s. One has a dating code that indicates a 1933 production. The rings in the bottom vary: two of that set have six (note the ivory example), while the others have only four around a 1½" plain center (like the one on the left). Photo by Harvey Linn, Jr.

**Plate 552**
*Blue Willow Covered Jar.*
HLC made an extensive line of Blue Willow dinnerware that is very collectible today. This matching Kitchen Kraft jar is a real prize. Photo courtesy Chuck Denlinger.

**Plate 553**
*7" Underplate.*

**Plate 554**
*Casserole.*

**Plates 553 and 554**
This unnamed, rare decal is only found on HLC shapes, causing speculation that it may have been the company's exclusive design. It was devised in three sizes, with the larger versions decorating larger items, the smallest the casserole lids, etc. Components in the primary decal include a lady, jug, teapot, and candlestick, with variations not only in size but also color, style, and placement. The lady stands in different poses, either with her hands empty or holding the bowl as seen in our examples. She was applied to all shapes, except for the lids to the covered jar and the refrigerator dish, Kitchen Kraft salt and pepper shakers, and Kitchen Kraft pie/cake server. Her yellow hat may be adorned with either a red band or a white flower garland, her shawl and blouse may be either yellow or red, and her skirt or apron may be dark blue or light green — the latter with a wide red border. There are two variations on the jug — it will either have a flat-top (in dark or light blue, the one most often encountered), or a pour spout (which is always dark blue). The teapot appears in one of two different locations. The medium teapot is always placed behind the jug with the handle of the teapot hidden. The large teapot is placed in front of the jug. The teapot and pour-spout jug decals were not used together. The candlestick in the medium size is always placed behind the flat-top jug while in the larger decal it is behind and to the right of the pour-spout jug or to the left in front of the flat-top jug. Two companion decals were also produced, each having only one size. One depicts a standing man wearing a matching hat and coat in either dark or light blue, with red and yellow flowers at his side. The second, flowers in red, yellow, and blue, varies in arrangement and was applied to all shapes. The primary and companion decals appear on twenty HLC shapes: covered casserole, 6" and 8"; large, medium, and small mixing bowls and jars; embossed OvenServe covered casserole, 6"; embossed OvenServe pie plate, 10"; Royal Chrome covered casserole, 8"; plates, 6" and 9" ; and the Brittany chop plate, 14". On rare occasions a platinum mark — KK335 — is stamped on the underside of the lids of both the 8" Kitchen Kraft/OvenServe casserole and the Royal Chrome casserole. Because the decal is rare, use the same price range recommended for Sun Porch. (Our thanks to J. T. Vaughn and Pat Bunetta for this in-depth information.)

# HARMONY LINES

The Kitchen Kraft in Plates 555, 556, and 557 is decorated in an Art Deco leaf pattern (N–260), one of the Harmony lines we told you about in the chapter entitled "The Story of Fiesta." This line was undiscovered until the sixth edition, and we were doubly excited to learn that a matching line of Kitchen Kraft had been produced. This, of course, is the line that coordinated with red Fiesta.

**Plate 555**
*Kitchen Kraft Jar; Nautilus Lug Cereal/Soup Bowl; 6½" and 7½" Plates; Cup and Saucer; Creamer and Sugar; Large Vegetable Bowl.*
It is interesting to note that collectors report finding several more Nautilus items than those that are listed in the Harmony assortment on page 11.

**Plate 556**
*Casserole; Mixing Bowl; Pie Plate; Spoon; Fork; Server.*

**Plate 557**
*Platter and Matching Glassware.*

**Plate 558**
*Nautilus Cup with Fiesta Saucer; Kitchen Kraft Individual Casserole; Nautilus Fruit Bowl; 6½" Plate; 7½" Fiesta Plate; Kitchen Kraft Shakers; Jug with Yellow Lid.*
This was designed to go with yellow Fiesta. Collectors have termed this pattern Shaggy Flower; it's the decal the company identified as N-258. You may find this decal on other HLC shapes.

# DECALED DINNERWARE PATTERNS AND SHAPES

## Americana

This very attractive set was made exclusively for Montgomery Ward who offered it for sale in its catalogs from 1944 through 1956. Each piece (thirty-one in all) carries a different design patterned after a Currier & Ives print. The rose-pink decorations suggestive of mulberry historical Staffordshire ware were "printed from fine copper engravings," so states the ad in the 1944 catalog.

Shapes from five different lines were selected for this pattern. These pieces were available: cup and saucer; plates, 10", 8½", 7", 6", and 8" square; dessert/fruit bowl; demitasse cup and saucer; coupe soup; creamer and sugar bowl with lid; sauce boat and stand; egg cup; teapot; oval platters, 11", 13", 15"; round platter, 13"; oval vegetable bowl; round vegetable bowls, 8", 9"; and vegetable bowl lid, 9".

**Plate 559**
*Americana Grouping.*

## American Provincial

The familiar shapes in this line are Rhythm, designed by Don Schreckengost. We know it best as the colored dinnerware line, but it was used as a basis for several decaled lines as well. Note the variations in the decal as well as the decoration — some items are trimmed with a red stripe while others have gold trim. The salt and pepper shakers are on the Jubilee shape. The large jug has never been reported in the solid colors of Rhythm.

**Plate 560**
*Salt and Pepper Shakers; Spoon Rest; Sugar Bowl; Large Jug; Sauce Boat.*

**Plate 561**
*Dessert Plate, 6"; Plate, 9"; Cake Plate, 10½"; Deep Plate, 8"; Cup and Saucer; Fruit Bowl.*

## Chinese Green Goddess

**Plate 562**
*Teapot.*
On the Swing shape, this pattern is very rare. Swing, introduced in 1938, was the first of HLC's shapes in the Eggshell weight. By 1945 it was identified only as Eggshell, not to be confused with Eggshell Nautilus, a lighter-weight version of the Nautilus shape, or Eggshell Georgian, a lightweight rendering of a classic English shape.

## Colonial Kitchen

**Plate 563**
*Plate.*
This is another line utilizing the Swing shape.

## Dogwood

Dogwood was produced in the early '60s. Among the hard-to-find items in this pattern are the 8" salad plate, the 10" dinner plate, the teapot, and the Kitchen Kraft mixing bowl set. This decal has also been reported on Rhythm shapes (except for the mixing bowl set); here the shape is Liberty.

**Plate 564**
*Teapot; Dinner Plate, 10"; Salad Plate, 8"; Mixing Bowl Set; Teacup and Saucer; Oval Vegetable Bowl; Fruit Bowl, 5".*

## English Garden

This lovely dinnerware is dated 1933, and the casserole is marked with the colorful Wells peacock trademark. The shape is Century; especially note the butter dish. This is actually the Century shape, one of only a few we've ever seen. In virtually every other instance, the one used in decaled lines on Century shapes is the Jade butter dish; you'll see more of the Jade shapes on the following pages.

**Plate 565**
*Egg Cup; Fast-Stand Gravy Boat; Plates, 10" and 8"; Platter, 12"; Covered Jug; Open Casserole; Gravy Boat; Syrup Pitcher; Sugar Bowl; Cream Soup; Butter Dish.*

## Historical America Subjects

Produced for the F. W. Woolworth Company who sold it through its retail stores, this line was aptly named. Each piece was decorated with a scene reproduced from the original works of Joseph Boggs Beale. All that has been reported to us has been in the rose-pink as shown here except for the 8" plate, which has also been found in blue. Scenes bear titles such as "Betsy Ross and the Flag," "Lincoln's Gettysburg Address," "George Washington Taking Command of the Army," "The First Thanksgiving," and "Paul Revere." Though very hard to find, there's a lot of enthusiasm for this line, and prices are already higher than for most decaled dinnerware. For a complete listing of available items, see "Suggested Values" in the back of this book.

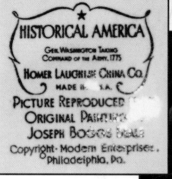

**Plate 566**
*Various Historical America Subjects Pieces.*

## La Hacienda

La Hacienda is the pattern name; the shape is called Jade. According to the dating code in the backstamp, it was made circa 1935. Although we always thought the stick butter dishes were on the Century shape because they were consistently found in Century-based Mexican lines, they're in fact Jade. (See Plate 565 for the round Century butter dish.)

**Plate 567**
*Creamer and Sugar Bowl; Century Platter, 12"; Casserole, 7½"; Plate, 8"; Tray, 9"; Sauce Boat.*

# Old Curiosity Shop

HLC's standard Nautilus shape is shown in this charming line. It was shown in the Mexicana lines and again as a basis for two of the Harmony lines. Though very hard to find, it is popular among dinnerware collectors.

**Plate 568**
*Cup and Saucer; Plate, 6½"; Deep Bowl; Casserole with Lid; Fruit Bowl; Platter, 11½"; Deep Plate; Plates, 9½"; Gravy Boat and Liner; Butter Dish (Jade Shape); Creamer and Sugar Bowl.*

# Priscilla

Favored by collectors, Priscilla is an extensive line and relatively easy to find. Two styles were produced — the regular line, simple round shapes on Eggshell (lightweight semiporcelain), and a second line that utilizes the Republic shape. In addition to the dinnerware, you'll find matching Kitchen Kraft. Among the harder-to-find items are the tall teapot (shape unknown) shown below to the far left, the Republic teapot, and these Kitchen Kraft items: the 9½" fruit bowl (far right), coffeepot, and the tab-handled platter. A more complete listing is offered in the "Suggested Values" section. (Note: Other items may be found in this pattern marked Universal China Company; these pieces are generally regarded as desirable enhancements to a HLC Priscilla collection.)

**Plate 569**
*Tall Teapot; Deep Plate, 8½"; Plates, 10" (the second is Republic); Kitchen Kraft Fruit Bowl; Republic Creamer and Sugar Bowl; Republic Teapot.*

**Plate 570**
*Kitchen Kraft Jug; Coffeepot; Regular Teapot; Republic Teapot; Mixing Bowls; Casserole.*

## Rhythm Rose

Rhythm is a shape designed by Don Schreckengost; it features a lovely rose design, and it was produced from the mid-'40s through the mid-'50s. Though we're most familiar with it as one of the colored dinnerware lines, it was the basis of several decaled lines as well. It is usually marked with the gold stamp: "Household Institute, Rhythm Rose."

**Plate 571**
*Open Jug; Cake Plate; Coffeepot; Teapot; Cup and Saucer; Creamer and Sugar Bowl; Cake Server; Pie Plate.*

# Sun Porch

**Plate 572**

*Covered Casserole.*

This line is a favorite with Fiesta collectors. It's called Sun Porch, and it's novel in that the decal depicts pieces of Fiesta dinnerware on the table under the umbrella. It's a hard-to-find line, and so far, only the two pieces on this page have been reported to us on the Century shape. It's most often found on items from the Kitchen Kraft line, and one piece has been reported on the Virginia Rose shape.

Photo courtesy Chuck Denlinger.

**Plate 573**

*Teapot.*

Both the casserole and this teapot are so rare we can't even suggest values for them, though advanced collectors would pay a hefty premium for either one.

**Plate 574**

*Tumblers with Fired-on Decoration.*

**Plate 575**

*Kitchen Kraft Individual Casserole and Salt and Pepper Shakers.*

These items came out of a New Jersey basement where, covered in soot, they were found together still in the original cardboard box stamped "4-Piece Range Set." This time the individual casserole is used as a drip jar.

## Virginia Rose

Virginia Rose was the name given to a line of standard HLC shapes which from 1929 until the early '70s was used as the basis for more than a dozen patterns of decaled or embossed dinnerware. The designer was Fredrick Rhead, and the name was chosen in honor of the daughter of Joseph Mahan Wells, granddaughter of Wm. E. Wells. Virginia Rose was one of the most popular shapes ever produced. Even after it was discontinued for use in the home, the shape was adopted by the hotel china division at HLC and became a bestseller in the field of hotel and institutional ware. Shown here is only a sampling of the many floral patterns you may find on pieces marked Virginia Rose. Among the harder-to-find items are the double egg cup, coffee mug, 8" tray with handles, and the salt and pepper shakers. A matching line of Kitchen Kraft is also available. Some of it is limited as well. The 12" pie plate, salt and pepper shakers, cake plate and server, straight-sided casserole, and 8" casserole with round sides are scarce. For a more complete listing of available items, see "Suggested Values" in the back of the book.

**Plate 576**
*JJ-59 Plates, 10", 8", 6"; Soups, 8" (one flanged); Salt and Pepper Shakers; Egg Cup; Oatmeal Bowl, 6"; Deep Bowl, 5".*
Also known as Moss Rose, this decal and Fluffy Rose (see Plate 581) are the most popular among collectors.

**Plate 577**
*JJ-59 Kitchen Kraft Salt and Pepper Shakers; Casserole; Tray, 8".*
The straight-sided casserole is harder to find than the style shown on the left in Plate 578. The small tray is very scarce and may have been used as an undertray for the casserole.

**Plate 578**
*JJ-59 Kitchen Kraft Covered Casseroles, 8½", 7½"; Daisy Chain Covered Casserole.*
The casserole on the right is very rare. Like the mugs in Plate 580, the darker decal indicates a '30s production. This piece is marked DC-714 under the lid and carries the HLC OvenServe logo.

**Plate 579**
*JJ-59 Water Pitcher, 7½"; Milk Pitcher, 5"; Kitchen Kraft Mixing Bowl Set.*

**Plate 580**
*JJ-59 Baltimore Coffee Mugs.*
All are dated 1930; they're very hard to find.

**Plate 581**
*VR-128 Covered Vegetable; Cake Set; Platter, 15"; Plate, 8"; Sauce Boat and Liner (9½" Platter); Butter Dish; Creamer and Sugar Bowl; Cup and Saucer; Kitchen Kraft Casserole, 8".*
Known as Fluffy Rose, this is one of the most collectible lines of Virginia Rose.

**Plate 582**

**Plate 583**

**Plate 584**

**Plate 585**

**Plates 582 – 585**
*Kitchen Kraft: Covered Jug, Covered Casserole, Ball Jars, Nested Mixing Bowl Set.*
This is pattern CAC-186, probably ranking #3 in the favor of Virginia Rose collectors, after VR-128 and JJ-59. It is also called Peony. A wide selection of dinnerware is available in this pattern. Some of the harder-to-find items include the ball jars; the covered pitcher; the spoon, cake lifter, and fork; and the stacking Kitchen Kraft refrigerator jars and lids. Photos courtesy Jack and Treva Hamlin.

## Western Dinnerware and Others

**Plate 587**
*Western Dinnerware.*
While we once thought the Western dinnerware was a child's set, we've since heard from a lady who received some as a wedding gift. She tells us that in addition to the place setting, there were serving pieces such as a creamer and sugar bowl, vegetable bowls, and platter. From another source, we've learned that there was even an ashtray to match; it was made for the Woolworth Company.

**Plate 586**
*After-Dinner (or Breakfast-in-Bed) Creamer; Cup and Saucer; Plate, 6".*
These are in an unnamed floral pattern; the shape is Swing.

**Plate 588**
*Casseroles.*
Floral decoration on the Swing shape. Photo © Adam Anik.

**Plate 589**
*Plate, 6"; Cup and Saucer; Deep Plate; Luncheon Plate; Fruit Bowl.*
When we first started collecting Depression-era glassware, folks would remark with disdain, "They used to give that stuff away at the movies." Well, here is a Century set that really was. Plates with the legend shown have been found in several northeastern states and at least one in the South. These pieces are never marked on the back, but they are unmistakably HLC.

# LAUGHLIN ART CHINA

In the early 1900s, perhaps in an attempt to compete with other companies that were doing so well in the art pottery field, HLC produced a unique line of art china. Many items were marked with an eagle and "Laughlin Art China." Some lines were stamped with the name of the pattern as well. Perhaps as many as eighty-nine shapes were utilized. Though by far the majority of the pieces are decaled, occasionally you'll find a hand-painted piece; on rare occasions you may discover an artist's signature. Some lines were produced until the mid-teens.

## Caledon

Caledon was introduced in 1908; today it's very hard to find. Characteristic of the line is this dog design on shaded background of yellow and brown.

**Plate 590**
*Plate, 9"; Mug.*
Photo courtesy Chuck Denlinger.

## Currant

The Currant pattern was the most extensive line of Art China. It was introduced in 1906 and featured a brown shaded background decorated with decals of berries and vines. There were several variations of the decals, and in Plate 609 you'll see and example with the background in white.

**Plate 591**
*Vase with Handles, 8".*

**Plate 592**
*Vase, 7".*

**Plate 593**
*Small Rose Bowl, 4¼".*
Photo courtesy Chuck Denlinger.

**Plate 594**
*Ruffled Salad Bowl, 2" x 10"; Plaque, 9½"; Scalloped Plate, 10".*

**Plate 596**
*Tobacco Jar.*
Photo courtesy Chuck Denlinger.

**Plate 595**
*Vase, 9½".*
This may be the #6 vase. It's very rare; this is the first one ever reported to us. Photo courtesy Chuck Denlinger.

**Plate 597**
*Fe Dora Bread Tray, 6½" x 12".*

**Plate 598**
*Cracker Jar.*
Photo courtesy Chuck Denlinger.

**Plate 599**
*Whiskey Jugs, 3½" and 5½".*
Photo courtesy Chuck Denlinger.

**Plate 602**
*Covered Dish.*

**Plate 601**
*Sugar Basket.*

**Plate 600**
*Pitcher, 10".*
Called "Dutch Jug" in old company records.

**Plate 603**
*Geisha Jug.*
Photo courtesy Craig Macaluso, Metairie, LA.

**Plate 604**
*Sapho Molasses Can.*
This is the only piece of Art China that utilizes a lid of another material. All other covered items have clay lids; this one is silver metal. Photo courtesy Chuck Denlinger.

**Plate 605**
*Vase, 12".*

**Plate 606**
*Vases, 9¾", 12", and 16"; Chocolate or After-Dinner Pot.*
Note the lovely after-dinner pot — it's 10" tall and very rare.

**Plate 607**
*Vase with Handles, 14".*

**Plate 608**
*Bulbous Pitcher, 6"; "Orange" Bowl with Handles, 12"; Straight-Sided Pitcher, 6½".*

**Plate 609**
*Orange Bowl in White.*
Though very similar in shape, the white example shown here is ½" smaller in diameter than the standard brown "Orange" bowl, and while the brown one is 5¼" tall, the white one is only 4⅛". It's decorated with smaller groupings of currants, and the handles are shaped similarly but with some minor differences.  Photo courtesy Chuck Denlinger.

.

## Delft

At first glance, one would think this is a piece of the very rare Holland line. But turning it over, we find it's marked "Laughlin's Delft." (See Plate 611.) This is an extremely rare item; HLC contacts tell us they've seen only one other piece with this mark. This is the #3 vase.

**Plate 610**
*Vase #3.*
Photo courtesy Chuck Denlinger.

**Plate 611**
*The Very Rare "Laughlin's Delft" Stamp.*
Photo courtesy Chuck Denlinger.

## Dreamland

Children feeding their pet goat, doing laundry, and playing follow the leader decorate this winsome line introduced by Homer Laughlin in 1906. The shaded brown-to-green-to-yellow backgrounds are characteristic of the line, examples of which are sometimes found with the "Laughlin's Dreamland" stamp shown below.

**Plate 612**
*Vase.*
This tiny vase is a mere 3½".

**Plate 613**
*Tankard Set.*
A collector has reported a variation of this set without the brown shading at the bottom; his is decorated with four different designs.

**Plate 614**
*Loving Cup, Three-Handled.*
**Extremely rare.** Photo courtesy Chuck Denlinger.

**Plate 615**
*Chop/Cake Plate, 10½".*
Note the closed handles. There is another style where the handles are open.

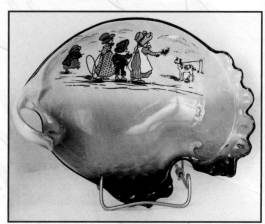

**Plate 617**
*Vase, 16".*

**Plate 616**
*Chocolate Pot.*
Photo courtesy Chuck Denlinger.

**Plate 618**
*Handled Nut Dish.*
Photo courtesy Chuck Denlinger.

**Plate 619**
*Plaque.*

**Plate 620**
*Jug, 6½".*
Photo courtesy Chuck
Denlinger.

**Plate 621**
*Rose Bowl, Large, 5".*
Photo courtesy Chuck Denlinger.

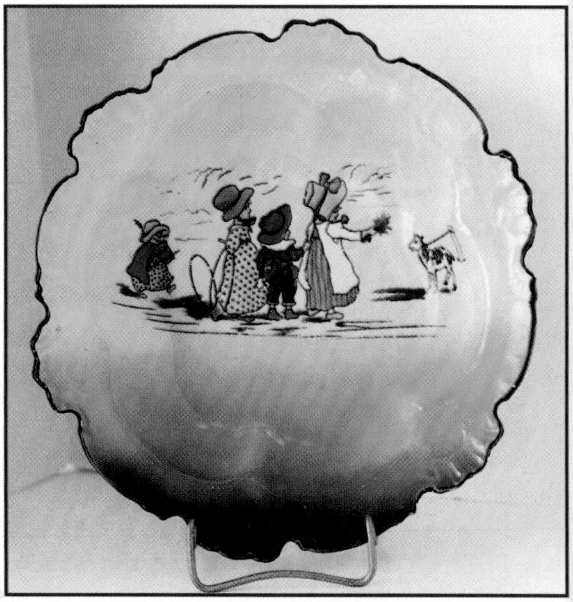

**Plate 623**
*Berry Bowl.*
Photo courtesy Chuck Denlinger.

**Plate 622**
*Ruffled Salad Bowl.*

## Golden Fleece

This unusual line is not readily available or highly collectible, compared to the other lines. It dates to about 1908.

**Plate 624**
*Tioga Creamer.*
Photo courtesy Chuck Denlinger.

**Plate 625**
*Tioga Sugar Basket.*
Photo courtesy Chuck Denlinger.

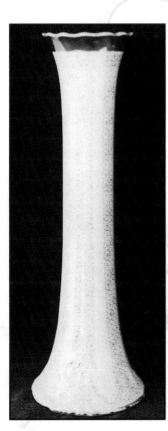

**Plate 626**
*Vase, 12".*
Photo courtesy Chuck Denlinger.

**Plate 627**
*Tankard and Staghorn Steins.*
Photo courtesy Chuck Denlinger.

## *Gypsy and Other Beauties*

**Plate 628**
*Gypsy Pear-Shaped Mug, Gold Eagle Mark, Rare.*
Photo courtesy Chuck Denlinger.

**Plate 629**
*Gypsy Plate, 10¼"; Geisha Jug with Rare Blue Trim.*
Photo courtesy Chuck Denlinger.

**Plate 630**
*Gypsy Plate, 6¼".*
Photo courtesy Chuck Denlinger.

**Plate 631**
*Gypsy Chocolate Pot.*
Photo courtesy Chuck Denlinger.

**Plate 632**
*Gypsy Tioga Sugar Basket and Creamer.*
Photo courtesy Chuck Denlinger.

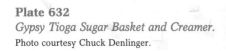

**Plate 633**
*Charger.*
Marked "American Beauty, Semi-vitreous China, 1900."

**Plate 634**
*Nut Dish.*

**Plate 635**
*Large Tankard and Mugs.*

## Holland

**Plate 636**
*Ewer, 15½".*

LAUGHLIN'S
HOLLAND

**Plate 637**
*Bowl, Fancy Salad (or Ruffled Salad).*
Photo courtesy Chuck Denlinger.

**Plate 638**
*Dutch Jug.*
Photo courtesy Chuck Denlinger.

**Plate 639**
*Bowl, Salad.*
Note the white exterior.

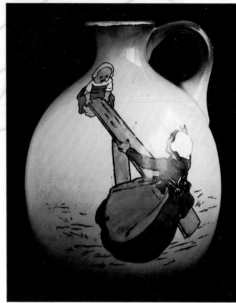

**Plate 641**
*Jug, 6½".*

**Plate 640**
*Rose Bowl.*

**Plate 642**
*Plate, 10½".*
Note the blue tones as opposed to the normal brown to yellow. This line was introduced in 1906.

# *Juno*

Named for the queen of the gods of ancient Rome, wife and sister of Jupiter, this line (circa 1905) is characterized by a full-length lady with either doves or a peacock and a multi-shaded brown-to-ivory background with areas of rose, blue, and green.

**Plate 643**
*Demitasse Cup and Saucer; Chocolate Pot.*

**Plate 644**
*Geisha Milk Jug.*

**Plate 645**
*Comport.*
Photo courtesy Chuck Denlinger.

**Plate 646**
*Bowl, Fancy Salad (or Ruffled Salad).*
Photo courtesy Chuck Denlinger.

**Plate 647**
*Orange Bowl.*
Photo courtesy Chuck Denlinger.

**Plate 648**
*Stein Ewer.*
Photo courtesy Chuck Denlinger.

**Plate 649**
*Tioga Salad Bowl.*
Photo courtesy Chuck Denlinger.

**Plate 650**
*Unidentified Piece, with Drain Hole and Underplate.*
Photo courtesy Chuck Denlinger.

## Laughlin Blue and Other Flow Blue Patterns

Laughlin Blue was made circa 1905 and is primarily characterized by vignettes of children in period attire. Most is gold trimmed. While the items in Plates 658, 659, and 660 may be from a line with a different name, we are including them here since they are decorated by the Flow Blue method.

**Plate 651**
*Jardineire, 10" x 14½".*
Photo courtesy Chuck Denlinger.

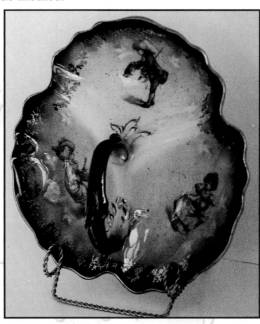

**Plate 652**
*Cabaret, Rare.*
Photo courtesy Chuck Denlinger.

**Plate 653**
*Tioga Cake Plate.*

**Plate 654**
*Vase, 12".*

**Plate 655**
*Tioga Cake Plate.*

**Plate 657**
*Cup and Saucer.*

**Plate 656**
*Spoon Tray, Small.*
Photo courtesy Chuck Denlinger.

**Plate 659**
*Staghorn Stein with Monk.*
Photo courtesy Jim Carpenter.

**Plate 658**
*Large Tankard with Monk.*

**Plate 660**
*Chocolate Cups.*
Gold Laughlin Art China eagle mark.
Photo courtesy Chuck Denlinger.

## Ruby, Silver Sienna

Circa 1905, Ruby is a line tinted all over in iridescent luster with broad bands of ruby luster and gold trim. Examples are extremely rare.

Introduced in 1908, the Silver Sienna line is characterized by brown backgrounds that feature dog subjects; it's finished off with silver bands and handles.

**Plate 662**
*Ruby Biscuit Jar.*
Photo courtesy Chuck Denlinger.

SILVER SIENNA

**Plate 661**
*Silver Sienna Mug (Unusual Shape); Dutch Jug; Plate, 10¼".*
Photo courtesy Chuck Denlinger.

## White Pets

White Pets is a line decorated with decals that have been over-painted predominately in white over pink to blue-gray. It was introduced in about 1907. Occasionally, one of these pieces will bear a decorator's name. Examples with cockatiels are especially hard to find.

**Plate 663**
*Comb and Brush Tray.*

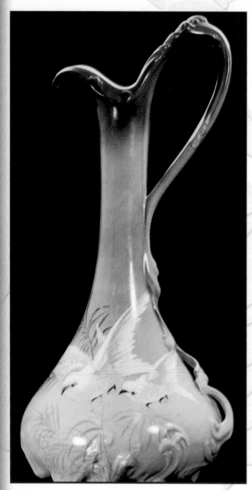

**Plate 665**
*Nut Dish, Unhandled.*
Photo courtesy Chuck Denlinger.

**Plate 666**
*Geisha Jug.*
Photo courtesy Jim Carpenter.

**Plate 664**
*Ewer, 15½".*

**Plate 667**
*Bread Tray, 13½".*
Photo courtesy Chuck Denlinger.

**Plate 668**
*Geisha Jug, 4".*
Smallest of five sizes.
Photo courtesy Chuck Denlinger.

**Plate 669**
*Geisha Jug, 4".*
Photo courtesy Chuck Denlinger.

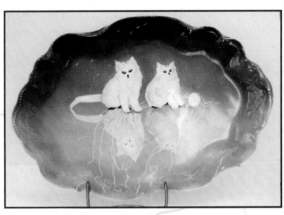

**Plate 670**
*Plate, 9½"; Stein Mug.*
Photo courtesy Chuck Denlinger.

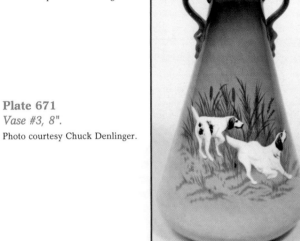

**Plate 671**
*Vase #3, 8".*
Photo courtesy Chuck Denlinger.

**Plate 672**
*Comb and Brush Tray.*
Photo courtesy Chuck Denlinger.

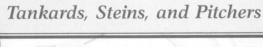

*Tankards, Steins, and Pitchers*

**Plate 674**
*Patriotic Staghorn Stein.*
Photo courtesy Chuck Denlinger.

**Plate 673**
*Patriotic Tankard.*

**Plate 675**

*Staghorn Stein.*

This stein was commissioned by a hardware company. It reads "Compliments of The Berger Manufacturing Company, Canton, Ohio, Everything in Sheet Metal," on the front, and on the back, "Ohio Hardware Association, February 27, 1928."

**Plate 676**

*Staghorn Stein.*

This one is inscribed "Copyright 1905 by the H.M. Suter Publishing Co."; the name John E. Sheridan is signed on the diagonal near the player's elbow.

**Plate 677**

*Pitcher from Toilet Set.*

This is marked with the gold eagle "Laughlin Art China" as well as the eagle over the lion with "Laughlin" in script. Photo courtesy Chuck Denlinger.

**Plate 678**

*Geisha Jug, 6"; with Mixed Fruit.*

**Plate 679**

*Geisha Jug, 6"; with Plums.*

**Plate 680**
*Staghorn Stein, Dutch Boy. Artist Signed.*
These may have been sold as blanks to hobbyists in the early 1900s when china painting was a popular pastime with the ladies.

**Plate 681**
*Tankard with Floral.*
Marked "American Floral."

**Plate 682**
*Staghorn Stein with Flowers.*
Photo courtesy Chuck Denlinger.

**Plate 683**
*Staghorn Stein with Plums.*
Photo courtesy Chuck Denlinger.

# WORLD'S FAIR: THE AMERICAN POTTER

As a tribute to the American Potter, six pottery companies united their efforts and jointly built and operated an actual working kiln at the 1939 – 1940 World's Fair in New York City. A variety of plates, vases, figural items, and bowls were produced and marked with an ink stamp "The American Potter, 1939 (or 1940), World's Fair Exhibit, Joint Exhibit of Capital and Labor." The Homer Laughlin China Company entry, designed by Fredrick Rhead, is shown in Plates 685 and 686. In the center of each plate are the Trylon and Perisphere, adopted symbols of the Fair. These plates have found favor not only with collectors of Homer Laughlin but also with World's Fair enthusiasts, and as a result of the strong Art Deco influence imparted by Rhead into their design, Art Deco aficionados vie to own them too.

**Plate 684**

*Assortment of World's Fair Vases.*
Potted, glazed, and fired right on the fairgrounds, these vases come in many sizes and shapes. None are very easy to find. Yellow seems to be the most common, but they were made in cobalt, turquoise, ivory, and light green as well — all being about equally difficult to locate. The vase on the far left is 7½", to give you an idea of scale. They are each marked with an ink stamp: "American Potter." You may also find bowls, individual creamers (see Plate 230), and ball-shaped candlesticks, but these are rare.

**Plate 685**

*Plates and Ashtray Designed by Fredrick Rhead.*
In Plate 686 you'll see the 1939 and the 1940 New York World's Fair plates. These are sought after not only by HLC and World's Fair collectors, but also by those who admire the wonderful Art Deco quality of the designs. Very rarely, one will bear this gold stamp: "Decorated by Charles Murphy, 150th Anniversary of George Washington as First President of the United States, 1789 – 1939." Plate 685 displays souvenirs of the Golden Gate International Exposition of 1939 and 1940. They're marked "Golden Gate Intern. Expo., Copyright License 63C, Homer Laughlin, Souvenir."

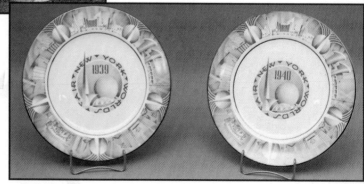

**Plate 686**

**Plate 687**
*Four Season Ashtrays.*
Each measures 4¼" in diameter. Spring shows a man fishing for trout; summer depicts a family picnicking; a man hunting with his dog represents autumn; and the winter plate has a skating scene. These sets are usually found in the colors shown, but a set with all four plates in turquoise has been reported, as well as a set in light green. Five autumn plates have been found in yellow, one winter in cobalt, and another winter in red.

**Plate 688**
*Zodiac Cup and Saucer.*
Very scarce in any color, turquoise is the color most often found. The green saucer is rare, and one set in ivory has been reported. Photo courtesy Becky Turner.

**Plates 689 through 692**
*(Right and top of page 242)*
*George and Martha Washington Pitchers.*
These were popular with fairgoers, since 1939 was the 150th anniversary of the inauguration of Washington as the first President of the United States. Martha is always the harder one to find. All shown measure 5", but some are only 2" tall. They're usually ivory — examples in cobalt are very rare. Mauve blue and Harlequin yellow have been reported as well as bisque (see Plate 692). George and Martha toothpick holders and salt and pepper shakers were also made, but

**Plate 689**

these are generally not marked. Three marks were used: "The American Potter, New York World's Fair," with the year on a raised disk superimposed over a Trylon; "First Edition For Collectors, New York's World's Fair, 1939"; or "Joint Exhibition of Capitol and Labor, American Pottery, NY WF, 1939."

**Plate 690**
*George Washington Mug.*
Photo courtesy Becky Turner.

**Plate 691**
*Martha Washington Pitcher.*

**Plate 692**
*George and Martha Washington Pitchers.*
These are the bisque Martha and George pitchers we mentioned previously. Interestingly enough, George is a little smaller than Martha, lighter in color, and the clay seems a bit harder, as though it may have been fired a second time. Though the small bisque Georges turn up on eBay every so often, bisque Martha is unique. Photo courtesy Steve Douglas/Becky Turner.

THIS BOX CONTAINS
**One "Potter's Wheel" Embossed Plate**
MANUFACTURED AT
**THE AMERICAN POTTER EXHIBIT**
— —
**Home Furnishings Building**
World's Fair ◆ 1939 ◆ New York

**Plate 693**
*Potter's Plates and Original Box.*
Here are the easiest of the World's Fair items to find. There are two plates — The Potter at His Wheel and The Artist Decorating the Vase. They've been found in turquoise as shown, light green, and ivory. They're scarce in the latter two colors, and we've seen a couple in tan/mocha shades. Four have been reported in bisque — the same hue as the Martha pitcher above. These plates are sometimes marked "First Edition For Collectors Limited to 100 Pieces, #85." What is rare, though, is the box these plates came in, shown above left.

**Plate 695**
*Edwin Knowles Marmalade.*

**Plate 694**
*Entries from Five Other Companies.*
Left to right: Cake set, "Cronin China Co., Minerva, O., National Brotherhood of Operative Potters"; bowl, "Paden City Pottery, Made in USA," 10"; plate, "Knowles, Joint Exhibit of Capital and Labor," 10¾"; marmalade bottom (shown complete with lid in Plate 695), embossed with the Trylon and Perisphere and "New York World's Fair," marked "Edwin M. Knowles China Co., Semi-Vitreous," 3"; Pitcher, marked "Porcelier Trade Mark, Vitreous Hand Decorated China, Made in U.S.A." The Porcelier pitcher was part of a seven-piece set that included teapots in three sizes, a sugar bowl, creamer, and a larger water pitcher. Some are shown in Plates 696 – 698. All are hard to find, especially the ashtray.

**Plate 696**

**Plate 697**

**Plate 698**

**Plate 699**

*Nude Vases and Donkey Ashtray.*

There is a continuing controversy over the nude vases in Plate 700 regarding their manufacturer. Shown glazed in a Fiesta-like red and ivory, the only mark they carry is "GAW," under the glaze, perhaps the initials of their creator. Along with the donkey, these were discovered near Newell, the property of an HLC supervisor. Four more colors have been found — rose, maroon, and spruce, as well as one in ivory with a rose drip. They may have been made by more than one pottery in the area, and they may not have been made by Homer Laughlin at all. Theories vary. Most certainly there were Japanese copies, inferior not only in modeling but also in glazing. The nude in Plate 700 is marked "USONA," a pottery that operated in the East Liverpool area during the '30s through the '50s. Note the differences in the mold.

**Plate 700**

The donkey shown here in red has also been found in green, and a mauve blue donkey figurine has been reported. Though first-hand examination by advanced HLC collectors has convinced them that this was an HLC product, not everyone agrees.

Photos courtesy Jim Carpenter.

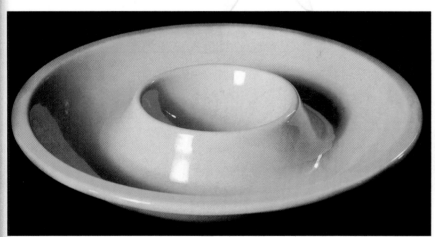

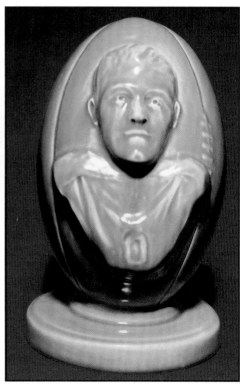

**Plates 701 and 702**

Shown here is an almost exact replica of the Kenilworth one-piece relish tray, differing only in color (yellow is not a Kenilworth color) and size. This one is 12" in diameter, while the Kenilworth piece is 10½". We're still betting that it was made at HLC. The football trophy in Plate 702 was produced in the early 1940s to commemorate Bill Booth, an Ohio State football star from East Liverpool who was tragically killed in an automobile accident. A very limited number of these trophies were made to present to his teammates. They've been reported in the light green shown here as well as yellow, ivory, and spruce green.

**Plate 702**

**Plate 703**

*Kraft Leaf Saucer.*

These were made by HLC for Swanky Swig glasses in the vintage Fiesta red glaze. They have been found in Fiesta light green, and a cobalt saucer was found in the morgue. They measure 7" in diameter by ¾" high. The back is completely glazed. Lids for the Swanky Swigs (they originally held cheese spread) are even harder to find than the plates. Photos courtesy Becky Turner.

**Plate 704**

*Lid.*

Advertising the leaf plate.

**Plate 705**

*Syrup.*

Though it's a little hard to believe considering the careful attention he paid to detail throughout the line, the syrup is the only piece of Fiesta that Rhead did not design. The mold was bought from the DripCut Company, who made the tops for HLC. (Other potteries, Vernon Kilns for one, also used this mold, and you'll find them in glass as well.) This blue one is molded of white ceramic and is marked "DripCut, Heatproof, L.A., Cal." Decades ago a tea company filled Fiesta syrup bases with tea leaves, added a cork stopper and its label, and unwittingly contributed to the frustration of today's collectors who have only a bottom. See the chapter entitled "Commercial Adaptations and Ephemera" for a photo.

**Plate 706**

*Plate.*

This red lid fits the Kitchen Kraft stacking units perfectly, and that's about all we know about it. It may even have been designed for some other purpose — a hot plate, for instance, for the regular Fiesta line (the band of rings does seem out of step in Kitchen Kraft). This is the only one that's ever been reported.

**Plate 707**

*Bowl and Mug.*

This is from the "other" Tom and Jerry set. But it's not done on Fiesta shapes, so it's not nearly as valuable as the one that is!

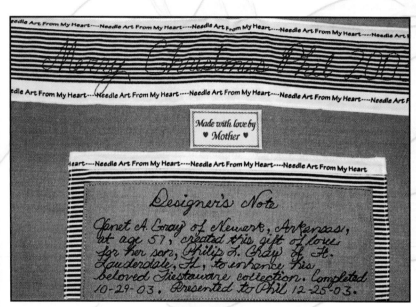

**Plate 708**
*Wall Hanging.*
The collector who was the recipient of this completely handmade wall hanging lovingly made for him by his mother is rightfully proud of it and wanted to share it with you. Each piece is layered, one upon the other; the "shine" is embroidered, and it's inscribed on the back — all done with a basic sewing machine, not a computerized one! I don't think she's taking orders, however! Photos courtesy Philip Gray.

**Plate 709**
*Demitasse Cup.*
There are few of these around — here's a demitasse cup with the original 25¢ store price sticker. Photo courtesy Jack Kunberger.

**Plate 710**
*Marked Washington Bicentennial, 1732 – 1932.*
These commemorative mugs are by HLC.

# SUGGESTED VALUES

Today's price structures are totally unpredictable and impossible to interpret. As one collector puts it, there are two "universes" when it comes to opinions on pricing vintage Fiesta — traditional sales vs. Internet sales. When we began our compilations, we were naive enough to believe that we could reconcile the two. Impossible! It just cannot be done. So even though we're sure you're going to love this edition — fantastic new photos, some new chapters, and a fresh look — we're very apprehensive about offering these suggested values. Without doubt, they will seem very high to many of you. Please remember, vintage Fiesta values are going to be geared to dealers' shows and shop pricing and will factor in the premium most collectors are happy to pay for the privilege of being able to see, inspect, and hold an item before having to purchase it. Most importantly, these values are for absolutely *mint condition* examples. Let's try to define *mint*: Obviously there must be no chips (fleabites, dings, or any other term that might instead be used), there must be no crazing, no hairlines, and no wear or scratches. The glaze must be strong, reasonably even, and shiny. A piece with prominent "curtains" or one that is noticeably light in color will not bring "high book" even if all the other criteria are met; neither will one with glaze misses or dark spots. It must not have been repaired. If an item takes a lid, both pieces must match color wise, and the lid must properly fit.

As for manufacturing flaws (pits, sand bumps, glaze skips, finger marks, etc.), this has become much more of an issue than it ever was when most of us started collecting thirty years ago. Because Fiesta is handcrafted, flaws are to be expected; and most collectors accept that. (Today, any Fiesta item with less than twelve minor manufacturing flaws is graded a "first.") So for our purposes here, in trying to establish standards for *mint condition*, we'll say that if a manufacturing flaw is in a prominent area and detracts from overall appearance, that piece will not be worth "high book." Some people are more tolerant than others, and obviously this is a subjective factor.

Now that we've addressed the "mint to high book" equation, where does that leave the other 80% or more of good vintage pieces with two or three manufacturing defects, a few more scratches than are acceptable on a mint condition item, or a "fleabite" on the foot ring, for example? If you track eBay sales (more about online auctions later), you know that if dealers have a flaw, wear, or even minimal damage they deem necessary to describe in order to safeguard their feedback rating, they have automatically rung the "death knell" for that sale (even when what they're describing fits into our definition of mint). The value of their item will fall from 30% to 50%, of course depending on the extent of the problem they're describing. For our purposes, common items with scratches, wear, or tiny dings should be discounted by half; a more desirable piece (one worth $75.00 and up) may bring 50% to 60% of its mint value if the damage is not particularly visual. A rare item may bring a slightly higher percentage. A chip on a plate or any other common item such as a bowl will render it virtually worthless — if it is a high-end, hard-to-find item, it may fare better, depending, naturally, on the chip. So for you who expect to see many prices lowered in this edition (of course, some prices for common items were lowered a bit), what you will see instead are perhaps higher standards being set for mint and a more realistic look at degraded values for less than perfect items.

Some colors are more prone to surface scratching than others, and after years of being stacked for storing, even plates and bowls not often used will display some scratches. Utensil marks are common; so are knife cuts. Any kind of wear degrades value. If such wear is *minimal* — no more than two or three short, *very superficial* scratches (those that you have to tilt in the light to see) — a 15% to 20% price reduction would be in order.

Decals, when present, must be complete, the colors well preserved, with little, if any, wear. When decals are worn, faded, or otherwise damaged, items should be sharply discounted.

In the end, the selling price depends on the standards of the buyer and how quickly the seller wants to regain his or her investment. Auctions on eBay generally run for seven days, and the end result depends on who is shopping during those few days and what they are willing to spend; while at a mall or shop, the dealer may keep the piece for weeks until the right person comes along who is willing to pay his price.

This is one reason we were reluctant to factor online auction values into our survey. Anyone that follows them knows how erratic sales can be. An item that sells for $50.00 one week may go for $100.00 the next. So many variables affect the selling price. It's very common for postage to cost from $8.00 to $10.00 or even more; cheaper items like plates and heavy items like chop plates and platters won't bring "book price" when postage can often add 35% to the overall price. As we've already mentioned, how flaws are perceived will depend on the individual. "Like new," "never used," and "mint except for ..." are phrases easily misinterpreted. Once stung, buyers tend to be more cautious about bidding an item up. So when you're trying to interpret the results of eBay sales, be sure to read the description thoroughly, study the photos, add in the shipping an handling costs, and do your sorting by "Completed Listings," "Price: highest first". It's also good to check to see how many bids were placed, and don't be afraid to ask questions of the seller.

Saggar pin marks on the undersides of many pieces are characteristic and result from the technique employed in stacking the ware for firing. These should in no way be considered damage. When buying odd lids and bases, remember that colors may vary, and some lids and openings will be just enough off-round that they will not properly fit together. If you do buy them separately, expect to pay 50% to 70% of listed values for lids and 30% to 40% for bases.

## Fiesta
### Pages 20 – 44

The first column of figures represents the range of values suggested for these colors: red, cobalt, and ivory. The second column contains values for yellow, turquoise (with exceptions), and light green. Collectors report that items discontinued in 1946 are generally harder to find in turquoise, since that color was not introduced until mid-1937, an entire year after the other colors. In the column on the far left, you'll notice that some of the items in the listings are followed by asterisks. These are the ones that were dropped in 1946. To evaluate these items in turquoise, use the first column of values (for red, cobalt, and ivory), generally the high end; for all other turquoise pieces, use the second column.

An original label such as the Kitchen Kraft label or the Royal Chrome label, for instance, will add from $100.00 to $150.00 to the value of the item that carries it. Pieces that are rarely marked, for instance the cup, salt and pepper shakers, juice tumblers, etc., can increase in value by as much as 400% to 500% when they are marked. Double-marked items (those with the ink stamp and the cast-indented mark) often sell at 25% over book price.

NEV — No Established Value
(*) – Use the values in the first column to price this item in turquoise.

| Vintage Fiesta | Red, Cobalt, Ivory | Yellow, Turquoise, Light Green | '50s Colors | Medium Green | As Specified |
|---|---|---|---|---|---|
| Ashtray | 45.00 – 60.00 | 35.00 – 50.00 | 55.00 – 75.00 | 175.00 – 200.00 | |
| Bowl, covered onion soup | | | | | |
|   cobalt or ivory | | | | | 600.00 – 675.00 |
|   red | | | | | 625.00 – 700.00 |
|   turquoise | | | | | 8,000.00+ |
|   yellow or lt. green | | | | | 525.00 – 625.00 |
| Bowl, cream soup | 45.00 – 60.00 | 30.00 – 45.00 | 60.00 – 75.00 | | 4,000.00+ |
| Bowl, dessert, 6" | 40.00 – 50.00 | 30.00 – 45.00 | 35.00 – 45.00 | 650.00 – 700.00 | |
| Bowl, footed salad* | 350.00 – 475.00 | 275.00 – 375.00 | | | |
| Bowl, fruit, 11¾"* | 250.00 – 300.00 | 225.00 – 275.00 | | | |
| Bowl, fruit, 4¾" | 25.00 – 30.00 | 20.00 – 25.00 | 30.00 – 35.00 | 550.00+ | |
| Bowl, fruit, 5½" | 25.00 – 30.00 | 20.00 – 25.00 | 35.00 – 40.00 | 65.00 – 70.00 | |
| Bowl, individual salad, 7½" | | | | 100.00 – 120.00 | |
|   red, turquoise, or yellow | | | | | 80.00 – 100.00 |
| Bowl, mixing, #1* | 275.00 – 300.00 | 220.00 – 250.00 | | | |
| Bowl, mixing, #2* | 125.00 – 150.00 | 100.00 – 125.00 | | | |
| Bowl, mixing, #3* | 125.00 – 150.00 | 110.00 – 140.00 | | | |
| Bowl, mixing, #4* | 150.00 – 185.00 | 110.00 – 145.00 | | | |
| Bowl, mixing, #5* | 190.00 – 235.00 | 175.00 – 200.00 | | | |
| Bowl, mixing, #6* | 260.00 – 300.00 | 230.00 – 265.00 | | | |
| Bowl, mixing, #7* | 400.00 – 500.00 | 325.00 – 450.00 | | | |
| Bowl, nappy, 8½"* | 45.00 – 50.00 | 30.00 – 35.00 | 50.00 – 60.00 | 150.00 | |
| Bowl, nappy, 9½"* | 60.00 – 70.00 | 55.00 – 60.00 | | | |
| Bowl, tricolator | | | | | |
|   any color | | | | | 260.00 – 310.00 |

| Vintage Fiesta | Red, Cobalt, Ivory | Yellow, Turquoise, Light Green | '50s Colors | Medium Green | As Specified |
|---|---|---|---|---|---|
| Bowl, unlisted salad, yellow | | | | | 80.00 – 100.00 |
| ivory, red, or cobalt* | | | | | 2,000.00+ |
| Candleholders, bulb, pr.* | 120.00 – 130.00 | 80.00 – 110.00 | | | |
| Candleholders, tripod, pr.* | 550.00 – 700.00 | 450.00 – 600.00 | | | |
| Carafe* | 275.00 – 300.00 | 250.00 – 285.00 | | | |
| Casserole | 180.00 – 200.00 | 150.00 – 175.00 | 250.00 – 275.00 | 1,000.00+ | |
| Casserole, French; yellow | | | | | 250.00 – 300.00 |
| other standard color | | | | | NEV |
| Casserole, promo complete, standard color | | | | | 150.00 – 160.00 |
| Coffeepot | 230.00 – 265.00 | 180.00 – 220.00 | 300.00 – 350.00 | | |
| gray | | | | 600.00+ | |
| Coffeepot, demitasse | 500.00 – 600.00 | 350.00 – 400.00 | | | |
| turquoise | | | | | 750.00+ |
| Comport, 12"* | 180.00 – 200.00 | 160.00 – 175.00 | | | |
| Comport, sweets* | 125.00 – 135.00 | 95.00 – 110.00 | | | |
| Creamer | 25.00 – 30.00 | 20.00 – 25.00 | 35.00 – 45.00 | 90.00 – 120.00 | |
| Creamer, ind.; in red turquoise or cobalt | | | | | 325.00+ |
| | | | | | NEV |
| yellow | | | | | 60.00 – 80.00 |
| Creamer, stick-handled* | 55.00 – 65.00 | 45.00 – 60.00 | | | |
| Cup, demitasse | 80.00 – 100.00 | 70.00 – 80.00 | 325.00 – 400.00 | | |
| Cup; See teacup. | | | | | |
| Egg cup | 60.00 – 70.00 | 55.00 – 65.00 | 140.00 – 160.00 | | |
| Lid, mixing bowls, #1 – 3 any color | | | | | 600.00 – 750.00 |
| Lid, mixing bowl, #4 any color | | | | | 1,000.00+ |
| Lid, mixing bowls, #5 – 6 | NEV | NEV | | | |
| Marmalade* | 365.00 – 400.00 | 350.00 – 375.00 | | | |
| Mug, Tom and Jerry | 70.00 – 80.00 | 50.00 – 60.00 | 80.00 – 90.00 | 125.00+ | |
| maroon | | | | | NEV |
| Mustard* | 250.00 – 300.00 | 240.00 – 275.00 | | | |
| Pitcher, disk juice; gray | | | | | 2,000.00+ |
| red | | | | | 550.00 – 650.00 |
| yellow | | | | | 45.00 – 50.00 |
| Harlequin yellow | | | | | 65.00 – 75.00 |
| celadon green | | | | | 165.00 – 175.00 |
| any other color | | | | | NEV |
| Pitcher, disk water | 150.00 – 175.00 | 100.00 – 125.00 | 200.00 – 275.00 | | 1,500.00+ |
| Pitcher, ice* | 130.00 – 145.00 | 110.00 – 125.00 | | | |
| Pitcher, 2-pt. jug | 95.00 – 105.00 | 70.00 – 80.00 | 120.00 – 140.00 | NEV | |
| Plate, cake* | 1,200.00 | 1,000.00 | | | |
| Plate, calendar, 1954, 10" | | | | | 50.00 – 55.00 |
| 1955, 9" | | | | | 45.00 – 50.00 |
| 1955, 10" | | | | | 45.00 – 50.00 |
| Plate, chop; 13" | 45.00 – 55.00 | 40.00 – 50.00 | 90.00 – 95.00 | 500.00 | |
| 15" | 90.00 – 100.00 | 70.00 – 80.00 | 135.00 – 150.00 | | |
| Plate, compartment, 10½" | 40.00 – 45.00 | 35.00 – 40.00 | 60.00 – 70.00 | | |
| 12" | 55.00 – 60.00 | 40.00 – 50.00 | | | |
| Plate, deep | 50.00 – 60.00 | 35.00 – 40.00 | 50.00 – 55.00 | 130.00 – 145.00 | |

| Vintage Fiesta | Red, Cobalt, Ivory | Yellow, Turquoise, Light Green | '50s Colors | Medium Green | As Specified |
|---|---|---|---|---|---|
| Plate, 6" | 5.00 – 7.00 | 4.00 – 6.00 | 7.00 – 10.00 | 30.00 – 45.00 | |
| Plate, 7" | 8.00 – 10.00 | 7.00 – 9.00 | 10.00 – 12.00 | 30.00 – 45.00 | |
| Plate, 9" | 15.00 – 20.00 | 10.00 – 15.00 | 20.00 – 25.00 | 60.00 – 75.00 | |
| Plate, 10" | 35.00 – 45.00 | 30.00 – 40.00 | 45.00 – 50.00 | 125.00+ | |
| Platter | 50.00 – 55.00 | 40.00 – 45.00 | 50.00 – 60.00 | 175.00 – 225.00 | |
| Salt & pepper shakers, pr. | 25.00 – 30.00 | 22.00 – 25.00 | 40.00 – 45.00 | 200.00 – 225.00 | |
| Sauce boat | 60.00 – 70.00 | 40.00 – 45.00 | 60.00 – 75.00 | 200.00 – 225.00 | |
| Sauce boat stand, Fiesta Ironstone, red | | | | | 100.00 – 150.00 |
| Saucer | 2.00 – 3.00 | 2.00 – 3.00 | 3.00 – 5.00 | 10.00 – 15.00 | |
| Saucer, demitasse | 15.00 – 20.00 | 15.00 – 20.00 | 70.00 – 110.00 | | |
| Sugar bowl with lid | 60.00 – 75.00 | 50.00 – 60.00 | 70.00 – 80.00 | 225.00 – 250.00 | |
| Sugar bowl, ind.; red | | | | | 375.00 – 400.00 |
| turquoise | | | | | 400.00 – 500.00 |
| yellow | | | | | 125.00 – 175.00 |
| Syrup* | 400.00 – 425.00 | 375.00 – 400.00 | | | |
| Teacup | 25.00 – 40.00 | 15.00 – 20.00 | 35.00 – 40.00 | 60.00 – 75.00 | |
| Teapot, large* | 300.00 – 350.00 | 250.00 – 300.00 | | | |
| Teapot, medium | 200.00 – 250.00 | 150.00 – 200.00 | 250.00 – 300.00 | 1,500.00+ | |
| Tom and Jerry, see Mug, Tom and Jerry | | | | | |
| Tom and Jerry bowl ivory w/gold letters | | | | | 250.00 – 265.00 |
| Tom and Jerry mug ivory w/gold letters | | | | | 55.00 – 65.00 |
| Tom and Jerry bowl, not on Fiesta mold | | | | | 35.00 – 40.00 |
| Tom and Jerry mug, not on Fiesta mold | | | | | 10.00 – 15.00 |
| Tray, figure-8; cobalt | | | | | 90.00 – 100.00 |
| turquoise | | | | | 350.00 – 400.00 |
| yellow | | | | | 500.00 – 600.00 |
| Tray, relish* center insert | 65.00 – 70.00 | 50.00 – 60.00 | | | |
| side insert | 50.00 – 60.00 | 45.00 – 55.00 | | | |
| relish base | 90.00 – 100.00 | 80.00 – 100.00 | | | |
| Tray, relish, gold decorated | | | | | 220.00 – 250.00 |
| Tray, utility* | 45.00 – 50.00 | 40.00 – 45.00 | | | |
| Tumbler, juice, | 45.00 – 50.00 | 40.00 – 45.00 | | | |
| rose | | | | | 55.00 – 60.00 |
| chartreuse or dark green | | | | | 750.00+ |
| Jubilee colors except gray | | | | | 45.00 – 50.00 |
| gray | | | | | 200.00 – 225.00 |
| maroon | | | | | NEV |
| Tumbler, water* | 80.00 – 90.00 | 70.00 – 80.00 | | | |
| Vase, bud* | 100.00 – 125.00 | 75.00 – 115.00 | | | |
| Vase, 8"* | 650.00 – 800.00 | 600.00 – 700.00 | | | |
| Vase, 10"* | 800.00 – 1,100.00 | 700.00 – 1,000.00 | | | |
| Vase, 12"* | 1,400.00 – 1,900.00 | 1,100.00 – 1,500.00 | | | |

## Kitchen Kraft
### Pages 44 – 50

When there is a range, use the high side to evaluate red and cobalt. See the Jubilee and Rhythm sections for information concerning the value of mixing bowls in the colors of those lines.

NEV — No Established Value

Bowl, mixing, 6" . . . . . . . . . . . . . . . . . . . . . . . .60.00
Bowl, mixing, 8" . . . . . . . . . . . . . . . . . . . . . . . .80.00
Bowl, mixing, 10" . . . . . . . . . . . .100.00 – 110.00
Cake plate . . . . . . . . . . . . . . . . . . . . . . . . . .35.00
Cake server . . . . . . . . . . . . . . . .150.00 – 175.00
Casserole, individual . . . . . . . . . . .150.00 – 160.00
Casserole, 7½" . . . . . . . . . . . . . . . . . . . . . .75.00
Casserole, 8½" . . . . . . . . . . . . . . . . . . . . . .85.00
Covered jar, large . . . . . . . . . . . . .350.00 – 375.00
Covered jar, medium . . . . . . . . . . .275.00 – 300.00
Covered jar, small . . . . . . . . . . . . .300.00 – 325.00
Covered jug, large . . . . . . . . . . . . .275.00 – 300.00
Covered jug, large in ivory . . . . . . . . . . . .1,400.00
Covered jug, small . . . . . . . . . . . . .300.00 – 320.00
Fork . . . . . . . . . . . . . . . . .150.00 – 160.00
Metal frame for platter . . . . . . . . . . . . . . . .15.00
Pie plate, 9" . . . . . . . . . . . . . . . . . . . . . . . .40.00
   with advertising in gold . . . . . . . . . . . . . . .NEV
Pie plate, 10" . . . . . . . . . . . . . . . . . . . . . . .40.00
   spruce green . . . . . . . . . . . . . . . . . . . . .150.00
Platter . . . . . . . . . . . . . . . . . .60.00 – 75.00
   mauve blue, minimum value . . . . . . . . . .600.00
   spruce green . . . . . . . . . . . . . . . . . . . . .150.00
Salt & pepper shakers, pr. . . . . . . .120.00 – 150.00
   ivory, very rare, minimum value . . . . . . . .500.00
Spoon . . . . . . . . . . . . . . . . . .150.00 – 200.00
Spoon, ivory, 12" . . . . . . . . . . . . .400.00 – 500.00
Stacking refrigerator lid . . . . . . . . . .90.00 – 100.00
   ivory . . . . . . . . . . . . . . . . . . . .210.00 – 225.00
Stacking refrigerator unit . . . . . . . . . .50.00 – 60.00
   ivory . . . . . . . . . . . . . . . . . . . .200.00 – 210.00

## Ironstone
### Page 51 – 52

Use the high side of the range to evaluate restyled red Ironstone. Items with an asterisk (*) were made only in Antique Gold.

Ashtray, rare . . . . . . . . . . . . . . . . .50.00 – 60.00
Coffee mug . . . . . . . . . . . . . . . . . .22.00 – 26.00
Coffee server* . . . . . . . . . . . . . . . .70.00 – 75.00
Covered casserole* . . . . . . . . . . . . .50.00 – 60.00
Creamer . . . . . . . . . . . . . . . . . . . .15.00 – 20.00
Fruit, small . . . . . . . . . . . . . . . . . . . .5.00 – 7.00
Fruit, small, red . . . . . . . . . . . . . . . .8.00 – 10.00
Marmalade . . . . . . . . . . . . . . . . . .45.00 – 55.00
Nappy, large . . . . . . . . . . . . . . . . .15.00 – 20.00

Pitcher, disk water* . . . . . . . . . . . . .60.00 – 75.00
Plate, 7" . . . . . . . . . . . . . . . . . . . . .3.00 – 4.00
Plate, 10". . . . . . . . . . . . . . . . . . .10.00 – 12.00
Platter, 13" . . . . . . . . . . . . . . . . . .20.00 – 25.00
Salad bowl, 10"* . . . . . . . . . . . . . .50.00 – 65.00
Salt & pepper shakers, pr. . . . . . . . .18.00 – 22.00
Sauce boat . . . . . . . . . . . . . . . . . .25.00 – 30.00
Sauce boat stand. . . . . . . . . . . . . .40.00 – 50.00
   red . . . . . . . . . . . . . . . . .200.00 – 225.00
Saucer . . . . . . . . . . . . . . . . . . . . .1.50 – 2.00
Soup/cereal . . . . . . . . . . . . . . . . . . .7.00 – 9.00
Soup plate . . . . . . . . . . . . . . . . . .10.00 – 14.00
Sugar bowl with lid . . . . . . . . . . . . .20.00 – 25.00
Teacup . . . . . . . . . . . . . . . . . . . . .6.00 – 8.00
Teapot, medium* . . . . . . . . . . . . . .60.00 – 75.00

## Amberstone
### Pages 52 – 54

Items marked with an asterisk (*) are decorated with the black Amberstone pattern. Collectors seem to prefer the plain brown hollow ware pieces over patterned items.

NEV — No Established Value

Ashtray, rare . . . . . . . . . . . . . . . . .50.00 – 60.00
Bowl, jumbo salad . . . . . . . . . . . . .40.00 – 45.00
Bowl, soup/cereal . . . . . . . . . . . . . . .5.00 – 8.00
Bowl, vegetable . . . . . . . . . . . . . . .15.00 – 20.00
Butter dish* . . . . . . . . . . . . . . . . . .20.00 – 25.00
Casserole . . . . . . . . . . . . . . . . . . .50.00 – 55.00
Coffee server . . . . . . . . . . . . . . . . .55.00 – 60.00
Covered jam jar . . . . . . . . . . . . . . .50.00 – 55.00
Covered mustard . . . . . . . . . . . . . .60.00 – 65.00
Creamer . . . . . . . . . . . . . . . . . . . . .7.00 – 8.00
Cup & saucer* . . . . . . . . . . . . . . . . .6.00 – 8.00
Deep plate/soup, 8"* . . . . . . . . . . .10.00 – 12.00
Dessert dish . . . . . . . . . . . . . . . . . . .5.00 – 6.50
Jumbo mug . . . . . . . . . . . . . . . . . . . . . . .NEV
Pie plate* . . . . . . . . . . . . . . . . . . .32.00 – 38.00
Pitcher, disk water . . . . . . . . . . . . . .60.00 – 80.00
Plate, bread & butter* . . . . . . . . . . . .1.50 – 2.50
Plate, salad* . . . . . . . . . . . . . . . . . .2.00 – 3.00
Plate, 10"* . . . . . . . . . . . . . . . . . . .5.00 – 7.00
Platter, oval* . . . . . . . . . . . . . . . . .12.00 – 16.00
Platter, round serving* . . . . . . . . . . .15.00 – 18.00
Relish tray, center handle* . . . . . . . .28.00 – 32.00
Salt & pepper shakers, pr. . . . . . . . .12.00 – 15.00
Sauce boat . . . . . . . . . . . . . . . . . .18.00 – 22.00
   with Fiesta mark . . . . . . . . . . . . .30.00 – 35.00
Sauce boat stand, rare . . . . . . . . . . .35.00 – 45.00
Sugar bowl with lid . . . . . . . . . . . . . .8.00 – 9.50
Tea server . . . . . . . . . . . . . . . . . . .55.00 – 60.00

## Casualstone
### Page 54

Items marked with an asterisk (*) are decorated with

the gold Casualstone pattern. There is little interest in this pattern at this time.

Ashtray, rare . . . . . . . . . . . . . . . . .12.00 – 15.00
Bowl, jumbo salad, 10" . . . . . . . . . .35.00 – 38.00
Bowl, round vegetable . . . . . . . . . . .12.00 – 15.00
Bowl, soup/cereal . . . . . . . . . . . . . . .4.00 – 6.00
Butter dish, stick* . . . . . . . . . . . . . .18.00 – 25.00
Casserole . . . . . . . . . . . . . . . . . . . .35.00 – 40.00
Coffee server . . . . . . . . . . . . . . . . .35.00 – 40.00
Creamer . . . . . . . . . . . . . . . . . . . . . .4.00 – 5.00
Cup & saucer* . . . . . . . . . . . . . . . . .6.00 – 8.00
Deep plate* . . . . . . . . . . . . . . . . . . .7.00 – 8.50
Dessert . . . . . . . . . . . . . . . . . . . . . .4.50 – 5.50
Jumbo mug . . . . . . . . . . . . . . . . . .12.00 – 18.00
Marmalade . . . . . . . . . . . . . . . . . .40.00 – 45.00
Pie plate* . . . . . . . . . . . . . . . . . . . .18.00 – 25.00
Pitcher, disk type . . . . . . . . . . . . . .35.00 – 40.00
Plate, bread & butter* . . . . . . . . . . . .2.50 – 3.50
Plate, dinner* . . . . . . . . . . . . . . . . . .6.00 – 8.00
Plate, salad* . . . . . . . . . . . . . . . . . . .3.50 – 4.50
Platter, oval, 13"* . . . . . . . . . . . . . .12.00 – 15.00
Platter, round* . . . . . . . . . . . . . . . .12.00 – 15.00
Relish tray* . . . . . . . . . . . . . . . . . .15.00 – 18.00
Salt & pepper shakers, pr. . . . . . . . .7.00 – 8.50
Sauce boat . . . . . . . . . . . . . . . . . . .13.00 – 17.00
Sugar bowl with lid . . . . . . . . . . . . .7.00 – 8.50
Tea server . . . . . . . . . . . . . . . . . . .25.00 – 30.00

## Casuals
### Pages 55 – 56

Because it is reported to be harder to find than Hawaiian Daisy, use the high side of the range to evaluate Carnation.

Plate, 7" . . . . . . . . . . . . . . . . . . . . . .8.00 – 12.00
Plate, 10" . . . . . . . . . . . . . . . . . . . .12.00 – 18.00
Platter, oval . . . . . . . . . . . . . . . . . . .40.00 – 50.00
Saucer . . . . . . . . . . . . . . . . . . . . . . .5.00 – 6.00

## Fiesta with Stripes
### Pages 56 – 59

Any Fiesta found with red or blue stripes is extremely rare. Both colors are of equal value. Because of the rarity, collectors and dealers should expect to pay a high dollar value for any item that is in excellent to mint condition. Red-striped values can range from five to fifteen times the value of ivory Fiesta. Nearly all items were in production when the line was initiated in November 1935. The ashtray and the 5½" fruit bowl entered into production in December of that year; the 10" vase in August.

Ashtray . . . . . . . . . . . . . . . . . . . . .650.00 – 780.00

Bowl, covered onion soup,
  minimum value . . . . . . . . . . . . . . .10,000.00
Bowl, cream soup . . . . . . . . . . . . .620.00 – 740.00
Bowl, dessert, 6" . . . . . . . . . . . . . .520.00 – 625.00
Bowl, footed salad . . . . . . . . . . .2,300.00 – 2,500.00
Bowl, fruit, 5½" . . . . . . . . . . . . . .375.00 – 425.00
Bowl, mixing, #1 . . . . . . . . . . . .1,540.00 – 1,850.00
Bowl, mixing, #2 . . . . . . . . . . . . .945.00 – 1,120.00
Bowl, mixing, #3 . . . . . . . . . . . . .980.00 – 1,120.00
Bowl, mixing, #4 . . . . . . . . . . . .1,120.00 – 1,260.00
Bowl, mixing, #5 . . . . . . . . . . . .1,190.00 – 1,435.00
Bowl, mixing, #6 . . . . . . . . . . . .1,750.00 – 2,135.00
Bowl, mixing, #7 . . . . . . . . . . . .3,000.00 – 3,500.00
Bowl, nappy, 8½" . . . . . . . . . . . .560.00 – 675.00
Bowl, nappy, 9" . . . . . . . . . . . . .650.00 – 725.00
Candleholders, bulb, pr. . . . . . . .600.00 – 840.00
Candleholders, tripod, pr. . . . . .3,000.00 – 3,500.00
Carafe . . . . . . . . . . . . . . . . . . .1,650.00 – 1,700.00
Casserole. . . . . . . . . . . . . . . . . .2,050.00 – 2,250.00
Coffeepot, demitasse . . . . . . . . .2,425.00 – 2,750.00
Coffeepot . . . . . . . . . . . . . . . . .1,175.00 – 1,275.00
Comport, 12" . . . . . . . . . . . . . .1,650.00 – 1,800.00
Creamer, stick-handled . . . . . . .1,050.00 – 1,200.00
Cup, demitasse . . . . . . . . . . . . .600.00 – 675.00
Mustard . . . . . . . . . . . . . . . . . .1,225.00 – 1,350.00
Pitcher, ice . . . . . . . . . . . . . . . .1,600.00 – 1,725.00
Plate, chop, 13" . . . . . . . . . . . . .450.00 – 575.00
Plate, chop, 15" . . . . . . . . . . . . .700.00 – 950.00
Plate, 6" . . . . . . . . . . . . . . . . . . .25.00 – 50.00
Plate, 7" . . . . . . . . . . . . . . . . . . .40.00 – 70.00
Plate, 9" . . . . . . . . . . . . . . . . . . .90.00 – 125.00
Plate, 10" . . . . . . . . . . . . . . . . .165.00 – 200.00
Salt and pepper shakers, pr. . . . . .375.00 – 500.00
Saucer, demitasse . . . . . . . . . . . .180.00 – 200.00
Saucer, teacup . . . . . . . . . . . . . . .60.00 – 85.00
Sugar bowl, with lid . . . . . . . . . .1,150.00 – 1,375.00
Teacup . . . . . . . . . . . . . . . . . . . .120.00 – 135.00
Teapot, large . . . . . . . . . . . . . . .1,700.00 – 1,825.00
Tray, relish, 6-pc., complete . . . .1,600.00 – 2,000.00
Vase, bud . . . . . . . . . . . . . . . . .1,200.00 – 1,350.00
Vase, 10", dated and decorated
  (one-of-a-kind), minimum value . . . . . . . .15,000.00
Vase, 10" . . . . . . . . . . . . . . . . .2,800.00 – 3,000.00

## Decals
### Pages 59 – 61

As for decaled items, they are generally valued at 50% more than red. It is short supply and market values are obviously hard to analyze. All of the following are Fiesta with the turkey decal.

Plate, 9½" . . . . . . . . . . . . . . . . . .100.00 – 110.00
Plate, cake: Kitchen Kraft . . . . . . .180.00 – 200.00
Plate, chop, 13" . . . . . . . . . . . . . .120.00 – 135.00
Plate, chop, 15" . . . . . . . . . . . . . .165.00 – 190.00

## Lustre
### Page 62

Because items of this nature are so rare, we have not attempted to establish a market value.

## New Fiesta — Post86
### Pages 63 – 96

We have attempted to list suggested values for only those secondary market pieces in the retired colors indicated. Lilac remains the "medium green" of the Post86 line. The market continues to grow for chartreuse, as it is one of the "hot" colors in decorating right now for the younger people. Sapphire is scarce, and prices are escalating. Juniper and pearl gray have been discontinued for several years and are starting to be priced at a premium over retail. (Remember that almost all stores discount Fiesta about 20% to 30% from the manufacturer's suggested retail price.) Apricot in anything less than mint condition is extremely plentiful, having been a top-selling color during the '80s, though prices are generally up from the last edition.

The trend we're seeing is that collectors may pass up an item in a rare and highly priced color in favor of one more reasonably priced in another color, which tends to keep the values of those rarer items more in line and relative in the Post86 Fiesta than the rare pieces of vintage Fiesta. But they prefer pieces in the place setting to match (as well as other items such as the mug, bouillon, or demitasse cup that are sometimes used to round it out); this gives those items a firmer rate of appreciation.

The ranges we used are for mint condition factory firsts (the market abounds with seconds), and the high end represents perfect examples or those with only the most insignificant factory flaws. Sapphire was only available in the items for which we've indicated a value. A place setting includes the 10½" dinner plate; the 7" salad plate; the 6⅞", 19-oz. bowl; and the cup and saucer.

Stick-handled demitasse cups range from $20.00 to $50.00, depending on color.

| | Lilac | Apricot | Sapphire | Chartreuse |
|---|---|---|---|---|
| Bowl, bouillon, 6¾" | 40.00 – 50.00 | 7.00 – 9.00 | 22.00 – 28.00 | 20.00 – 25.00 |
| Bowl, chili, 18-oz | 40.00 – 50.00 | 18.00 – 22.00 | | |
| Bowl, fruit, 5⅜", 6-oz. | 30.00 – 40.00 | | | 12.00 – 16.00 |
| Bowl, medium, 6⅞", 19-oz. | 40.00 – 50.00 | 10.00 – 15.00 | 35.00 – 42.00 | 24.00 – 38.00 |
| Bowl, mixing, 44-oz. | | | | 25.00 – 30.00 |
| Bowl, mixing, 60-oz. | | | | 30.00 – 40.00 |
| Bowl, pasta, 12" | 75.00 – 90.00 | 15.00 – 20.00 | | 30.00 – 35.00 |
| Bowl, pedestal | | | | 50.00 – 60.00 |
| Bowl, presentation | | | | 50.00 – 75.00 |
| Bowl, rim soup, 9" | 40.00 – 50.00 | 15.00 – 20.00 | | 22.00 – 28.00 |
| Bowl, small, 5⅝", 14-oz. | 25.00 – 35.00 | 10.00 – 15.00 | | 18.00 – 22.00 |
| Bowl, stacking cereal, 6½" | 25.00 – 35.00 | 15.00 – 18.00 | | 20.00 – 25.00 |
| Bowl, vegetable, large, 39-oz. | 75.00 – 90.00 | 18.00 – 28.00 | 60.00 – 70.00 | 25.00 – 35.00 |
| Butter dish | 50.00 – 65.00 | 25.00 – 30.00 | | 25.00 – 32.00 |
| Candle bowl | | | | 25.00 |
| Candleholders, 6½", pr. | | | | 30.00 – 40.00 |
| Candlesticks, pyramid, ea. | 275.00 – 300.00 | 25.00 – 35.00 | | 28.00 – 32.00 |
| Candlesticks, round (bulb), ea. | 75.00 – 90.00 | | | 10.00 – 15.00 |
| Carafe | | 40.00 – 50.00 | 65.00 – 80.00 | 65.00 – 80.00 |
| Casserole with lid | 125.00 – 140.00 | 45.00 – 55.00 | | 70.00 – 80.00 |
| Clock | | | 50.00 – 70.00 | 100.00 –125.00 |
| Coffee server, 36-oz. | 150.00 – 160.00 | 50.00 – 60.00 | | |
| Creamer, covered sugar and tray set | 70.00 – 85.00 | 35.00 – 45.00 | | |
| Creamer, individual, 7-oz. | | 9.00 – 12.00 | | 25.00 – 30.00 |
| Cup, A.D., with saucer | 45.00 – 55.00 | 25.00 – 35.00 | 22.00 – 28.00 | 30.00 – 40.00 |

| | Lilac | Apricot | Sapphire | Chartreuse |
|---|---|---|---|---|
| Cup, jumbo, 18-oz. | 100.00 – 125.00 | 20.00 – 25.00 | 22.00 – 28.00 | 25.00 – 30.00 |
| Cup, regular, with saucer | 30.00 – 35.00 | 15.00 – 20.00 | 40.00 – 48.00 | 20.00 – 25.00 |
| Hostess set, 4-pc. | | 18.00 – 22.00 | | |
| Lamp** | | 150.00 – 165.00 | | |
| Mug, 10-oz. | 35.00 – 40.00 | 15.00 – 20.00 | | 40.00 – 55.00 |
| Napkin rings, 4-pc. set | 135.00 – 150.00 | 40.00 – 50.00 | | 16.00 – 22.00 |
| Pie baker, deep dish, 10⅛" | 60.00 – 75.00 | 22.00 – 28.00 | | 25.00 – 30.00 |
| Pitcher, disk, large | 110.00 – 130.00 | 45.00 – 60.00 | 85.00 – 100.00 | 50.00 – 60.00 |
|   with anniversary logo | 60.00 – 75.00 | | 60.00 – 75.00 | 50.00 – 60.00 |
| Pitcher, disk, mini | 45.00 – 55.00 | 25.00 – 30.00 | | 12.00 – 15.00 |
| Pitcher, disk, small (juice) | 85.00 – 100.00 | 35.00 – 45.00 | | 32.00 – 38.00 |
| Pitcher, disk, large, with<br>  Millennium 2000 | | | | 40.00 – 50.00 |
| Place setting, 5-pc. | 175.00 – 225.00 | 60.00 – 85.00 | 150.00 – 180.00 | 45.00 – 60.00 |
| Place setting of flatware,<br>  5-pc. | 30.00 – 40.00 | 20.00 – 25.00 | 22.00 – 28.00 | 20.00 – 25.00 |
| Plate, bread and butter,<br>  6⅛" | 25.00 – 35.00 | 4.00 – 7.00 | | 14.00 – 18.00 |
| Plate, chop, 11¾" | 50.00 – 60.00 | 25.00 – 30.00 | | 30.00 – 35.00 |
| Plate, dinner, 10½" | 40.00 – 50.00 | 25.00 – 30.00 | 50.00 – 60.00 | 22.00 – 25.00 |
| Plate, luncheon, 9" | 65.00 – 75.00 | 18.00 – 22.00 | | 20.00 – 25.00 |
| Plate, salad, 7" | 35.00 – 40.00 | 8.00 – 12.00 | 15.00 – 22.00 | 15.00 – 18.00 |
| Platter, #6, 9⅝" | 50.00 – 60.00 | 22.00 – 30.00 | | 42.00 – 48.00 |
| Platter, #8, 11⅝" | 60.00 – 75.00 | 22.00 – 30.00 | | |
| Platter, #10, 13⅝" | 60.00 – 70.00 | 30.00 – 38.00 | 50.00 – 60.00 | 32.00 – 36.00 |
| Salt and pepper shakers,<br>  2¼", pr. | 35.00 – 45.00 | 22.00 – 28.00 | | 20.00 – 25.00 |
| Salt and pepper shakers,<br>  range, pr. | | | | 35.00 – 40.00 |
| Sauce boat | 35.00 – 50.00 | 25.00 – 35.00 | 100.00 – 125.00 | 40.00 – 45.00 |
| Saucer, jumbo, 6¾" | 15.00 – 20.00 | 8.00 – 10.00 | 9.00 – 12.00 | 12.00 – 16.00 |
| Skillet | | 22.00 – 28.00 | | |
| Steak knife set | | 15.00 – 20.00 | | |
| Sugar caddy | 45.00 – 50.00 | 12.00 – 18.00 | | |
| Sugar, 8½-oz., individual,<br>  with lid | 50.00 – 60.00 | 15.00 – 18.00 | | 35.00 – 40.00 |
| Teapot, 2-cup | | | | 30.00 – 40.00 |
| Teapot, 44-oz.* | 125.00 – 145.00 | 45.00 – 60.00 | | |
| Tray, relish<br>  (corn-on-the-cob) | 60.00 – 70.00 | | | 18.00 – 22.00 |
| Tray, round serving,<br>  with handles, 11" | 350.00 – 375.00 | 25.00 – 35.00 | 50.00 – 65.00 | 35.00 – 40.00 |
| Tumbler | 30.00 – 40.00 | 10.00 – 15.00 | 25.00 – 30.00 | 14.00 – 20.00 |
| Vase, bud, 6" | 80.00 – 100.00 | 15.00 – 20.00 | | 18.00 – 22.00 |
| Vase, medium, 9⅝" | 200.00 – 250.00 | 35.00 – 45.00 | 150.00 – 175.00 | 40.00 – 50.00 |
| Vase, Millennium | | | | 125.00 – 150.00 |
| Vase, Millennium II,<br>  9" x 7½" | | | | 35.00 – 45.00 |
| Vase, Millennium III | | | | 25.00 – 35.00 |

\* The lid must match the base well to bring these prices.

\*\* Made in only the first nine colors (no lilac); all are worth $150.00 – 165.00.

## *Holiday Fiesta*
### *Page 81*

Bowl, 6⅞" . . . . . . . . . . . . . . . . . . . . . . . . .7.00 – 9.00
Candleholders, 2½", pr. . . . . . . . . . . . .25.00 – 30.00
Creamer, covered sugar, and tray,
   set . . . . . . . . . . . . . . . . . . . . . . . .35.00 – 40.00
Cup, jumbo, with saucer . . . . . . . . . . .18.00 – 22.00
Cup, regular, with saucer . . . . . . . . . .12.00 – 15.00
Mug . . . . . . . . . . . . . . . . . . . . . . . . . . .9.00 – 12.00
Pitcher, disk, juice . . . . . . . . . . . . . . .20.00 – 25.00
Pitcher, disk, mini . . . . . . . . . . . . . . .15.00 – 18.00
Pitcher, disk, water . . . . . . . . . . . . . . .25.00 – 30.00
Place setting . . . . . . . . . . . . . . . . . . . .40.00 – 50.00
Place setting of flatware, 5-pc. . . . . . .40.00 – 45.00
Plate, chop . . . . . . . . . . . . . . . . . . . . .15.00 – 18.00
Plate, dinner . . . . . . . . . . . . . . . . . . . .12.00 – 15.00
Plate, salad; 7" . . . . . . . . . . . . . . . . . . .8.00 – 10.00
Platter, #8 . . . . . . . . . . . . . . . . . . . . . .15.00 – 18.00
Salt and pepper shakers, range, pr. . . . .30.00 – 35.00
Sauce boat . . . . . . . . . . . . . . . . . . . . . .20.00 – 25.00
Sauce boat stand (white) . . . . . . . . . . . .7.00 – 9.00
Sugar bowl, individual, with lid . . . . .20.00 – 25.00
Teapot, 36-oz. . . . . . . . . . . . . . . . . . . .50.00 – 55.00
Tray, round serving, with handles,
   11" . . . . . . . . . . . . . . . . . . . . . . . . .20.00 – 25.00

## *HLCCA Exclusives & Auction Items*— *Pages 91 – 93*

**Member Exclusives:**
(1998) 1930 Chrysler Building juice pitcher,
   gray . . . . . . . . . . . . . . . . . . . . . . . .95.00 – 295.00
(1999) 1931 Dick Tracy juice pitcher,
   white . . . . . . . . . . . . . . . . . . . . . . . .55.00 – 125.00
(2000) 1932 Golden Age of Radio juice pitcher,
   yellow . . . . . . . . . . . . . . . . . . . . . . .50.00 – 125.00
(2001) 1933 Chicago World's Fair
   Century of Progress, black . . . . . . .75.00 – 150.00
(2002) 1934 Ocean Liner, juniper . . .100.00 – 150.00
   periwinkle . . . . . . . . . . . . . . . . . . . .50.00 – 85.00
(2003) 1935 Dish Night at the Movies,
   plum . . . . . . . . . . . . . . . . . . . . . . . .55.00 – 125.00
(2004) 1936 Rhead and the
   Introduction of Fiesta, tangerine . . .50.00 – 165.00

**HLCCA Conference Exclusives:**
2001 Conference Geo Bowl, HLCCA decal, sunflower
   (ltd. edition of 144) . . . . . . . . . . . . .35.00 – 55.00

2002 Conference utensil crock, New Orleans decal
   (ltd. edition of 35) . . . . . . . . . . . . .95.00 – 145.00
2002 Conference 8" pie baker, New Orleans decal
   (ltd. edition of 144) . . . . . . . . . . . . .35.00 – 55.00
2003 5th Anniversary baseball teapot
   (ltd. edition of 40) . . . . . . . . . . . . .175.00 – 265.00
2003 5th Anniversary baseball covered sugar
   (ltd. edition of 144) . . . . . . . . . . . . .35.00 – 75.00
2004 Conference carafe, Phoenix decal
   (ltd. edition of 40) . . . . . . . . . . . . .200.00 – 250.00
2004 Conference bread tray, Phoenix decal
   (ltd. edition of 144) . . . . . . . . . . . . .45.00 – 75.00

**HLCCA Conference Auction Items:**
1999 Dick Tracy disk pitcher,
   white (2) . . . . . . . . . . . . . . . . . . . . . .1,000.00 +
2000 HLC Millennium III vase,
   sunflower (1) . . . . . . . . . . . . . . . . . . .1,000.00 +
2001 sample Chicago World's Fair Century of
   Progress, juice pitcher, juniper (2) . . . . . .1,000.00 +
2001 Fiestaware 2000 charger,
   sample in sea mist (1) . . . . . . . . . . . . . .1,000.00 +
2002 sample Ocean Liner juice pitcher, turquoise, sea
   mist green (1 ea.) . . . . . . . . . . . . . . . . .500.00 +
2003 Limited edition of ten trivets, experimental black
   metallic glaze, ea . . . . . . . . . . . . . 300.00 – 450.00
2002 HLC prototype animals (donkey, fish, duck, cat)
   in cobalt, plum, yellow, persimmon,
   cinnabar, ea. . . . . . . . . . . . . .275.00 – 1,200.00 +
2003 sample Dish Night at the Movies juice pitcher in
   shamrock, turquoise, sunflower, plum, test metallic
   black (2 ea.) . . . . . . . . . . . . . . .400.00 – 700.00
2004 Royalty vase, Phoenix decal,
   matte terra cotta . . . . . . . . . . . . . .500.00 – 600.00
2004 Royalty vase, Rhead bookplate,
   matte terra cotta . . . . . . . . . . . . . .500.00 – 600.00
2004 Utensil crock, Phoenix decal,
   matte terra cotta . . . . . . . . . . . . . .500.00 – 600.00
2004 Utensil crock, Rhead bookplate,
   matte terra cotta . . . . . . . . . . . . . .500.00 – 600.00
2004 Pizza trays, designed by HLC
   for 2004 Conference . . . . . . . . . . . . . . . .400.00
2004 Java mug, scarlet first fire mug
   (March 2004) . . . . . . . . . . . . . . . . . . . . .NEV

**Betty Crocker Exclusives:**
All of these items are shown online with current market prices at www.bettycrocker.com.

## Harlequin
### Pages 97 – 109

Notice that we have regrouped the colors for this edition. As the antiques and collectibles market in general has been hard hit by economic factors as well as Internet competition, prices for this line have softened dramatically, except for the very rare and desirable items. Though the collector base for Harlequin may be somewhat limited and thus prices for this line always trail well behind Fiesta's, there is still an active market. In most cases, prices have remained fairly stable, but some of the rare and more desirable pieces have risen in value. Medium green Harlequin is even scarcer than medium green Fiesta, and as seasoned collectors vie with each other for these rarities, prices have remained stable; in some instances they're even higher than in the last edition. Based on this activity, values are suggested individually for many medium green items; when no specific value is given, we suggest that you at least double the upper side of the highest range.

NEV — No established value

| | Maroon, Dk. Green, Gray, Spruce, Chartreuse | Mauve Blue, Rose, Red, Lt. Green | Yellow, Turquoise | Medium Green | As Specified |
|---|---|---|---|---|---|
| Ashtray, basketweave | 45.00 – 50.00 | 25.00 – 35.00 | 20.00 – 30.00 | 200.00 + | |
| Ashtray, regular | 45.00 – 50.00 | 35.00 – 45.00 | 25.00 – 35.00 | | |
|   light green | | | | | 175.00 + |
|   with HLCo USA mark | | | | | 100.00 |
| Ashtray, saucer | 100.00 – 125.00 | 85.00 – 100.00 | 65.00 – 75.00 | | |
|   ivory | | | | | 225.00 + |
|   with advertising | | | | | 200.00 |
| Bowl, cream soup | 35.00 – 40.00 | 25.00 – 35.00 | 15.00 – 20.00 | 1,200.00 + | |
| Bowl, fruit, 5½" | 9.00 – 11.00 | 8.00 – 10.00 | 5.00 – 7.00 | 40.00 – 50.00 | |
| Bowl, individual salad | 25.00 – 30.00 | 20.00 – 25.00 | 15.00 – 20.00 | 75.00 – 100.00 | |
| Bowl, mixing, KK, 6" | | | | | |
|   light green | | | | | 60.00 – 80.00 |
|   red | | | | | 125.00 – 150.00 |
| Bowl, mixing, KK, 8" | | | | | |
|   mauve blue | | | | | 75.00 – 100.00 |
| Bowl, mixing, KK, 10" | | | 110.00 – 125.00 | | |
|   mauve blue | | | | | NEV |
|   yellow | | | | | 110.00 – 125.00 |
| Bowl, nappy | 35.00 – 45.00 | 25.00 – 30.00 | 20.00 – 25.00 | 90.00 – 100.00 | |
| Bowl, oval baker | 30.00 – 35.00 | 25.00 – 30.00 | 20.00 – 25.00 | | |
| Bowl, 36s | 35.00 – 45.00 | 30.00 – 40.00 | 20.00 – 30.00 | 125.00 – 150.00 | |
|   spruce or maroon | | | | | 75.00 – 95.00 |
| Bowl, 36s oatmeal | 15.00 – 20.00 | 10.00 – 15.00 | 7.00 – 10.00 | 50.00 – 60.00 | |
|   maroon | | | | | 125.00 + |
| Butter dish, ½-lb. | 95.00 – 125.00 | 80.00 – 100.00 | 65.00 – 85.00 | | |
|   cobalt | | | | | 135.00 – 150.00 |
|   Fiesta yellow | | | | | 225.00 + |
| Candleholders, pr., | | | | | |
|   spruce, maroon | | | | | 250.00 – 300.00 |
|   yellow, mauve blue, red | | | | | 250.00 – 300.00 |
|   rose | | | | | 500.00 + |
|   light green | | | | | NEV |
| Casserole | 150.00 – 175.00 | 100.00 – 125.00 | 60.00 – 90.00 | NEV | |
| Creamer, high lip, | | | | | |
|   any color | | | | | 125.00 – 165.00 |
| Creamer, individual, | 35.00 – 40.00 | 25.00 – 30.00 | 15.00 – 20.00 | | |
|   light green | | | | | 65.00 – 80.00 |

| | Maroon, Dk. Green, Gray, Spruce, Chartreuse | Harlequin Blue, Rose, Red, Lt. Green | Yellow, Turquoise | Medium Green | As Specified |
|---|---|---|---|---|---|
| Creamer, novelty | 25.00 – 35.00 | 20.00 – 30.00 | 15.00 – 20.00 | NEV | |
| Creamer, regular | 15.00 – 20.00 | 10.00 – 15.00 | 7.00 – 10.00 | 65.00 – 75.00 | |
| Cup, demitasse | 75.00 – 95.00 | 55.00 – 75.00 | 35.00 – 40.00 | 450.00+ | |
|   gray, chartreuse, or dark green | | | | | 100.00 – 200.00 |
| Cup, large (Epicure body), any color but medium green | | | | | 175.00 – 225.00 |
| Egg cup, double | 25.00 – 35.00 | 20.00 – 30.00 | 15.00 – 20.00 | 1,300.00+ | |
| Egg cup, single | 25.00 – 35.00 | 20.00 – 30.00 | 15.00 – 20.00 | | |
|   light green | | | | | 350.00+ |
| Marmalade | 275.00 – 300.00 | 250.00 – 275.00 | 220.00 – 250.00 | | |
|   rose | | | | | 400.00+ |
|   light green | | | | | 500.00+ |
| Nut dish, basketweave | 45.00 – 55.00 | 30.00 – 45.00 | 20.00 – 30.00 | | |
|   rose | | | | | 55.00 – 65.00 |
|   light green | | | | | 65.00 – 75.00 |
| Perfume bottle, either size, either color | | | | | 975.00+ |
| Pitcher, service water (Plate 221) | 75.00 – 90.00 | 55.00 – 75.00 | 50.00 – 60.00 | 3,000.00+ | NEV |
| Pitcher, 22-oz. jug | 50.00 – 65.00 | 45.00 – 50.00 | 25.00 – 35.00 | 1,500.00+ | |
| Plate, deep | 15.00 – 20.00 | 10.00 – 15.00 | 7.00 – 10.00 | 95.00+ | |
| Plate, 6" | 7.00 – 9.00 | 6.00 – 8.00 | 4.00 – 6.00 | 25.00 – 30.00 | |
| Plate, 7" | 9.00 – 11.00 | 8.00 – 10.00 | 6.00 – 8.00 | 25.00 – 30.00 | |
| Plate, 9" | 12.00 – 15.00 | 11.00 – 13.00 | 7.00 – 10.00 | 35.00 – 45.00 | |
| Plate, 10" | 25.00 – 30.00 | 20.00 – 25.00 | 15.00 – 20.00 | 100.00+ | |
| Platter, 11" | 20.00 – 25.00 | 15.00 – 20.00 | 10.00 – 15.00 | 300.00+ | |
| Platter, 13" | 25.00 – 35.00 | 20.00 – 25.00 | 15.00 – 20.00 | 375.00+ | |
| Relish tray | | | | | |
|   mixed colors | | | | | 365.00+ |
|   base only, turquoise | | | | | 80.00 – 100.00 |
|   insert: red, mauve blue, yellow, maroon | | | | | 75.00 – 90.00 |
|   insert: rose, turquoise, spruce | | | | | NEV |
| Salt and pepper shakers, pr. | 50.00 – 70.00 | 30.00 – 40.00 | 20.00 – 30.00 | 240.00+ | |
| Sauce boat | 25.00 – 30.00 | 20.00 – 25.00 | 15.00 – 20.00 | 250.00+ | |
| Saucer | 4.00 – 5.00 | 3.00 – 4.00 | 2.00 – 3.00 | 15.00 – 20.00 | |
| Saucer, demitasse | 20.00 – 25.00 | 15.00 – 20.00 | 10.00 – 15.00 | 175.00+ | |
|   gray, chartreuse, or dark green | | | | | 75.00 – 125.00 |
| Saucer, for large cup | | | | | NEV |
| Souvenirs (Plate 230), any | | | | | 60.00 – 100.00 |
| Spoon rest, | | | | | |
|   dark green, yellow, or turquoise - See Rhythm | | | | | |
|   red | | | | | NEV |
| Sugar bowl, with lid | 30.00 – 40.00 | 25.00 – 30.00 | 20.00 – 25.00 | 135.00+ | |
| Syrup | | 225.00 – 275.00 | | | |
|   spruce, mauve blue, or red | | | | | 300.00 – 375.00 |
|   yellow | | | | | 225.00 – 275.00 |

| | Maroon, Dk. Green, Gray, Spruce, Chartreuse | Mauve Blue, Rose, Red, Lt. Green | Yellow, Turquoise | Medium Green | As Specified |
|---|---|---|---|---|---|
| Teacup | 8.00 – 12.00 | 6.00 – 10.00 | 4.00 – 8.00 | 35.00 – 45.00 | |
| Teapot | 75.00 – 125.00 | 65.00 – 90.00 | 40.00 – 60.00 | NEV | |
| cobalt | | | | | NEV |
| Tumbler | 35.00 – 50.00 | 30.00 – 40.00 | 25.00 – 35.00 | | |
| ivory | | | | NEV | |
| with car decal | | | | | 40.00+ |
| boxed set with brochure | | | | | NEV |

## Harlequin Animals
### Pages 110 – 111

Price the donkey and cat at the high end of the range given for standard colors, the penguin and lamb at mid-range, and the duck and fish at the low end.

Standard colors . . . . . . . . . . . . . . .125.00 – 225.00
Non-standard colors, minimum value . . . . . . . 500.00
Mavericks, near full size, with or
   without gold . . . . . . . . . . . . . . . . . . .40.00 – 60.00
   smaller, in porcelain . . . . . . . . . . . .12.00 – 20.00
Duck, turquoise . . . . . . . . . . . . . . . . . . . . . . . . .NEV

## Harlequin Reissue
### Page 109

This is the first time we've listed values for the 1979 reissue, but now that it's been on the market for 25 years, collectors are beginning to take notice of it as well, especially anything in a non-standard color.

Bowl, 36s oatmeal . . . . . . . . . . . . . . . . . .5.00 – 10.00
Bowl, nappy, reissue green . . . . . . . . . .20.00 – 25.00
Creamer, turquoise . . . . . . . . . . . . . . . . .5.00 – 10.00
Plate, 7" . . . . . . . . . . . . . . . . . . . . . . . . . .5.00 – 10.00
Plate, 10", four standard colors . . . . . . . .15.00 – 20.00
   clear glaze over clay body . . . . . . . . .25.00 – 45.00
   other non-standard solid colors (apricot, lilac, and
   chartreuse known to be in collectors' hands),
   minimum value . . . . . . . . . . . . . . . . . .95.00
Platter, round, coral . . . . . . . . . . . . . . .35.00 – 45.00
   yellow, minimum value . . . . . . . . . . . . . . . .75.00
Saucer . . . . . . . . . . . . . . . . . . . . . . . . . .2.00 – 3.00
Sugar bowl, with lid, yellow . . . . . . . .15.00 – 25.00
Teacup, four standard colors . . . . . . . . . .4.00 – 6.00
   powder blue . . . . . . . . . . . . . . . . . . . .65.00 – 85.00

## Riviera and Ivory Century
### Pages 112 – 119

NEV — No Established Value

Batter set, standard colors . . . . . . . .175.00 – 225.00

with decals . . . . . . . . . . . . . . . . . . .140.00 – 160.00
red . . . . . . . . . . . . . . . . . . . . . . . . . . . . . . .NEV
ivory, with covered sugar bowl
   and 11½" square platter . . . . . . . . . . . . . . . .NEV
Bowl, baker, 9" . . . . . . . . . . . . . . . . . . . .15.00 – 20.00
Bowl, cream soup, with liner, ivory . . . .40.00 – 50.00
   liner only . . . . . . . . . . . . . . . . . . . . . . .10.00 – 15.00
Bowl, fruit, 5½" . . . . . . . . . . . . . . . . . . . . .6.00 – 10.00
   cobalt . . . . . . . . . . . . . . . . . . . . . . . . .20.00 – 25.00
Bowl, nappy, 7¼" . . . . . . . . . . . . . . . . . . .20.00 – 25.00
Bowl, oatmeal, 6" . . . . . . . . . . . . . . . . . . .25.00 – 32.00
Bowl, utility, ivory . . . . . . . . . . . . . . . . . .32.00 – 35.00
Butter dish, ¼-lb. . . . . . . . . . . . . . . . .100.00 – 140.00
   ivory . . . . . . . . . . . . . . . . . . . . . . . . .120.00 – 150.00
   turquoise . . . . . . . . . . . . . . . . . . . . . .225.00 – 250.00
   cobalt . . . . . . . . . . . . . . . . . . . . . . . . .200.00 – 250.00
Butter dish, ½-lb., other Riviera
   colors . . . . . . . . . . . . . . . . . . . . . . . .100.00 – 125.00
   cobalt, ½-lb. . . . . . . . . . . . . . . . . . . .125.00 – 150.00
Casserole . . . . . . . . . . . . . . . . . . . . . . .85.00 – 100.00
Creamer . . . . . . . . . . . . . . . . . . . . . . . .11.00 – 13.00
Cup & saucer, demitasse, ivory . . . . . . .40.00 – 50.00
Jug, covered . . . . . . . . . . . . . . . . . . . . .90.00 – 110.00
Jug, open . . . . . . . . . . . . . . . . . . . . . . . .65.00 – 80.00
Jug, open, 4½", ivory . . . . . . . . . . . . . . . . . . . . .NEV
Pitcher, juice, yellow . . . . . . . . . . . . . .75.00 – 90.00
Pitcher, juice, mauve blue . . . . . . . . .100.00 – 130.00
Pitcher, juice, red . . . . . . . . . . . . . . . .120.00 – 145.00
Plate, compartment . . . . . . . . . . . . . . . . . . . . . .NEV
Plate, deep . . . . . . . . . . . . . . . . . . . . . .15.00 – 20.00
Plate, 6" . . . . . . . . . . . . . . . . . . . . . . . . . .3.00 – 5.00
Plate, 7" . . . . . . . . . . . . . . . . . . . . . . . . . .4.00 – 8.00
   cobalt . . . . . . . . . . . . . . . . . . . . . . . . .20.00 – 25.00
Plate, 9" . . . . . . . . . . . . . . . . . . . . . . . . .15.00 – 18.00
Plate, 10" . . . . . . . . . . . . . . . . . . . . . . . .50.00 – 60.00
Platter, 11½", oval well . . . . . . . . . . . .15.00 – 22.00
Platter, 11¼", closed handles . . . . . . . .20.00 – 25.00
Platter, 11½", square well . . . . . . . . . . . . . . . . .NEV
Platter, 12", cobalt . . . . . . . . . . . . . . . .60.00 – 75.00
Platter, 15", oval well . . . . . . . . . . . . . .40.00 – 50.00
Plater, 15", rectangular well . . . . . . . . .50.00 – 60.00
Salt & pepper shakers, pr. . . . . . . . . . .15.00 – 20.00
Sauce boat . . . . . . . . . . . . . . . . . . . . . . .18.00 – 20.00
Sauce boat, fast-stand . . . . . . . . . . . . . .50.00 – 60.00
Saucer . . . . . . . . . . . . . . . . . . . . . . . . . .2.00 – 4.00
Sugar bowl with lid . . . . . . . . . . . . . . . .18.00 – 20.00
Syrup with lid . . . . . . . . . . . . . . . . . .100.00 – 150.00

Teacup . . . . . . . . . . . . . . . . . . . . . . . . .6.00 – 9.00
Teapot . . . . . . . . . . . . . . . . . . . .125.00 – 150.00
Tidbit, 2-tier, ivory . . . . . . . . . . . . . .40.00 – 50.00
Tumbler, handled . . . . . . . . . . . . . . .35.00 – 50.00
  ivory . . . . . . . . . . . . . . . . . . . . . .95.00 – 110.00
  spruce green . . . . . . . . . . . . . . . . . . . . . . . .NEV
Tumbler, juice . . . . . . . . . . . . . . . . . .25.00 –35.00

## Carnival
### Page 120

Use the low range of values for these colors: gray, light green, yellow, and dark green. The high side represents values for cobalt, red, ivory, and turquoise.

Fruit, small . . . . . . . . . . . . . . . . . . . . . . .5.00 – 7.00
Oatmeal . . . . . . . . . . . . . . . . . . . . . . . . .5.00 – 7.00
Plate, 6½" . . . . . . . . . . . . . . . . . . . . . . . .3.00 – 5.00
Saucer . . . . . . . . . . . . . . . . . . . . . . . . . . .1.00 – 2.00
Teacup . . . . . . . . . . . . . . . . . . . . . . . . . .5.00 – 7.00
Oats box, carnival/mother's . . . . . . . . . .60.00 – 90.00

## Epicure
### Pages 121 – 122

Though there are relatively few Epicure collectors, those that like its sleek '50s designer styling are loyal.

    Little of it is sold through eBay, so our values have been suggested by those fans who follow the market. One reports that since eBay has flattened the regional distribution issues (originally the line sold better in California and the Midwest than it did in the East), prices have softened.

NEV — No Established Value

Ashtray* . . . . . . . . . . . . . . . . . . . . . . . . . . . NEV
Bowl, coupe soup, 8" . . . . . . . . . . .30.00 – 35.00
Bowl, covered vegetable . . . . . . . . . .70.00 – 80.00
Bowl, cereal, 6" . . . . . . . . . . . . . . .15.00 – 18.00
Bowl, nappy, 8¾" . . . . . . . . . . . . . .35.00 – 45.00
Casserole, individual . . . . . . . . . . .100.00 – 125.00
Coffeepot, 10" . . . . . . . . . . . . . . .400.00 – 450.00
Creamer . . . . . . . . . . . . . . . . . . . .20.00 – 25.00
Gravy bowl . . . . . . . . . . . . . . . . . . .30.00 – 35.00
Ladle, 5½" . . . . . . . . . . . . . . . . . . .75.00 – 95.00
Nut dish/sample, 4"
    turquoise . . . . . . . . . . . . . . . . . . .32.00 – 38.00

other colors . . . . . . . . . . . . . . . . .100.00 – 125.00
Pickle (small oval platter) . . . . . . . . . . .30.00 – 35.00
Plate, 6½" . . . . . . . . . . . . . . . . . . . . . . . .6.00 – 8.00
Plate, 8" . . . . . . . . . . . . . . . . . . . . . .22.00 – 25.00
Plate, 10" . . . . . . . . . . . . . . . . . . . . .20.00 – 22.00
Platter, 12" . . . . . . . . . . . . . . . . . . . .30.00 – 35.00
Salt and pepper shakers, pr. . . . . . . . .25.00 – 30.00
Sugar bowl, with lid . . . . . . . . . . . . .22.00 – 28.00
Teacup and saucer . . . . . . . . . . . . . .35.00 – 40.00
Tidbit, 2-tier, original, white . . . . . .150.00 – 175.00

* One sold in 2004 for $3,000.00.

## Jubilee
### Pages 122 – 123

After years of confusion, we finally came to realize that the only gray 10" mixing bowl known to man came from one of the Jubilee three-piece bowl sets. There are no gray 6" or 8" bowls.

NEV — No Established Value

Bowl, cereal/soup . . . . . . . . . . . . . . . . .6.00 – 8.00
Bowl, fruit . . . . . . . . . . . . . . . . . . . . .4.00 – 5.00
Bowl, mixing, Kitchen Kraft, 6" . . . . . .90.00 – 110.00
Bowl, mixing, Kitchen Kraft, 8" . . . . .100.00 – 120.00
Bowl, mixing, Kitchen Kraft, 10" . . . .150.00 – 180.00
Bowl, nappy, 8¾" . . . . . . . . . . . . . . . .7.00 – 9.00
Casserole . . . . . . . . . . . . . . . . . . . .35.00 – 45.00
Coffeepot . . . . . . . . . . . . . . . . . . . .45.00 – 55.00
Creamer . . . . . . . . . . . . . . . . . . . . . .5.00 – 6.50
Cup & saucer . . . . . . . . . . . . . . . . . . .6.00 – 8.00
Cup & saucer, after-dinner . . . . . . . . . .12.00 – 15.00
Egg cup . . . . . . . . . . . . . . . . . . . . . .7.00 – 11.00
Fiesta juice tumbler, see Fiesta pricing
Fiesta juice pitcher, see Fiesta pricing
Plate, 6" . . . . . . . . . . . . . . . . . . . . . .1.50 – 2.50
Plate, 7" . . . . . . . . . . . . . . . . . . . . . .4.00 – 6.00
Plate, 9" . . . . . . . . . . . . . . . . . . . . . .5.00 – 7.00
Plate, 10" . . . . . . . . . . . . . . . . . . . . .8.00 – 10.00
Plate, calendar, cream, 1953 . . . . . . . .20.00 – 25.00
Plate, chop . . . . . . . . . . . . . . . . . . . .14.00 – 17.00
Platter, 11" . . . . . . . . . . . . . . . . . . . .8.00 – 10.00
Platter, 13" . . . . . . . . . . . . . . . . . . .10.00 – 14.00
Salt & pepper shakers, pr. . . . . . . . . . . .6.00 – 10.00
Sauce boat . . . . . . . . . . . . . . . . . . . . .9.00 – 12.00
Sugar bowl with lid . . . . . . . . . . . . . . .7.00 – 10.00
Teapot . . . . . . . . . . . . . . . . . . . . . . .45.00 – 55.00

## Kenilworth
### Pages 123 – 130

Interest in this line continues to grow. Pink and black are highly valued by collectors. Use the high side of the range to evaluate black Kenilworth. Add 50% to the value of any piece having gold, decals, or two-color glazing. Values are listed for pieces that are complete — lid, handle, and base ring or stand must be present if that item was originally designed to have them. See the color photos for detailed information.

NEV - No Established Value
(*) - Items marked with an asterisk are rare.

| | White or Turquoise | Pink or Black | Green | NEV |
|---|---|---|---|---|
| Ashtray, fluted* | | | | NEV |
| Bowl, 3¼" x 10¼", complete | 25.00 – 35.00 | 40.00 – 95.00 | | |
| Bowl, 3¼" x 10¼", with fork & spoon | 50.00 – 75.00 | 75.00 – 100.00 | | |
| Bowl, chowder/cereal, Rhythm, 5½" | 25.00 – 30.00 | 40.00 – 50.00 | 40.00 – 50.00 | |
| Bowl, nappy, round, Rhythm, 3¾" x 9¼" | 65.00 – 75.00 | | | |
| Bowl, nappy, oval, 9¾" x 10⅜", complete with brass wire foot, white | 75.00 – 80.00 | | | |
| Carafe, 10⅛" x 6", complete[1] | 100.00 – 110.00 | 125.00 – 175.00 | 350.00+ | |
| Carafe, complete in original box | 200.00 – 220.00 | 250.00 – 275.00 | | |
| Casserole, small, 3½" x 8¼", complete with lid, white | 70.00 – 80.00 | | | |
| Casserole, large, 3¼" x 10¼", complete with lid, white* | 125.00 – 150.00 | | | |
| Casserole, OvenServe, 11¼", complete with lid, white* | 175.00 – 200.00 | | | |
| Casserole lid, OvenServe, 11¼", white* | 100.00 – 110.00 | | | |
| Chip & dip set, 10¼", complete | 75.00 – 100.00 | 150.00 – 200.00 | | |
| Chip & dip set, 11", complete, white | 125.00 – 150.00 | | | |
| Coffeepot, 10½" x 5", complete, white | 75.00 – 95.00 | | | |
| turquoise, very rare | | | | NEV |
| Comport, 2" x 11⅛", complete, white | 95.00 – 110.00 | | | |
| Creamer, 4½" x 3⅜", white | 20.00 – 25.00 | | | |
| Ice bucket, 8" x 8½", complete with brass lid & stand, glass liner, white* | 125.00 – 150.00 | | | |
| Pie plate, 10¼", white* | 75.00 – 80.00 | | | |
| Platter, rectangular, 11" x 15", white* | 90.00 – 110.00 | | | |
| Platter, rectangular, 11" x 15", white, complete with stand* | 100.00 – 125.00 | | | |
| Relish tray, round, 1-pc., 1¾" x 10½"* | | | | NEV |
| Relish tray, round, 6 pie-wedge pieces* | | | | NEV |
| Salt & pepper shakers, Charm House, 2½" x 2½", pr. | | 35.00 – 50.00 | 75.00 – 100.00 | |
| Sauce boat, Rhythm, 2½" x 9" | 30.00 – 35.00 | 50.00 – 75.00 | | |
| Serving tray, round, brass collar, white ceramic center, 15" | 75.00 – 95.00 | | | |
| Soup tureen, complete, 8" x 8½", white* | 150.00 – 175.00 | | | |
| Spoon rest, Rhythm, 8¼" x 6", turquoise | 350.00 – 400.00 | | | |
| white | 120.00 – 130.00 | | | |
| Sugar bowl, with lid, 3⅜" x 3⅝", white | 30.00 – 35.00 | | | |

[1]Two carafes in Fiesta light green, not a standard Kenilworth color, are known to exist. One sold on eBay several years ago, and the other is in a private collection.

## Pastel Nautilus
### Page 131

Bowl, cream soup . . . . . . . . . . . . . . . . .9.00 – 11.00
Bowl, flat soup (deep plate) . . . . . . .7.00 – 10.00
Bowl, footed oatmeal, 6" . . . . . . . . . . . .6.00 – 8.50
Bowl, fruit, 5" . . . . . . . . . . . . . . . . . . . .5.00 – 6.50
Bowl, tab-handled, soup/cereal . . . . . .9.00 – 12.00
Bowl, oval vegetable . . . . . . . . . . . . . .9.00 – 12.00
Bowl, round nappy . . . . . . . . . . . . . . . .9.00 – 12.00
Casserole with lid . . . . . . . . . . . . . . .40.00 – 45.00
Creamer . . . . . . . . . . . . . . . . . . . . . .7.00 – 8.50
Cup & saucer . . . . . . . . . . . . . . . . .10.00 – 12.00
Egg cup, double . . . . . . . . . . . . . . . .12.00 – 15.00
Gravy boat . . . . . . . . . . . . . . . . . . .12.00 – 16.00
Plate, 6" . . . . . . . . . . . . . . . . . . . . . . .2.50 – 3.50
Plate, 7" . . . . . . . . . . . . . . . . . . . . . . .5.00 – 6.50
Plate, 8" . . . . . . . . . . . . . . . . . . . . . . .5.00 – 6.50
Plate, 9" . . . . . . . . . . . . . . . . . . . . . . .6.00 – 8.00
Plate, 10" . . . . . . . . . . . . . . . . . . . . .9.00 – 12.00
Platter, 13" . . . . . . . . . . . . . . . . . . .12.00 – 16.00
Platter, 11" . . . . . . . . . . . . . . . . . . . .9.00 – 12.00
Platter/gravy boat liner, 9" . . . . . . . . . .9.00 – 12.00
Sugar bowl with lid . . . . . . . . . . . . . .10.00 – 15.00

## Rhythm
### Pages 132 – 135

Bowl, footed cereal/chowder . . . . . . . . . .8.00 – 9.00
Bowl, fruit, 5½" . . . . . . . . . . . . . . . . . .3.00 – 5.00
Bowl, mixing, Kitchen Kraft, 6" . . . . . .50.00 – 70.00
Bowl, mixing, Kitchen Kraft, 8" . . . . . .60.00 – 85.00
Bowl, mixing, Kitchen Kraft, 10" . . . . .90.00 – 120.00
Bowl, nappy . . . . . . . . . . . . . . . . . . . .9.00 – 14.00
Bowl, salad, large . . . . . . . . . . . . . . .55.00 – 65.00
Casserole lid (bottom is nappy) . . . . . .50.00 – 60.00
Creamer, 2¾" . . . . . . . . . . . . . . . . . 7.00 – 9.00
Cup & saucer . . . . . . . . . . . . . . . . . . .7.00 – 9.00
Cup & saucer, after-dinner, rare . . . . .200.00 – 235.00
    marked, very rare . . . . . . . . . . . .325.00 – 350.00
Plate, 6" . . . . . . . . . . . . . . . . . . . . . . .3.00 – 4.00
Plate, 7" . . . . . . . . . . . . . . . . . . . . . . 5.00 – 7.00
Plate, 9" . . . . . . . . . . . . . . . . . . . . . . 6.00 – 9.00
Plate, 10" . . . . . . . . . . . . . . . . . . . . .10.00 – 12.00
Plate, calendar . . . . . . . . . . . . . . . . .12.00 – 15.00
Plate, snack . . . . . . . . . . . . . . . . . . .28.00 – 32.00
    maroon . . . . . . . . . . . . . . . . . . . .120.00 – 135.00
Platter, 11½" . . . . . . . . . . . . . . . . . .12.00 – 14.00
Platter, 13½" . . . . . . . . . . . . . . . . . .15.00 – 20.00
Salt & pepper shakers, pr. . . . . . . . . .10.00 – 15.00
Sauce boat . . . . . . . . . . . . . . . . . . .12.00 – 16.00
Sauce boat stand . . . . . . . . . . . . . . .10.00 – 14.00
Spoon rest, colors other than white . .350.00 – 400.00
    white . . . . . . . . . . . . . . . . . . . . .120.00 – 130.00
Sugar bowl, with lid . . . . . . . . . . . . .12.00 – 15.00
Teapot . . . . . . . . . . . . . . . . . . . . . .50.00 – 60.00
Tidbit, 3-tier . . . . . . . . . . . . . . . . . .38.00 – 42.00

## Seller's Line
### Page 135

Very rare . . . . . . . . . . . . . . . . . . . . . . .NEV

## Serenade
### Pages 136 – 137

Bowl, fruit . . . . . . . . . . . . . . . . . . . . .6.00 – 9.00
Bowl, lug soup . . . . . . . . . . . . . . . . .20.00 – 25.00
Bowl, nappy, 9" . . . . . . . . . . . . . . . .18.00 – 22.00
Casserole . . . . . . . . . . . . . . . . . . . .55.00 – 70.00
Casserole base, Kitchen Kraft . . . . . . .55.00 – 65.00
    matching lid . . . . . . . . . . . . . . . .90.00 – 100.00
    non-standard color . . . . . . . . . . .300.00 – 350.00
Creamer . . . . . . . . . . . . . . . . . . . . . .9.00 – 14.00
Pickle dish . . . . . . . . . . . . . . . . . . .12.00 – 18.00
Plate, 6" . . . . . . . . . . . . . . . . . . . . . .4.00 – 5.00
Plate, 7" . . . . . . . . . . . . . . . . . . . . . .7.00 – 9.00
Plate, 9" . . . . . . . . . . . . . . . . . . . . . .9.00 – 12.00
Plate, 10" . . . . . . . . . . . . . . . . . . . .12.00 – 16.00
Plate, chop . . . . . . . . . . . . . . . . . . .20.00 – 25.00
Plate, deep . . . . . . . . . . . . . . . . . . .15.00 – 18.00
Platter, 12½" . . . . . . . . . . . . . . . . .15.00 – 20.00
Salt & pepper shakers, pr. . . . . . . . . .14.00 – 18.00
Sauce boat . . . . . . . . . . . . . . . . . . .18.00 – 22.00
Sugar bowl with lid . . . . . . . . . . . . .12.00 – 18.00
Teacup & saucer . . . . . . . . . . . . . . . .9.00 – 12.00
Teapot . . . . . . . . . . . . . . . . . . . . . .70.00 – 95.00

## Skytone/Suntone
### Pages 138 – 139

Use values for Jubilee to price these lines.

## Tango
### Page 139

Use the high side of the range to evaluate red, spruce
green, and maroon items. Though many collectors like
the shapes and colors of this line, dealers tell us that
because it's so hard to find, most don't really attempt to
collect it, and unless they can offer several items for
sale at once, it's hard to sell. So while they may do well
to sell the lone plate at 50% of book price, a lot of several items or an incomplete set might bring from 25%
to 50% more than our suggested values.

Bowl, fruit, 5¾" . . . . . . . . . . . . . . . . .5.00 – 7.00
Bowl, nappy, 8¾" . . . . . . . . . . . . . . . .9.00 – 12.00
Bowl, oval baker, 9" . . . . . . . . . . . . . .9.00 – 12.00
Casserole . . . . . . . . . . . . . . . . . . . .60.00 – 70.00
Creamer . . . . . . . . . . . . . . . . . . . . . .6.00 – 8.00
Cup & saucer . . . . . . . . . . . . . . . . . . .7.00 – 9.00
Plate, 6" . . . . . . . . . . . . . . . . . . . . . .3.00 – 4.00

| | |
|---|---|
| Plate, 7" | 3.00 – 4.50 |
| Plate, 9" | 6.00 – 8.00 |
| Plate, 10" | 9.00 – 11.00 |
| Plate, deep | 8.00 – 11.00 |
| Platter, 11¾" | 9.00 – 12.00 |
| Salt & pepper shakers, pr. | 10.00 – 15.00 |
| Saucer | 1.50 – 2.50 |
| Sugar bowl with lid | 12.00 – 15.00 |

## Wells Art Glaze
### Pages 140 – 142

| | |
|---|---|
| Batter set, 3-pc. | 200.00 – 235.00 |
| Bowl, cream soup | 25.00 – 30.00 |
| Bowl, fruit, 5" | 10.00 – 12.00 |
| Bowl, nappy, 8" | 22.00 – 28.00 |
| Bowl, oatmeal 36s | 22.00 – 28.00 |
| Bowl, oval baker, 8" | 20.00 – 25.00 |
| Bowl, oval baker, 9" | 22.00 – 28.00 |
| Casserole | 65.00 – 75.00 |
| Coffeepot, demitasse | 125.00 – 150.00 |
| Covered jug, 9" | 150.00 – 165.00 |
| Covered jug, with decals | 70.00 – 80.00 |
| Covered muffin | 70.00 – 80.00 |
| Cream soup stand | 12.00 – 17.00 |
| Creamer | 18.00 – 25.00 |
| Creamer, individual | 18.00 – 22.00 |
| Cup, bouillon, with handles | 22.00 – 26.00 |
| Cup & saucer | 16.00 – 20.00 |
| Cup & saucer, after-dinner | 30.00 – 35.00 |
| Egg cup, double | 22.00 – 26.00 |
| Mug, coffee, 4¾" | 25.00 – 30.00 |
| Nut dish/butter pat | 12.00 – 15.00 |
| Pickle dish with handles | 20.00 – 25.00 |
| Plate, 6" | 6.00 – 9.00 |
| Plate, 7" | 8.00 – 10.00 |
| Plate, 9" | 12.00 – 15.00 |
| Plate, 10" | 20.00 – 25.00 |
| Plate, chop, with handles | 24.00 – 28.00 |
| Plate, deep | 12.00 – 15.00 |
| Plate, square, 6" | 15.00 – 18.00 |
| Platter, oval, 11½" | 18.00 – 22.00 |
| Platter, oval, 13½" | 25.00 – 30.00 |
| Platter, oval, 15½" | 30.00 – 40.00 |
| Sauce boat | 25.00 – 30.00 |
| Sauce boat, fast-stand | 32.00 – 38.00 |
| Sauce boat liner with handles | 18.00 – 22.00 |
| Sugar bowl, individual, open | 15.00 – 20.00 |
| Sugar bowl with lid | 25.00 – 30.00 |
| Syrup | 120.00 – 135.00 |
| Syrup, with decals | 62.00 – 68.00 |
| Teapot, Empress, rare | 325.00 – 350.00 |
| Teapot, regular | 110.00 – 125.00 |

## Mexican Decaled Lines
### Conchita, Hacienda, Mexicana, and Max-i-cana
### Pages 143 – 151

To simplify the problem of evaluating these lines, we have compiled a general listing that basically will apply to the first three patterns mentioned above (on Century shapes) and Max-i-cana on Yellowstone. Not all of these items have been found in every pattern. Letter codes have been used to indicate pieces that so far are known to exist in only the coded patterns: H — Hacienda; Me — Mexicana; Ma — Max-i-cana. Remember that prices given are for pieces with mint decals. Examples with worn or scratched decals are worth no more than chipped ones.

| | |
|---|---|
| Bell (H) | 90.00 – 98.00 |
| Bowl, baker, 9" | 28.00 – 32.00 |
| Bowl, cream soup, rare (H, Ma, Me) | 60.00 – 68.00 |
| Bowl, deep, 2½" x 5" (Me) | 40.00 – 44.00 |
| Bowl, fruit, 5" | 12.00 – 14.00 |
| Bowl, lug soup, 4½" (Ma, Me) | 38.00 – 42.00 |
| Bowl, oatmeal, 6" | 28.00 – 32.00 |
| Bowl, vegetable, 8½" | 25.00 – 30.00 |
| Bowl, vegetable, 9½" | 28.00 – 32.00 |
| Butter dish, ½-lb. (H, Ma) | 135.00 – 150.00 |
| round (H) | 220.00 – 235.00 |
| Casserole | 140.00 – 165.00 |
| Creamer | 15.00 – 20.00 |
| Creamer, large (Ma) | 22.00 – 26.00 |
| Cup & saucer | 18.00 – 22.00 |
| Egg cup, rolled edge (Me, Ma) | 40.00 – 45.00 |
| Egg cup, torpedo shape (Me, Ma) | 32.00 – 38.00 |
| Plate, 6" | 10.00 – 12.00 |
| Plate, 7" | 12.00 – 14.00 |
| Plate, 9" | 20.00 – 25.00 |
| Plate, 9½" (10") | 42.00 – 46.00 |
| Plate, deep, 8" | 25.00 – 30.00 |
| Platter, 10" | 30.00 – 34.00 |
| Platter, oval or rectangular well, 11½" | 35.00 – 40.00 |
| Platter, oval or rectangular well, 13½" | 48.00 – 52.00 |
| Platter, rectangular well, 15" | 48.00 – 52.00 |
| Sauce boat | 30.00 – 35.00 |
| Sauce boat liner (Me, Ma) | 28.00 – 32.00 |
| Sugar bowl with lid | 28.00 – 32.00 |
| Sugar bowl, large (Ma) | 28.00 – 33.00 |
| Syrup jug, covered, Century (H, Me)* | 375.00 – 425.00 |
| Tall covered jug, Century (H, Me)* | 425.00 – 475.00 |
| Teapot, rare (H, Me) | 145.00 – 165.00 |
| Tumbler, fired-on design, 6-oz | 12.00 – 15.00 |
| Tumbler, fired-on design, 8-oz | 14.00 – 18.00 |
| Tumbler, fired-on design, 10-oz | 18.00 – 20.00 |

*Jugs with missing lids are worth one-third to one-half as much as those with lids.

## Kitchen Kraft Conchita & Mexicana
### Pages 144, 145, and 148

Bowl, mixing, 6" . . . . . . . . . . . . . . .30.00 – 35.00
Bowl, mixing, 8" . . . . . . . . . . . . . . .35.00 – 40.00
Bowl, mixing, 10" . . . . . . . . . . . . . .40.00 – 50.00
Cake plate, 10½" . . . . . . . . . . . . . .35.00 – 40.00
Cake server . . . . . . . . . . . . . . . . . .65.00 – 75.00
Casserole, individual . . . . . . . . . . .90.00 – 105.00
Casserole, 7½" . . . . . . . . . . . . . . . .80.00 – 85.00
Casserole, 8½" . . . . . . . . . . . . . . . .82.00 – 88.00
   OvenServe, Handy Andy . . . . . .55.00 – 62.00
   metal base . . . . . . . . . . . . . . . .15.00 – 20.00
Covered jar, large . . . . . . . . . . . . .155.00 – 175.00
Covered jar, medium . . . . . . . . . . .135.00 – 145.00
Covered jar, small . . . . . . . . . . . . .125.00 – 135.00
Covered jug . . . . . . . . . . . . . . . . .160.00 – 175.00
Fork . . . . . . . . . . . . . . . . . . . . . . .70.00 – 75.00
Pie plate . . . . . . . . . . . . . . . . . . . .32.00 – 38.00
Refrigerator stack unit . . . . . . . . . .45.00 – 50.00
   lid . . . . . . . . . . . . . . . . . . . . . . .50.00 – 60.00
Salt & pepper shakers, pr. . . . . . . .50.00 – 60.00
Spoon . . . . . . . . . . . . . . . . . . . . . .65.00 – 75.00
Underplate, 9" . . . . . . . . . . . . . . . .40.00 – 45.00
Underplate, 6" (rare) . . . . . . . . . . .45.00 – 50.00

## Max-i-cana (Fiesta)
### Page 150

This line is so rare that even very advanced collectors tell us they've never seen a piece.

Cup & saucer . . . . . . . . . . . . . . . . .52.00 – 58.00
Fruit, 5½" . . . . . . . . . . . . . . . . . . .40.00 – 45.00
Nappy, 8½" . . . . . . . . . . . . . . . . . .65.00 – 72.00
Plate, 6" . . . . . . . . . . . . . . . . . . . .16.00 – 20.00
Plate, 10" . . . . . . . . . . . . . . . . . . .45.00 – 52.00
Platter . . . . . . . . . . . . . . . . . . . . . .68.00 – 72.00

## Mexicali, Arizona, Pueblo
### Pages 152 – 154

Values for these seldom-seen lines are estimated as follows. Use the low end of the range for berry bowls and similar items and the high end for the casseroles (other than Kitchen Kraft), covered pitchers or jugs, teapots, and butter dishes.

Mexicali . . . . . . . . . . . . . . . . . . . .15.00 – 250.00
Arizona, rare . . . . . . . . . . . . . . . . .25.00 – 400.00
Pueblo, extremely rare . . . . . . . . . .40.00 – 1,000.00

## Ranchero & Other Mexican Lines
### Page 153

These lines are difficult to evaluate in this format. Some variations, even of the more common patterns, are more valuable than others. For example, a 9" plate in Mexicana on the Virginia Rose shape would bring $30.00 – 35.00, whereas in Mexicana on the Century shape, it would be worth $20.00 – 25.00. The rarer patterns such as Sleeping Mexican (Plate 371), Ranchera, etc.) and the different variations of the more common patterns on unusual shapes (Virginia Rose, Marigold, Nautilus, etc.) may increase the price by 50% and in some instances as much as 75% compared to a similar piece on a Century shape.

## Go-Alongs
### Pages 155 – 167

Values are for examples in excellent to mint condition.

NEV — No Established Value

Plate 375:   Tumbler with fired-on Fiesta
                     dancing lady . . . . . . . .40.00 – 50.00
Plate 376:   Pitcher with fired-on figures .45.00 – 50.00
                     Tumblers, ea. . . . . . . . . .12.00 – 16.00
Plate 377:   Tumblers, ea. . . . . . . . . .12.00 – 16.00
Plate 378:   Napkin rings, set of 4 . . . .25.00 – 30.00
                     Placecard holders, set of 6 .50.00 – 60.00
                     Tumbler, cord-wrapped, ea. .18.00 – 22.00
                     Coaster set . . . . . . . . . . .16.00 – 20.00
Plate 379:   Boxed Fiesta Ensemble,
                     complete . . . . . . . . . .650.00 – 725.00
                     Tumblers, 6-oz., ea. . . . . . . . . . . .15.00
                     Tumblers, 8-oz., ea. . . . . . . . . . . .18.00
                     Tumblers,10-oz., ea. . . . . . . . . . . .20.00
Plate 380:   Ensemble Go-Alongs:
                     Catalin-handled flatware,
                        3-pc. place setting . . . . .15.00 – 18.00
                     Glass ashtray/coaster . . . .12.00 – 15.00
                     Glass individual salt & pepper shakers,
                        pr. . . . . . . . . . . . . . . . .17.00 – 20.00
                     Glass stirrers, set of 8 (4 colors) . . .50.00
Plate 381:   Tumblers, ea. . . . . . . . . .20.00 – 25.00
Plate 382:   Sherbet . . . . . . . . . . . . .15.00 – 20.00
Plate 383:   Rattan tumbler holders, ea. .10.00 – 15.00
Plate 384:   Quikut flatware set, MIB .125.00 – 135.00
Plate 385:   Chef's Set, Quikut, MIB . . . . . . . . .NEV
Plate 386:   Metal frame for Fiesta jam set
                     (cream soup bowl) . . . .85.00 – 100.00
                     Metal frame for Fiesta marmalade, very
                     rare . . . . . . . . . . . . . . .100.00 – 150.00
                     Metal frame for Fiesta
                     chop plate . . . . . . . . . . .50.00 – 60.00
Plate 387:   Metal frame for Fiesta double tidbit set
                     with folding stand . . . .135.00 – 145.00
Plate 388:   Metal frame for Fiesta promotional
                     casserole . . . . . . . . . . . .40.00 – 50.00
Plate 389:   Metal frame for Fiesta salad service set,
                     very rare . . . . . . . . . . .135.00 – 145.00
Plate 390:   Metal frame for Fiesta 3-pc. condiment
                     set, chrome or enameled,
                     very rare . . . . . . . . . .110.00 – 125.00

Plate 392: Metal handle for Fiesta mixing bowl/ ice bucket . . . . . . . . . . .70.00 – 80.00

Plate 393: Fiesta 3-tier tidbit tray (in mixed colors) . . . . . . . . . . . .100.00 – 125.00 (Add 10% for each plate in red or cobalt — 20% for each plate in the '50s colors)

Plate 394: Century nut dish in ivory . .55.00 – 62.00

Plate 395: Ash stand . . . . . . . . . . .125.00 – 150.00

Plate 396: Frame for Fiesta ice-lip pitcher & tumblers (watch for repros) .90.00 – 100.00

Plate 397: Century 2-tier tidbit tray in ivory . . . . . . . . . . . .70.00 – 75.00

Plate 398: Harlequin nut dish . . . . . .45.00 – 52.00

Plate 399: Metal holder for Harlequin tumbler . . . . . . . . . . . .22.00 – 25.00

Not shown: Metal frame for Fiesta mustard and marmalade, very rare . .100.00 – 150.00

Metal frame for Fiesta cake plate . . . . . . . . . . .45.00 – 50.00

Metal revolving base for Fiesta relish tray . . . . . . . . . . . . . .30.00 – 35.00

Metal holder for Kitchen Kraft platter . . . . . . . . . . . .22.00 – 25.00

Metal holder for Kitchen Kraft pie plate . . . . . . . . . . . . .18.00 – 22.00

Metal holder for Kitchen Kraft casserole . . . . . . . . . . .18.00 – 22.00

Plate 400: Fiesta-Wood salad bowl .100.00 – 125.00

Plate 401: Metal holder for Fiesta nappy .16.00 – 20.00

Metal dripolator insert for Fiesta teapot . . . . . . . . . . . . . .12.00 – 19.00

Metal frame for Fiesta jam set .85.00 – 100.00

Wireware holder for Fiesta water set . . . . . . . . . . . . . .80.00 – 90.00

Sta Bright flatware, 3-pc. place setting . . . . . .15.00 – 18.00

Fiesta-Wood tray with glass insert . . . . . . . . . . . .120.00 – 135.00

Glass insert for Fiesta-Wood tray 22.00 – 28.00

Plate 402: Fiesta-Wood hors d'oeuvres tray . . . . . . . . . . . . . .100.00 – 110.00

Plate 403: Wooden tray/metal base for Fiesta chop plate . . . . . . . . . . . . .70.00 – 75.00

Plate 404: Fiesta-Wood hors d'oeuvres tray . . . . . . . . . . . . . .100.00 – 110.00

Plate 405: Metal Kitchenware bread box .60.00 – 70.00

Metal Kitchenware garbage can .75.00 – 85.00

Plate 406: Metal Kitchenware canister set, 4-pc. . . . . . . . . . . . .100.00 – 115.00

Metal Kitchenware napkin holder . . . . . . . . . . . .52.00 – 64.00

Plate 407: Metal Kitchenware wastebasket .60.00 – 70.00

Plate 408: Metal Kitchenware bread box .85.00 – 95.00

Plate 409: Popcorn set in original box . . . . . . .NEV

Not shown: Metal popcorn bowl set, 5-pc., excellent paint . . . . . . .85.00 – 95.00

Plate 410: Metal 3-part tidbit set, excellent paint . . . . . . . . . . . . . .72.00 – 77.00

Plate 411: Hankscraft egg cup . . . . . . .6.00 – 8.00

Hankscraft egg poacher with glass insert . . . . . . . . . . . . .50.00 – 60.00

Plate 412: Fiestacraft paper, MIB . . . .25.00 – 35.00

Plate 413: Paper tablecloth, napkins . .15.00 – 20.00

Plate 414: Cabinet . . . . . . . . . . . . . . . . . . . . .NEV

Plate 416: Sheet of decals . . . . . . . . .40.00 – 70.00

Plate 417: Japan tea set: pot, sugar & creamer, 6 plates, 6 cups & saucers .100.00 – 125.00

Not shown: Luncheon set, tablecloth & 4 napkins, c. 1930s – 1940s, color & design compatible . . . . . . . . . . .40.00 – 50.00

## Commercial Adaptations and Ephemera
### Pages 168 – 173

NEV — No Established Value

**Company Price Lists**

Plates 418 –
422: Fiesta price lists
Undated (1936) . . . . . .200.00 – 225.00
Undated (1936), showing mixing bowl lids . . . . . . . . . . . . .700.00 – 750.00
1936 – 1939 . . . . . . . . . . .40.00 – 50.00
1940 – 1949 . . . . . . . . . . .30.00 – 40.00
1950 – 1959 . . . . . . . . . . .25.00 – 30.00
1960 – 1968 . . . . . . . . . . .15.00 – 20.00

Plate 423: Harlequin price list . . . .125.00 – 175.00

Plate 424: Riviera price list . . . . . . . . . . . . . . .NEV

Plate 425: Jubilee price list . . . . . . .35.00 – 45.00

Plates 426 &
427: Epicure price list . . . . . . .90.00 – 105.00

Plate 428: Fiesta store display, complete (variations exist, large and small), near mint . . . . . . .1,400.00 – 1,650.00

Plate 429: Fiesta carton for dinnerware set . . . . . . . . . . . . .150.00 – 180.00

Plate 430: Fiesta carton, dancing girl logo, small to large . . . . . . . . . . . . .45.00 – 52.00

Plate 431: Fiesta carton (no dancing girl logo) . . . . . . . . . . . . . . .38.00 – 42.00

Plate 432: Harlequin reissue 45-pc. set, MIB . .NEV

Plate 433: Amberstone packaging. Add 100% to minimum value of item packaged

Not shown: Riviera carton for "Juanita" dinnerware set . . . . . . . . . . . . . . . . . . . . .250.00

## Catalog and Newspaper Ads
### Pages 173 – 183

Plates 434,
435, 436,
& 437 Ads from catalogs . . . .150.00 – 225.00

Plates 438 –
440:       Newspaper ads,
              full page . . . . . . . . . .700.00 – 1,500.00
Plates 441 &
442:       Ensemble ad, insert flyer, two sides
              printed, very rare . . . . . . . . . .3,000.00
Plates 443 –
448:       Advertising pieces, add 25% to 35% to
              standard values
Plate 444:  Kitchen Kraft pie plate, in spruce
              green . . . . . . . . . . . .300.00 – 325.00
Plate 449:  Fiesta syrup with Dutchess
              tea . . . . . . . . . . . . . . .175.00 – 200.00
Plates 450 –
453:       Can labels, seed packets featuring HLC
              lines . . . . . . . . . . . . .12.00 – 15.00
Plate 454:  Rolled Oats box . . . . . . .50.00 – 80.00
Plate 455:  National Dairy Council punch-outs, as
              shown (watch for repros) .130.00 – 140.00
Plate 456:  Flour sack . . . . . . . . . . . . . . . . . . .NEV
Plate 457:  Ice cream parlor decoration . .25.00 – 35.00
Plate 458:  Restaurant soup menu . . . . . . . . . .NEV
Plate 459:  Fiesta Tom & Jerry mugs in white (or
              color inside), 1-color
              advertising . . . . . . . . . .40.00 – 45.00
              2-color advertising . . . . .50.00 – 55.00
              3-color advertising . . . . .60.00 – 65.00
              4-color advertising . . . . .70.00 – 75.00
Plate 460:  Fiesta Tom & Jerry mugs, color inside, no
              advertising . . . . . . . . . .30.00 – 35.00
              Matching Sit n' Sip coasters .20.00 – 25.00
Plate 461:  New Fiesta mug . . . . . . . .20.00 – 25.00
Plate 462:  Buick ashtray . . . . . . . . .75.00 – 82.00
Plate 463:  Buick Tom & Jerry mugs,
              ea. . . . . . . . . . . . . . . .75.00 – 80.00
              Buick coasters . . . . . . . .30.00 – 35.00
Plates 464 –
473:       Trade card calendars
              Fiesta . . . . . . . . . . . . .35.00 – 40.00
              Harlequin . . . . . . . . . .25.00 – 35.00
              Illustrated with factory . . .6.00 – 10.00
              Others . . . . . . . . . . . .6.00 – 20.00,
              depending on collectiblility of the line
              pictured.

## Experimentals
### Pages 189 – 195

Most of the items shown in this chapter are one-of-a-kind or at least extremely rare, making them difficult if not impossible to evaluate. A minimum value of $8,000.00 each has been suggested for the ivory individual teapot, French casserole, and footed mixing bowl. However, as with any rare, possibly unique item, they will be worth whatever the market will bear.

## Lamps
### Pages 196 – 197

Fiesta lamp with fabricated body . . . .700.00 – 850.00
Harlequin lamp with fabricated body .600.00 – 750.00
Syrup lamp base . . . . . . . . . . . . . . .400.00 – 600.00
  with original shade, add . . . . . . . . . .30.00 – 35.00

## Apple Tree Bowls
### Page 198

Add 10% for colors other than turquoise, 30% for striped examples.

Set of six . . . . . . . . . . . . . . . . . . . . .250.00 – 275.00

## Children's Dishes
### Page 199 – 202

NEV — No Established Value

Plate 524:  Lunch time for teddy, bowl .50.00 – 60.00
Plate 525:  My Own Plate, baby's plate .80.00 – 90.00
Plate 526:  Animal characters on Fiesta shapes,
              ea. pc. . . . . . . . . . . . . .225.00 – 250.00
              on HLC shapes other than Fiesta,
              ea. pc. . . . . . . . . . . . . . .50.00 – 60.00
Plate 527:  Eggshell Nautilus set, very
              rare . . . . . . . . . . . . . . . . . . . . . . .NEV
Plate 528:  Rabbit family on Fiesta
              Mug . . . . . . . . . . . . .175.00 – 200.00
              Plate, divided . . . . . . . .75.00 – 90.00
Plate 529:  Tom & the Butterfly set
              Plate . . . . . . . . . . . . .140.00 – 150.00
              Bowl . . . . . . . . . . . . . .55.00 – 60.00
              Mug . . . . . . . . . . . . . . .55.00 – 60.00
Plate 530:  Western plate, Best China .75.00 – 90.00
Plate 531:  Dick Tracy set
              Plate . . . . . . . . . . . . .140.00 – 150.00
              Soup/cereal bowl . . . .150.00 – 160.00
              Mug . . . . . . . . . . . . . .150.00 – 160.00
Plates 532 &
533:       Art Deco children,
              Bowl, 6½" . . . . . . . . . .40.00 – 50.00
              Mug . . . . . . . . . . . . . . .40.00 – 50.00
Plates 534 –
536:       Empress shape with comic kids
              Bowl, 5½" . . . . . . . . . .35.00 – 40.00
              Bowl, 8" . . . . . . . . . . .65.00 – 70.00
              Cup . . . . . . . . . . . . . . .45.00 – 50.00
              Pitcher, Genesee shape,
                3½" . . . . . . . . . . . . .75.00 – 80.00
              Plate, 9" . . . . . . . . . . .45.00 – 50.00
              Plate, 6" (not shown) . . .30.00 – 35.00
Plate 537 –
538:       Nursery Rhymes line, Yellowstone shape
              Plate, 6½" . . . . . . . . . .35.00 – 45.00

Platter, 9" . . . . . . . . . .65.00 – 75.00
Plate 539:    Ralston Purina bowl . . . . .50.00 – 60.00
Plate 540:    Orphan Annie mug . . . . . .50.00 – 60.00

## Kitchen Kraft
### Pages 203 – 206

Add at least 50% to these values for the more collectible lines such as Sun Porch, Lady with Jug, Blue Willow, etc.

Bowl, mixing, 6" . . . . . . . . . . . . . .22.00 – 26.00
Bowl, mixing, 8" . . . . . . . . . . . . . .22.00 – 28.00
Bowl, mixing, 10" . . . . . . . . . . . . .35.00 – 40.00
Cake plate . . . . . . . . . . . . . . . . . .32.00 – 38.00
Cake server . . . . . . . . . . . . . . . . .40.00 – 45.00
Casserole, individual . . . . . . . . . . .60.00 – 70.00
Casserole, 6" . . . . . . . . . . . . . . . .38.00 – 42.00
Casserole, 8½" . . . . . . . . . . . . . . .40.00 – 45.00
  Metal base . . . . . . . . . . . . . . . . .15.00 – 20.00
Covered jar, large . . . . . . . . . . . . .110.00 – 125.00
Covered jar, medium . . . . . . . . . . .90.00 – 105.00
Covered jar, small . . . . . . . . . . . . .75.00 – 85.00
Covered jug . . . . . . . . . . . . . . . . .100.00 – 110.00
Pie plate . . . . . . . . . . . . . . . . . . .35.00 – 40.00
Platter . . . . . . . . . . . . . . . . . . . . .40.00 – 45.00
Metal base . . . . . . . . . . . . . . . . . .20.00 – 25.00
Salt and pepper shakers, pr. . . . . . . .40.00 – 45.00
Spoon . . . . . . . . . . . . . . . . . . . . .38.00 – 42.00
Stacking refrigerator lid . . . . . . . . . .30.00 – 35.00
Stacking refrigerator unit . . . . . . . . .22.00 – 28.00
Underplate . . . . . . . . . . . . . . . . . .20.00 – 25.00

## Embossed OvenServe Lines
### Pages 204 – 205

Add 50% when decals are present.

Ashtray . . . . . . . . . . . . . . . . . . . .50.00 – 60.00
Batter pitcher . . . . . . . . . . . . . . . .65.00 – 75.00
Bean pot, 4" x 4½" . . . . . . . . . . . . .20.00 – 25.00
Bean pot, 4¼" x 5½" . . . . . . . . . . . .25.00 – 30.00
Bowl, 4" . . . . . . . . . . . . . . . . . . . .4.00 – 5.50
Bowl, fruit, 5½" . . . . . . . . . . . . . . .8.00 – 10.00
Bowl, mixing, 6¼" . . . . . . . . . . . . .12.00 – 15.00
Bowl, mixing, 7¼" . . . . . . . . . . . . .15.00 – 20.00
Bowl, mixing, 8½" . . . . . . . . . . . . .20.00 – 25.00
Bowl, mixing, 12" . . . . . . . . . . . . .50.00 – 60.00
Bowl, oval baker, 6½" . . . . . . . . . . .8.00 – 10.00
Bowl, oval baker, 8½" . . . . . . . . . . .10.00 – 14.00
Bowl, oval baker, 11" . . . . . . . . . . .18.00 – 22.00
Bowl, ramekin, handled, 4½" . . . . . .8.00 – 10.00
Bowl, tab-handled, soup, 7" . . . . . . .9.00 – 12.00
Casserole, 6" . . . . . . . . . . . . . . . .12.00 – 15.00
Casserole, 7½" . . . . . . . . . . . . . . .22.00 – 28.00
Casserole, 8½" . . . . . . . . . . . . . . .28.00 – 32.00

Casserole, 10" . . . . . . . . . . . . . . .40.00 – 45.00
Creamer, rare . . . . . . . . . . . . . . . .70.00 – 85.00
Cup, 3¾", rare . . . . . . . . . . . . . . .20.00 – 25.00
Custard cup, 3½" . . . . . . . . . . . . . .4.00 – 5.00
Pie plate, 9" . . . . . . . . . . . . . . . . .16.00 – 20.00
Pie plate, 10½" . . . . . . . . . . . . . . .22.00 – 28.00
Plate, 7" . . . . . . . . . . . . . . . . . . . .5.00 – 7.00
Plate, 10" . . . . . . . . . . . . . . . . . .12.00 – 15.00
Platter, deep, oval, 8" . . . . . . . . . . .12.00 – 15.00
Platter, deep, oval, 12" . . . . . . . . . .15.00 – 18.00
Sauce boat, rare . . . . . . . . . . . . . . . . . .200.00
Saucer, 5¾" . . . . . . . . . . . . . . . . . .5.00 – 8.00
Spoon, long handle, minimum value . . . . . . .200.00
Sugar bowl base . . . . . . . . . . . . . .70.00 – 85.00
Sugar bowl lid, minimum value . . . . . . . . .85.00
Teapot, two sizes/two shapes,
  very rare . . . . . . . . . . . . . . . . . . .350.00 – 500.00

## Harmony Lines
### Page 207

For Kitchen Kraft items not listed here, use the high side of the range of values suggested for Kitchen Kraft.

Bowl, cereal/soup . . . . . . . . . . . . .12.00 – 14.00
Bowl, fruit, 5½" . . . . . . . . . . . . . . .6.00 – 8.00
Bowl, mixing, Kitchen Kraft, 10" . . . . .40.00 – 45.00
Bowl, nappy, 9" . . . . . . . . . . . . . . .15.00 – 20.00
Bowl, oval baker, 10" . . . . . . . . . . .16.00 – 22.00
Cake server, Kitchen Kraft . . . . . . . .50.00 – 55.00
Casserole, Kitchen Kraft, 8" . . . . . . .45.00 – 50.00
Cup & saucer . . . . . . . . . . . . . . . .10.00 – 14.00
Fork, Kitchen Kraft, . . . . . . . . . . . .50.00 – 55.00
Pie plate, Kitchen Kraft, 10" . . . . . . .35.00 – 40.00
Plate, 6" . . . . . . . . . . . . . . . . . . . .3.00 – 4.00
Plate, 7" . . . . . . . . . . . . . . . . . . . .6.00 – 9.00
Plate, 9" . . . . . . . . . . . . . . . . . . . .9.00 – 12.00
Spoon, Kitchen Kraft . . . . . . . . . . . .50.00 – 55.00

## Decaled Dinnerware Patterns and Shapes
### Page 208

Because it is impossible to list every decaled dinnerware line produced by HLC, we offer these suggestions to help you determine approximately how much you should expect to pay for the following:

1) For place-setting items (plates, cups and saucers, small bowls, etc.) purchased one at a time in a very simple pattern, use Carnival prices.
2) For place-setting items purchased one at a time in a more desirable pattern (for example, Sun Porch, English Garden, La Hacienda, American Provincial, Old Curiosity Shop, Rhythm Rose, Colonial Kitchen, etc.), use 50% of the Mexicana prices.
3) For larger serving pieces or purchases of larger lots

of a very simple pattern, use 50% of Mexicana prices.
4) For larger serving pieces or purchases of larger lots of a more desirable pattern, use 75% of Mexicana prices.

## Americana
### Page 208

| | |
|---|---|
| Bowl, coupe soup | 15.00 – 20.00 |
| Bowl, cream soup | 70.00 – 80.00 |
| Bowl, dessert/fruit | 9.00 – 12.00 |
| Bowl, oval vegetable, 8½" | 25.00 – 32.00 |
| Bowl, round vegetable, 8" | 25.00 – 32.00 |
| Bowl, round vegetable, 9" | 25.00 – 32.00 |
| Bowl lid, 9" | 50.00 – 55.00 |
| Creamer | 15.00 – 18.00 |
| Cup & saucer | 20.00 – 25.00 |
| Cup & saucer, after-dinner | 35.00 – 40.00 |
| Egg cup | 25.00 – 32.00 |
| Plate, 6" | 4.00 – 5.00 |
| Plate, 7" | 6.00 – 8.00 |
| Plate, 8" square | 15.00 – 20.00 |
| Plate, 8½" | 15.00 – 20.00 |
| Plate, 10" | 25.00 – 30.00 |
| Platter, 11" | 20.00 – 25.00 |
| Platter, 13" | 25.00 – 32.00 |
| Platter, 15" | 65.00 – 75.00 |
| Platter, round, 13" | 38.00 – 45.00 |
| Sauce boat | 18.00 – 24.00 |
| Sauce boat stand | 45.00 – 60.00 |
| Sugar bowl with lid | 18.00 – 25.00 |
| Teapot | 100.00 – 120.00 |

## American Provincial
### Page 209

Values for this line may be computed by using the suggestions under Decaled Dinnerware Patterns and Shapes.

| | |
|---|---|
| Spoon rest | 100.00 – 125.00 |

## Chinese Green Goddess
### Page 210

| | |
|---|---|
| Teapot | NEV |

## Colonial Kitchen
### Page 210

Values for this line may be computed by using the suggestions under Decaled Dinnerware Patterns and Shapes.

## Dogwood
### Page 211

Values are given for pieces with excellent gold trim.

| | |
|---|---|
| Bowl, cereal, 6" | 10.00 – 13.00 |
| Bowl, fruit, 5¾" | 6.00 – 8.00 |
| Bowl, mixing, Kitchen Kraft, 6½" | 38.00 – 48.00 |
| Bowl, mixing, Kitchen Kraft, 8¾" | 38.00 – 48.00 |
| Bowl, mixing, Kitchen Kraft, 10½" | 38.00 – 48.00 |
| Bowl, oval vegetable, 9½" | 22.00 – 28.00 |
| Bowl, round vegetable, 8¾" | 22.00 – 28.00 |
| Bowl, soup, 8" | 12.00 – 15.00 |
| Creamer | 12.00 – 15.00 |
| Cup & saucer | 10.00 – 13.00 |
| Plate, 6" | 4.00 – 5.00 |
| Plate, 7" | 10.00 – 12.00 |
| Plate, 8", scarce | 15.00 – 18.00 |
| Plate, 9" | 8.00 – 10.00 |
| Plate, 10", scarce | 14.00 – 16.00 |
| Platter, 11¾" | 22.00 – 28.00 |
| Platter, 13½" | 28.00 – 35.00 |
| Sauce boat | 22.00 – 28.00 |
| Sauce boat liner, 8½" | 28.00 – 32.00 |
| Sugar bowl with lid | 12.00 – 15.00 |
| Teapot | 82.00 – 90.00 |

## English Garden
### Page 211

Values for this line may be computed by using the suggestions under Decaled Dinnerware Patterns and Shapes.

## Historical America Subjects
### Page 212

| | |
|---|---|
| Bowl, cereal/soup | 14.00 – 18.00 |
| Bowl, dessert/fruit, 5¾" | 9.00 – 12.00 |
| Bowl, vegetable, 8¾" | 25.00 – 32.00 |
| Bowl, vegetable, oval, 9½" | 25.00 – 32.00 |
| Bowl, rim soup, 8½" | 15.00 – 20.00 |
| Creamer | 15.00 – 18.00 |
| Cup & saucer | 20.00 – 25.00 |
| Plate, 7" | 6.00 – 8.00 |
| Plate, 8" | 15.00 – 20.00 |
| Plate, 9" | 18.00 – 22.00 |
| Plate, 10" | 25.00 – 30.00 |
| Platter, 11" | 20.00 – 25.00 |
| Platter, 13" | 25.00 – 32.00 |
| Sauce boat | 18.00 – 24.00 |
| Sauce boat stand | 45.00 – 60.00 |
| Sugar bowl | 18.00 – 24.00 |
| Teapot | 100.00 – 120.00 |

## La Hacienda
### Page 212

Values for this line may be computed by using the suggestions under Decaled Dinnerware Patterns and Shapes.

## Old Curiosity Shop
### Page 213

Values for this line may be computed by using the suggestions under Decaled Dinnerware Patterns and Shapes.

## Priscilla
### Pages 213 – 214

Reports from dealers are that Priscilla sells well for them. This line was also made by Universal China, which is marked like HLC's, and Priscilla aficionados find that these pieces add dimension to their collections. Values are given for pieces with excellent gold trim.

| | |
|---|---|
| Bowl, fruit, 5" | 7.00 – 8.00 |
| Bowl, fruit, Kitchen Kraft, 9½", scarce | 35.00 – 40.00 |
| Bowl, mixing, small, Kitchen Kraft, 6" | 38.00 – 42.00 |
| Bowl, mixing, medium, Kitchen Kraft, 8" | 40.00 – 45.00 |
| Bowl, mixing, large, Kitchen Kraft, 10" | 45.00 – 50.00 |
| Bowl, oval vegetable, 9" | 22.00 – 28.00 |
| Bowl, round vegetable, 8" | 22.00 – 28.00 |
| Bowl, soup, 8" | 12.00 – 15.00 |
| Cake plate, Kitchen Kraft, 11" | 22.00 – 28.00 |
| Casserole, round, Kitchen Kraft, 8½" | 38.00 – 42.00 |
| Coffeepot, Kitchen Kraft | 100.00 – 110.00 |
| Creamer | 15.00 – 20.00 |
| Cup & saucer | 12.00 – 18.00 |
| Pie plate, Kitchen Kraft, 9½" | 25.00 – 30.00 |
| Pitcher, water, Kitchen Kraft | 35.00 – 40.00 |
| Plate, 6" | 6.00 – 7.00 |
| Plate, 7" | 8.00 – 10.00 |
| Plate, 8" | 9.00 – 10.00 |
| Plate, 9" | 9.00 – 10.00 |
| Plate, 10" | 12.00 – 15.00 |
| Platter, tab-handled, made by Universal | 28.00 – 32.00 |
| Platter, 9" | 20.00 – 25.00 |
| Platter, 13½" | 28.00 – 32.00 |
| Sauce boat | 22.00 – 28.00 |
| Sugar bowl with lid | 20.00 – 25.00 |
| Teapot, regular | 90.00 – 100.00 |
| Teapot, Republic, hard to find | 90.00 – 100.00 |
| Teapot, tall, hard to find, made by Universal | 90.00 – 100.00 |

## Rhythm Rose
### Page 214

Values for this line may be computed by using the suggestions under Decaled Dinnerware Patterns and Shapes.

## Sun Porch
### Page 215

Values for this line may be computed by using the suggestions under Decaled Dinnerware Patterns and Shapes, with these exceptions:

| | |
|---|---|
| Casserole, Century shape | NEV |
| Teapot, Century shape | NEV |
| Tumblers, each | 25.00 – 30.00 |

## Virginia Rose
### Pages 216 – 218

Of the various patterns on Virginia Rose, the two most popular are Moss Rose (#JJ59) and Fluffy Rose (VR128). The Moss Rose decal was used by the company on other lines as early as eleven years before it was used on Virigina Rose in 1933. Other Virginia Rose florals sell for 66% of these prices, simply due to lack of demand. Values are for examples with excellent gold or silver trim.

| | |
|---|---|
| Bowl, cereal, 6" | 15.00 |
| Bowl, deep, 6" | 40.00 |
| Bowl, fruit, 5½" | 8.00 |
| Bowl, soup, flanged, 8½" | 20.00 |
| Bowl, soup, no flange, 8½" | 20.00 |
| Bowl, mixing, 6½" | 50.00 |
| Bowl, mixing, 8½" | 50.00 |
| Bowl, mixing, 10½" | 50.00 |
| Bowl, vegetable, oval, 8¼" | 35.00 |
| Bowl, vegetable, oval, 9¼" | 25.00 |
| Bowl, vegetable, oval, 10¼" | 30.00 |
| Bowl, vegetable, round, 7¾" | 35.00 |
| Bowl, vegetable, round, 8¾" | 25.00 |
| Bowl, vegetable, round, 9¾" | 30.00 |
| Bowl, vegetable, with lid, 8½" | 100.00 |
| Butter dish, ½-lb. | 125.00 |
| Cake lifter | 150.00 |
| Cake plate, flat, 10¾" | 150.00 |
| Cake plate, Kitchen Kraft, 10" | 125.00 |
| Casserole, 7½" | 100.00 |
| Casserole, 8½" | 100.00 |
| Casserole, Daisy Chain | 500.00 |

Casserole, straight sides, 8" . . . . . . . . . . . . . .250.00
Creamer . . . . . . . . . . . . . . . . . . . . . . . . . . . . .20.00
Cup . . . . . . . . . . . . . . . . . . . . . . . . . . . . . . . .10.00
Egg cup, double, 3¾" . . . . . . . . . . . . . . . . . .150.00
Egg cup, double, 4¾" . . . . . . . . . . . . . . . . . .100.00
Jar, ball, sm., 17½" circumference . . . . . . . .150.00
Jar, ball, med., 22" circumference . . . . . . . . .150.00
Jar, ball, lg., 27½" circumference . . . . . . . . . .250.00
Mug, Baltimore, 3½" . . . . . . . . . . . . . . . . . . .125.00
Pie plate, 9½" . . . . . . . . . . . . . . . . . . . . . . . . .40.00
Pie plate, 12" . . . . . . . . . . . . . . . . . . . . . . . . .75.00
Pitcher, 5¼" . . . . . . . . . . . . . . . . . . . . . . . . . .150.00
Pitcher, 7½" . . . . . . . . . . . . . . . . . . . . . . . . . .250.00
Plate, 6¼" . . . . . . . . . . . . . . . . . . . . . . . . . . . .6.00
Plate, 7" . . . . . . . . . . . . . . . . . . . . . . . . . . . . .15.00
Plate, 8¼" . . . . . . . . . . . . . . . . . . . . . . . . . . . .25.00
Plate, 9¼" . . . . . . . . . . . . . . . . . . . . . . . . . . . .10.00
Plate, 10" . . . . . . . . . . . . . . . . . . . . . . . . . . . .18.00
Platter, 9¼" . . . . . . . . . . . . . . . . . . . . . . . . . .30.00
Platter, 10½" . . . . . . . . . . . . . . . . . . . . . . . . .35.00
Platter, 11½" . . . . . . . . . . . . . . . . . . . . . . . . .25.00
Platter, 13" . . . . . . . . . . . . . . . . . . . . . . . . . .40.00
Platter, 15¼" . . . . . . . . . . . . . . . . . . . . . . . . .75.00
Salt & pepper shakers, Debutante, pr. . . . . . .150.00
Salt & pepper shakers, Kitchen Kraft, lg. . . . .100.00
Salt & pepper shakers, Swing, pr. . . . . . . . . . .75.00
Sauce boat . . . . . . . . . . . . . . . . . . . . . . . . . . .30.00
Saucer . . . . . . . . . . . . . . . . . . . . . . . . . . . . . . .5.00
Sugar bowl . . . . . . . . . . . . . . . . . . . . . . . . . . .25.00
Tray, with handles, 8¼" . . . . . . . . . . . . . . . . .200.00

## Western Dinnerware
### Page 219

Bowl, fruit . . . . . . . . . . . . . . . . . . . . . . .25.00 – 30.00
Bowl, vegetable . . . . . . . . . . . . . . . . . . .50.00 – 60.00
Cup & saucer . . . . . . . . . . . . . . . . . . . . .30.00 – 35.00
Plate, 9" . . . . . . . . . . . . . . . . . . . . . . . . .28.00 – 32.00

## Caledon
### Page 220

Mug, 9" . . . . . . . . . . . . . . . . . . . . . . . .165.00 – 200.00

## Currant
### Pages 220 – 223

Plate 591:   Vase with handles, 8" . . .125.00 – 140.00
Plate 592:   Vase, 7" . . . . . . . . . . . .110.00 – 125.00
Plate 593:   Rose bowl, small, 4¼" . . .350.00 – 375.00
Plate 594:   Ruffled bowl, salad, 2" x 10" .165.00 – 180.00
             Plate, 9½" . . . . . . . . . . . .75.00 – 85.00
             Plate, scalloped, 10" . . . .90.00 – 110.00

Plate 595:   Vase, 9½" . . . . . . . . . . . . . . . . . .NEV
Plate 596:   Tobacco jar . . . . . . . . .225.00 – 250.00
Plate 597:   Bread tray, 6½" x 12" . . . .75.00 – 85.00
Plate 598:   Cracker jar . . . . . . . . . .550.00 – 600.00
Plate 599:   Whiskey jug, small, 3½" . .350.00 – 375.00
             Large, 5½" . . . . . . .300.00 – 325.00
Plate 600:   Pitcher, Dutch jug, 10" . .165.00 – 185.00
Plate 601:   Sugar basket . . . . . . . .200.00 – 225.00
Plate 602:   Covered dish . . . . . . . .210.00 – 230.00
Plate 603:   Geisha jug, large . . . . .125.00 – 140.00
Plate 604:   Sapho molasses can . . . .350.00 – 375.00
Plate 605:   Vase, 12" . . . . . . . . . . .210.00 – 230.00
Plate 606:   Vase, 9¾" . . . . . . . . . .165.00 – 185.00
             Vase, slim form, 12" . . .155.00 – 175.00
             Vase, slim form, 16" . . .250.00 – 275.00
             Chocolate/AD pot, 10" . .300.00 – 325.00
Plate 607:   Vase with handles, 14" .325.00 – 350.00
Plate 608:   Bulbous Pitcher, 6" . . . .110.00 – 135.00
             Orange bowl with
               handles . . . . . . . . .200.00 – 225.00
             pitcher, straight-sided .120.00 – 140.00
Plate 609:   Orange bowl in white . . . . . . . . . .NEV

## Delft
### Page 224

Plate 610:   Vase #3 . . . . . . . . . . . . . . . . . . . .NEV

## Dreamland
### Pages 224 – 226

Plate 612:   Vase, 3½" . . . . . . . . . . .225.00 – 250.00
Plate 613:   Staghorn Stein . . . . . . .245.00 – 265.00
             Tankard . . . . . . . . . . .400.00 – 450.00
Plate 614:   Loving cup . . . . . . . . . .750.00 – 800.00
Plate 615:   Chop/cake plate, 10½" . .250.00 – 300.00
Plate 616:   Chocolate pot . . . . . . .375.00 – 400.00
Plate 617:   Vase, 16" . . . . . . . . . . .425.00 – 475.00
Plate 618:   Nut dish, handled . . . . .300.00 – 325.00
Plate 619:   Plaque . . . . . . . . . . . .225.00 – 250.00
Plate 620:   Jug, 6½" . . . . . . . . . . .275.00 – 250.00
Plate 621:   Rose bowl, large, 5" . . . .350.00 – 425.00
Plate 622:   Ruffled salad bowl . . . . .275.00 – 325.00
Plate 623:   Berry bowl . . . . . . . . . .375.00 – 400.00

## Golden Fleece
### Page 227

Plate 624:   Tioga creamer . . . . . . . .175.00 – 200.00
Plate 625:   Tioga sugar basket . . . . .250.00 – 275.00
Plate 626:   Vase, 12" . . . . . . . . . . .225.00 – 250.00
Plate 627:   Staghorn Stein . . . . . . .150.00 – 175.00
             Tankard . . . . . . . . . . .225.00 – 250.00

## Gypsy and Other Beauties
### Pages 228 – 229

Plate 628:  Gypsy pear-shaped mug . . . . . . . . .NEV
Plate 629:  Gypsy plate, 10¼" . . . . .200.00 – 225.00
               Geisha jug with rare blue
               trim . . . . . . . . . . . .250.00 – 275.00
Plate 630:  Gypsy plate, 6¼" . . . . . .75.00 – 100.00
Plate 631:  Gypsy chocolate pot . . .300.00 – 325.00
Plate 632:  Gypsy Tioga sugar basket and
               creamer . . . . . . . . . .275.00 – 300.00
Plate 633:  Charger, marked "American
               Beauty" . . . . . . . . . . .150.00 – 165.00
Plate 634:  Nut dish . . . . . . . . . . .350.00 – 375.00
Plate 635:  Tankard . . . . . . . . . . .360.00 – 390.00
               Mug . . . . . . . . . . . . . .125.00 – 140.00

## Holland
### Pages 229 – 230

Plate 636:  Ewer . . . . . . . . . . . . .625.00 – 725.00
Plate 637:  Ruffled salad bowl . . . . .325.00 – 375.00
Plate 638:  Dutch jug . . . . . . . . . .450.00 – 475.00
Plate 639:  Bowl, white interior . . . .475.00 – 500.00
Plate 640:  Rose bowl . . . . . . . . . .475.00 – 525.00
Plate 641:  Jug, 6½" . . . . . . . . . . .450.00 – 475.00
Plate 642:  Plate, 10½", unusual colors .350.00 – 400.00

## Juno
### Pages 231 – 232

Plate 643:  Chocolate pot . . . . . . . .375.00 – 400.00
               Demitasse cup & saucer .195.00 – 225.00
Plate 644:  Geisha milk jug . . . . . .350.00 – 375.00
Plate 645:  Comport . . . . . . . . . . .275.00 – 300.00
Plate 646:  Tioga salad bowl . . . . .225.00 – 250.00
Plate 647:  Orange bowl . . . . . . . .375.00 – 400.00
Plate 648:  Stein ewer . . . . . . . . .250.00 – 275.00
Plate 649:  Tioga salad bowl . . . . .275.00 – 300.00
Plate 650:  Unidentified piece with drain hole and
               underplate . . . . . . . . . . . . . . . .NEV

## Laughlin Blue and Other Flow Blue Patterns
### Pages 233 – 234

Plate 651:  Jardiniere, 10" x 14" . . . .700.00 – 750.00
Plate 652:  Cabaret, rare . . . . . . . .200.00 – 250.00
Plate 653:  Tioga cake plate . . . . . .180.00 – 200.00
Plate 654:  Vase, 12" . . . . . . . . . . .350.00 – 385.00
Plate 655:  Tioga cake plate . . . . . .180.00 – 200.00
Plate 656:  Spoon tray, small . . . . .275.00 – 300.00
Plate 657:  Cup & saucer . . . . . . . .180.00 – 200.00
Plate 658:  Tankard with Monk, large . .275.00 – 300.00
Plate 659:  Staghorn Stein with Monk 180.00 – 200.00

Plate 660:  Chocolate cup . . . . . . .180.00 – 200.00

## Ruby, Silver Sienna
### Page 235

Plate 661:  Mug . . . . . . . . . . . . . .175.00 – 200.00
               Dutch jug, 10¼" . . . . . .375.00 – 400.00
               Plate 10¼" . . . . . . . . . .200.00 – 225.00
Plate 662:  Biscuit jar . . . . . . . . . . . . . . . . . .NEV

## White Pets
### Pages 235 – 237

Plate 663:  Comb & brush tray . . . .225.00 – 250.00
Plate 664:  Ewer, 15½" . . . . . . . . .425.00 – 450.00
Plate 665:  Nut dish . . . . . . . . . . .200.00 – 225.00
Plate 666:  Geisha jug, large . . . . .350.00 – 400.00
Plate 667:  Bread tray, 13½" . . . . . .175.00 – 200.00
Plate 668:  Geisha jug, 4" . . . . . . .275.00 – 300.00
Plate 669:  Vase #3 . . . . . . . . . . . .325.00 – 350.00
Plate 670:  Plate, 9½" . . . . . . . . . .175.00 – 200.00
               Staghorn Stein . . . . . . .180.00 – 200.00
Plate 671:  Vase with handles, 8" . .275.00 – 300.00
Plate 672:  Comb & brush tray . . . .225.00 – 250.00

## Tankards, Steins, and Pitchers
### Pages 237 – 239

Plate 673:  Patriotic tankard . . . . . .380.00 – 400.00
Plate 674:  Patriotic staghorn stein .175.00 – 200.00
Plate 675:  Staghorn stein, advertising . .220.00 – 245.00
Plate 676:  Staghorn stein, football player .325.00 – 350.00
Plate 677:  Pitcher from toilet set . . . . . . . . . . .NEV
Plate 678:  Geisha jug, 6" . . . . . . .165.00 – 185.00
Plate 679:  Geisha jug, 6" . . . . . . .165.00 – 185.00
Plate 680:  Staghorn stein, Dutch boy .125.00 – 150.00
Plate 681:  Tankard, American Floral .345.00 – 360.00
Plate 682:  Staghorn stein with flowers .190.00 – 210.00
Plate 683:  Staghorn stein with plums .190.00 – 210.00

## World's Fair: The American Potter
### Pages 240 – 243

NEV — No Established Value

Plate 684:  Vases, yellow is the most common color
               Vase, under 5" . . . . . .125.00 – 175.00
               Vase, 5" . . . . . . . . . . .175.00 – 250.00
               Vase, 6" . . . . . . . . . . .275.00 – 350.00
               Vase, 7" – 8" . . . . . . . .375.00 – 450.00
               Candleholders, rare, ea. . .225.00 – 250.00
               Bowl, extremely rare . . .265.00 – 300.00
               Individual Harlequin creamer .90.00 – 100.00

Plate 685: Plate, Golden Gate Expo, either
year . . . . . . . . . . . . . .135.00 – 150.00
Ashtray, Golden Gate Expo .100.00 – 125.00

Plate 686: Plate, HLC World's Fair, either
year . . . . . . . . . . . . .150.00 – 200.00

Plate 687: Ashtray, Four Seasons, turquoise,
ea. . . . . . . . . . . . . . . .90.00 – 100.00
other colors . . . . . . . . . . . . . . . . .NEV

Plate 688: Cup & saucer, Zodiac,
turquoise . . . . . . . . . .100.00 – 125.00

Plates 689 &
690: Pitchers, George & Martha Washington,
yellow or cobalt, 5", extremely
rare . . . . . . . . . . . . . . . . . . . . . . .NEV

Plate 691: Pitcher, Martha Washington, ivory
5" . . . . . . . . . . . . . . . .$70.00 – 80.00

Plate 692: Pitchers, George & Martha Washington,
bisque . . . . . . . . . . . . . . . . . . . . .NEV

Plate 693: Potters' plates, either view,
turquoise . . . . . . . . . . .40.00 – 45.00
ivory or green . . . . . . .120.00 – 140.00
tan/mocha . . . . . . . . .135.00 – 145.00
bisque . . . . . . . . . . . . . . . . . . . .NEV
box only . . . . . . . . . . .75.00 – 100.00

Plate 694: Cake set, Cronin China Co. .125.00 – 150.00
Bowl, Paden City Pottery, 10" .125.00 – 150.00
Plate, Knowles, 10¾" . . .100.00 – 135.00
Marmalade (see Plate 695 for value of
complete example) shown here with no
lid
Juice pitcher, Porcelier . .175.00 – 200.00

Plate 695: Marmalade, complete, Edwin Knowles,
very rare . . . . . . . . . .300.00 – 400.00

Plate 696: Ashtray, Porcelier . . . . .125.00 – 130.00

Plate 697: Teapot, large, Porcelier .290.00 – 325.00
Teapot, medium, Porcelier,
not shown . . . . . . . . .285.00 – 320.00
Teapot, small, Porcelier .325.00 – 350.00

Plate 698: Water pitcher, Porcelier .250.00 – 300.00

Creamer, Porcelier . . . .125.00 – 150.00
Sugar bowl, Porcelier,
not shown . . . . . . . . .150.00 – 175.00

## Miscellaneous
### Pages 244 – 246

Plate 699: Not HLC . . . . . . . . . . . . . . . . . . . .NEV
Plate 700: Too controversial . . . . . . . . . . . . . .NEV
Plate 701: Chip & dip, 12" . . . . . . . . . . . . . . .NEV
Plate 702: Bill Booth football . .1,100.00 – 1,400.00
Plate 703: Leaf saucers, 7"
red, minimum value . . . . . . . . .200.00
green, minimum value . . . . . .125.00
Plate 704: Lid, rare, minimum value . . . . . .150.00
Plate 705: Syrup, not HLC . . . . . . . . . . . . . . .NEV
Plate 706: Plate . . . . . . . . . . . . . . . . . . . . . . .NEV
Plate 707: Tom & Jerry bowl . . . . . . .35.00 – 45.00
Tom & Jerry mug . . . . . . .10.00 – 15.00

Values for Our Early Editions

The earlier editions of our Fiesta books have themselves become sought-after collectibles. However,
online auctions have made more of them available than
they once were, and values have gone down dramatically. Remember that condition is important, and values are given for copies in very fine condition.

First edition . . . . . . . . . . . . . . . . . . .50.00 – 85.00
Second edition . . . . . . . . . . . . . . . . .40.00 – 70.00
Third edition . . . . . . . . . . . . . . . . . .30.00 – 50.00
Fourth edition . . . . . . . . . . . . . . . . .25.00 – 30.00
Fifth edition . . . . . . . . . . . . . . . . . .20.00 – 25.00
Sixth edition . . . . . . . . . . . . . . . . . .15.00 – 20.00

# BIBLIOGRAPHY

Cunningham, Jo. *Collector's Encyclopedia of American Dinnerware, Second Edition*. Schroeder Publishing Company, Collector Books: Paducah, KY, 2005.

Cunningham, Jo. *Homer Laughlin, A Giant Among Dishes, 1873 – 1949*. Schiffer Publishing: Atglen, PA, 1998.

*The Homer Laughlin China Collector's Association Guide: Fiesta, Harlequin, and Kitchen Kraft Dinnerware*. Schiffer Publishing: Atglen, PA, 2000.

Jasper, Joanne. *Collector's Encyclopedia of Homer Laughlin China*. Schroeder Publishing Company, Collector Books: Paducah, KY, 2002.

Racheter, Richard. *Post86 Fiesta*. Schroeder Publishing Company, Collector Books: Paducah, KY, 2000.